W9-CMJ-233

THE FIELDS OF LIGHT

THE FIELDS OF LIGHT

An Experiment in Critical Reading

REUBEN ARTHUR BROWER

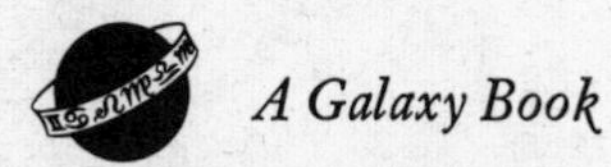

A Galaxy Book

NEW YORK · OXFORD UNIVERSITY PRESS · 1962

FIRST PUBLISHED AS A GALAXY BOOK, 1962

Much of the material of two chapters (on Jane Austen and on E. M. Forster) originally appeared in *Scrutiny* and the *Chicago Review,* and I wish to thank the publishers of both journals for their permission to use it here.

For kind permission of authors and publishers to reprint selections from various works, I wish to make acknowledgment as follows:

A Way Out by Robert Frost, copyright 1917, 1929 by Robert Frost; 'Education by Poetry' by Robert Frost, 'The Amherst Graduates' Quarterly', XX (1931); used by permission of the author. 'Once by the Pacific' by Robert Frost from *West-Running Brook,* copyright 1928 by Henry Holt and Company, Inc.; used by permission of the publisher.

Mrs. Dalloway by Virginia Woolf, copyright 1925 by Harcourt, Brace & Company; *A Passage to India* by E. M. Forster, copyright 1924 by Harcourt, Brace & Company; used by permission of the publisher.

'Roses Only' by Marianne Moore from *Selected Poems,* copyright 1935 by Marianne Moore; 'Two Songs from a Play' by W. B. Yeats from *The Tower,* copyright 1928 by the Macmillan Company; both used by permission of the Macmillan Company and A. P. Watt and Son.

Ideas of Good and Evil by W. B. Yeats, copyright 1903 by the Macmillan Company; used by permission of the Macmillan Company.

The Art of the Novel by Henry James, copyright 1934 by Charles Scribner's Sons.

'Thou Art Indeed Just, Lord, If I Contend' by Gerard Manley Hopkins from *Poems,* copyright 1948 by Oxford University Press, Inc.; used by permission of the publisher.

PRINTED IN THE UNITED STATES OF AMERICA

TO HELEN AND J. E. R.

PREFACE

This book might well be dedicated to my fellow teachers and my students in courses that I have taught at Amherst College and the Bread Loaf School of English. I owe a more particular debt to Theodore Baird and G. Armour Craig, and to all my Amherst colleagues who have made with me various experiments in critical reading of literature. Although they are not responsible for the methods or conclusions of this book, they will see at many points how much I have learned from their teaching. To Elizabeth Drew of Smith College I am indebted for generous encouragement in the initial stages of writing and for most helpful criticisms of the completed manuscript.

I am also glad to record an earlier and continuing obligation to talks with Robert Frost, who first showed me 'the figure a poem makes,' to the teaching of F. R. Leavis, of Cambridge University, who introduced me to 'practical criticism,' and to the critical writings of I. A. Richards, now of Harvard University. My indebtedness to Mr. Richards appears with the first sentence of the book and is evident on many pages that follow. It should be noted that in taking over terms from *The Principles of Literary Criticism* and other works I have often radically altered their original meanings to fit a quite different point of view.

For various kinds of assistance I stand in debt to: Professors Wendell V. Clausen, Francis H. Fobes, Newton F. McKeon, John A. Moore, and George F. Whicher, of Amherst College; to Professor Harry Levin and the late Professor F. O. Matthiessen, of Harvard University.

I wish to express my warm appreciation to President Charles W. Cole, of Amherst College, for his considerate help in arranging a sabbatical leave and for securing the grant of a Sherman Pratt Faculty Fellowship, which made it possible for me to complete the writing of the book. I am very grateful to the Librarian and staff of the Stanford University Library for the many courtesies they extended to me during my stay in California.

I am greatly indebted to Mrs. Evelyn Cooley for accurate typing and retyping of the manuscript.

I owe much that was pleasant and interesting during the months in which I wrote this book to my friends in the Western fields of light, in Boulder Creek, California, and in El Porvenir, New Mexico.

R. A. B.

Amherst, Mass.
February, 1951

CONTENTS

TO THE READER

Whatever one reads with close attention to the words and also to the things the words mean is the instrument of a liberal culture; whatever one reads otherwise, whether philosophy or history or poetry, is not.

LEO STEIN

In a complete and successful work there are hidden masses of implications, a veritable world which reveals itself to those whom it may concern, which means: to those who deserve it.

LE CORBUSIER

This is a book to read with, an experiment in critical reading. While writing it, I have always been thinking of literature as *read* by someone, as an active engagement between the reader and the printed page. My aim has been twofold: to demonstrate some methods of reading analysis and to use them in discovering designs of imaginative organization in particular poems, plays, and novels. A book of this sort necessarily calls for active participation if the experiment is to be even moderately successful. The ideal reader of the chapters that follow will stop to read a poem more than once, or come back to a chapter a second time after he has reread the novel or play that is being discussed. He will on occasion want to read a poem or a passage of prose aloud. Above all he will not forget that he is making an experiment, that he is learning to do something, rather than passively viewing a series of more or less revolutionary interpretations on which he is to vote 'Yes' or 'No.' I shall not measure the success of this book by whether the reader agrees or disagrees with my interpretations, but by the way in which he interprets the next poem or the next novel he reads. If by adopting some of the methods I have used he discovers relations he had missed before, then he may agree with me that the experiment has been successful.

In spite of the ugly associations attached to such terms as method and analysis the responsible critic is obliged to give an account of what he is doing, of how he works. He will not succeed, of course, since no one, including the technologist, ever describes exactly what he does. However conscious the operator may be, there is always some point at which he becomes inarticulate; some indispensable act of perception, of co-ordination of eye and hand, always lies beyond expression. The brief and generalized account of method in the first chapter of this book certainly does not escape the limitations common to all similar accounts. But the ideal reader (perhaps he is beginning to seem impossibly ideal) will take it as a rough chart and move on as quickly as possible to what is done. Others may wish to omit it until the last; still others may omit it altogether.

Readers of every variety should perhaps be warned that in some instances I shall work my methods for all they are worth, that I shall push interpretation just as far as I dare. But that is part of the fun: to see what can be done and what can be discovered. I feel certain that the seasoned reader will regard my gymnastics with a tolerant eye. He will realize that I most certainly do not recommend reading every book with the same closeness of attention, that I am far from suggesting that we make a complete analysis of every book we read. But there is a therapeutic value in occasional experiments in slow reading. For in reading, as in other arts, there is a mental form and awareness to be fostered and improved by directed practice. Most of us are not in much danger of reading too closely or with too fine a response too much of the time.

There is no simple and certain way of defending critical reading, as there is no simple way of defending any educational activity. Two sorts of justification are suggested by the two quotations at the head of this introductory note. Practice in defining the meanings of words in literature is an 'instrument of liberal culture' since it is practice in making discriminations. Practice in discovering the 'masses of implications' in a work of literary art is practice in finding relationships, in finding order in experience. These are among the primary activities of civilized men.

THE FIELDS OF LIGHT

The seer and speaker under the descent of the god is the 'poet,' whatever his form, and he ceases to be one only when his form, whatever else it may nominally or superficially or vulgarly be, is unworthy of the god: in which event, we promptly submit, he isn't worth talking of at all. He becomes so worth it, and the god so adopts him, and so confirms his charming office and name, in the degree in which his impulse and passion are general and comprehensive—a definitional provision for them that makes but a mouthful of so minor a distinction, in the fields of light, as that between verse and prose.

HENRY JAMES: Preface to *The Golden Bowl*

Introduction

THE BEAUTIFUL GATE OF ENJOYMENT

. . . *analytic appreciation . . . the Beautiful Gate itself of enjoyment.**

HENRY JAMES

Perhaps I can best introduce the kind of critical activity I have in mind and its larger aims by a parable or rough analogy from painting. Suppose that I am looking at a domestic scene by de Hooch, one of a type familiar in Dutch art, a picture of a woman spinning. Even with a Pater's command of nuance, I cannot define exactly the peculiar sense of life, the complete fullness and warmth, which is conveyed to me by de Hooch's picture. Nor shall I be very successful in showing anyone else what I mean by complete fullness and warmth or in convincing him that it has anything to do with seeing the picture, unless I direct his attention to lines and colors, lights and shadows which I can locate and which we both can see. I can point out, for example, the use in this picture of rounded forms which are similar in curve and convexity, in color and light, and which recur distinctly in the spinning wheel the woman is turning, in a copper pot, and in the woman's knee pressed against the wheel. All are painted in light of the same blurred intensity, the color of each form showing a similar blend of coppery grayish-brown. By pointing out this motif and indicating how it is related to other forms in the picture through harmonizing lines and colors, I can at least communicate some more particular meaning for 'complete fullness and warmth.' I can say to my fellow viewer, 'I am talking about our response to

* From the Preface to *The Lesson of the Master*.

that design, to that relationship of lines, colors, and lights.' (I take for granted some community of response, an assumption on which all group activities, including the use of all languages, is dependent.) We may conclude later that a more adequate label than fullness and warmth is needed to express the *felt* structure of this picture. But what matters for the business of criticism is that by turning our attention to the medium, to the language of the painting, we have found a way of describing to someone else the character of the experience. Still more important, we can go on to another picture and make use of this experiment in looking and defining. If at a first viewing we have only a sense of confusion, if no particularized sense of life emerges, we may turn again to the medium and discover some design that will give us a cue to what we have missed.

As this parable suggests, any critical method presumes and in fact defines an end. We looked at our picture in a certain way in order to discover pictorial design. Similarly, to read in a certain way means to read for a certain object. In this book we are reading to discover and describe certain designs of imaginative organization in particular works of literature. In Part I, The Discovery of Design, I introduce my reading methods by tracing a number of designs (such as imagery, metaphor, irony) in short poems or passages of poetry. In Part II, In Large Letters, I trace the same designs in a group of longer works—a play by Shakespeare, a satire by Pope, and novels by three different writers. The reader is asked to give to the more extensive literary forms the close attention he ordinarily reserves for short poems.

In the last chapter of the book I shall try to show what we mean by integrity of imagination, especially as the term is applied to longer works of literature. I hardly expect to produce a neat definition for this haunting idea of literary criticism, but by reviewing the analyses that have been made I can at least outline a distinguishable order of meanings. The reader can then say with me, 'By integrity of imagination we mean what we have seen in this poem and this play and this novel.' And in the potential realm that extends beyond fruitful discussion, in which reader and writer go on to further reading and communication, we both may find other similar instances and meanings. Since the works read are not 'perfect specimens,' we may also learn something about limitations and comparative failures in the working of imagination, we may gain a heightened sense of the nature of imaginative design and of how it is realized through language.

In each of the chapters on Discovery of Design, I define a type of design and show by example how we can examine a poet's language to discover it. The definitions and the analyses are inseparable; I often begin by analyzing a poem and only later state the definition that has been applied: the definition of tone follows an account of how in a particular lyric the poet speaks to his auditor. The general statements defining metaphor or irony or any other design should be read as indications of practice, not as a complete or in any sense final account of the 'truth' about any one of these literary designs. If the reader can see what I look for and how I go about interpreting a metaphor or the poet's tone, he will be well enough prepared to follow this experiment in reading.

Each design calls for its own modes of analysis, and each poem demands slight variations in the approach of the interpreter. While aiming at some uniformity of method, I have tried to respect the uniqueness of the poetic experience, to test my statements by what I experienced in reading a particular poem or passage. Two basic methods can be traced throughout: full and exact definition by context and comparison of similar expressions. So described these methods sound naïve enough and certainly not revolutionary; but there is perhaps some novelty in my critical application of them. As for naïveté, one of my aims is to show that naïveté of a certain sort is indispensable in criticism and pays. The critic should start from what the writer says and what he means 'here' and 'here' and 'here' in the text. Then he may safely go on to make as large relationships as he wishes, providing he never goes contrary to these initial findings.

But we may postpone further talk of methods until we have a more exact notion of the aim for which they are to be used—to discover and describe designs of imaginative organization. What do I mean by imaginative organization and design? I am tempted to say that the meaning of both expressions is defined by the whole book, that the last chapter rather than the first is the place to look for an answer to this question. However, in this as in any investigation we need at least a rough idea of what we are looking for, in order to recognize it when it is found. I shall try to outline the meaning of these notoriously ambiguous terms from the reading of a single familiar lyric:

THE SICK ROSE

O ROSE, thou art sick!
The invisible worm,
That flies in the night,
In the howling storm,

Has found out thy bed
Of crimson joy;
And his dark secret love
Does thy life destroy.

WILLIAM BLAKE

In saying that Blake's poem is imaginatively organized, I mean that we have a sense of extraordinary interconnectedness among a relatively large number of different items of experience. A random list will suggest their number and variety: a sick rose, a rose eaten by a worm, flying in the night, a storm sound, an invisible worm (reminding us of 'that false worm,' Satan), a sensation of dark red, a hint of illicit love, the exclamatory voice of the discoverer of evil ('O Rose!'), heard line and phrase units, rhyming sounds, and so on. The term 'item of experience' is used here to name any response whatsoever that a printed word may stand for: that is, sounds made in pronouncing it; rhythmic stress; grammatical connection; and meanings of any sort, from the most obscure organic disturbance to images of sensations, to the most distinct reference to an object or person. We can best measure the fullness of interconnection among the items by reviewing some of the kinds of relationship we perceive in reading the single word 'worm.' We take it, for instance, as a subject in anticipation of a verb, a relation that is never completed until we reach 'destroy.' We read it in the sense of 'rose worm' and make a causal connection with 'sick' (botanically) and 'rose.' This relationship also extends throughout the poem. We also place 'worm' (as a cause) in a chronological sequence that runs from 'art sick' (present) to 'has found' (past) to 'does destroy' (very nearly future).

Though only Sir Thomas Browne might ask and answer the question 'What does an "invisible worm" look like?', many readers will agree that some shadow of physical form is evoked by the expression. This vague sensation is one in a whole merging series of movements, sights, and sounds from 'flies in the night' to 'howling storm' to 'crimson' (which belongs to 'bed' as well as 'joy') to 'dark.' We get an over-all impression of a magical nocturnal creature swiftly moving against a background of ugly sound, lurid light and darkness. The 'worm' that has found the rose's 'bed' and whose 'secret love' destroys her 'life' belongs to still another order of relations, one that includes the Rose-person of the opening line, the dying beloved in her 'bed of crimson joy.' 'Invisible,' as we have noted, reminds us of Satan, of some evil spiritual power, perhaps of Milton's 'undying Worm.' The language elsewhere recalls the ninety-first Psalm: 'Thou shalt not be afraid for the terror by night; nor for the arrow that flieth by day. Nor for the pestilence that walketh in darkness . . .' The worm's evil love and killing power symbolize the corruption that permeates nature. The poem is a 'Song of Experience,' and the worm is a symbol comparable to the 'tiger' and the 'poison tree.'

If we read the poem through aloud, we note that 'worm' enters into another set of connections. It is heard as stressed and completing the line, as rhyming oddly with storm, as a single element in the long wave of fluctuating stresses, pauses, and sonorities which is never completely broken until the final syllable of the poem.

With almost Miltonic 'labour and difficulty' I have been trying to display the network of connections through which we move while reading a single word in Blake's lyric. The printed word 'worm' stands not for one but for half a dozen or more items of experience: thinking of a rose-worm and a lover and Satan, a blending of sense impressions, the sounds made in reading the word aloud, and so on. More important for the purposes of definition is what we learned by selecting one item and asking what connections we could make with it. In every instance we found a whole set of homogeneous relationships, often extending throughout the poem. The sets may be roughly labeled grammatical, logical, chronological, imaginal, dramatic, metaphorical, and rhythmic. Any such set of homogeneous relationships experienced by the reader is a design. (The list includes all of the types referred to later, except ironic. I shall use the term 'design' only in speaking of these types or in referring to key designs * and total designs. As a matter of convenience I use the term 'pattern' for a set of relationships included within a single design.)

What do we now mean by 'imaginatively organized'? We mean that in reading Blake's words we are impelled to make multiple relationships, which occur in sets or designs. Imaginative organization therefore implies a certain sort of response to words and certain ways of using them, single words frequently being used so as to have multiple significance. Not only 'worm' but many other words in the poem invite responses that are similarly various and similarly ordered. We may call this use of language either poetic or imaginative, the terms being interchangeable in the present discussion. I cannot emphasize too strongly the point that this is a minimal account of imaginative organization, that it serves only as a guide to what we shall be looking for. In later chapters I shall try to extend and refine this basic definition by bringing the reader to a more particular sense of interconnection in a number of different works.

Imaginative organization is certainly not limited to short works of literature in verse, as much of this book will attempt to prove: in 'the fields of light' the distinction between prose and verse is a minor one. Multiple response to words and perception of design is not peculiar to our reading of verse or of literature composed in one of the conventionally recognized forms. The *Decline and Fall of the Roman Empire* is not without a high degree of imaginative order, although it is a rarity among historical works written in English. But admittedly we more often find a high degree of imaginative organization in works of 'literature' than in other sorts of writing. Nor are there uses of language or designs that are intrinsically nonpoetic. Blake's poem has its logical and chronological designs as well as metaphorical and rhythmical ones.

We can, however, distinguish between degrees of imaginative organization. A crude example may be helpful in bringing out this distinction. Set beside 'The Sick Rose' the words of a gardener to his helper:

> This rose is diseased. The petals have been eaten by a flying worm, which is killing it.

* See chapter III.

If we look for interconnection here of the sort we found in Blake's lyric, we can easily point out similar sets of grammatical, logical, and chronological relationships for 'worm,' and we may also record our awareness that 'worm' is a stressed sound in a series of sounds making up a sentence. But if we look for other and further connections, nothing happens. 'Worm' can be read as the flying pest that eats the rose; and that is all. Neither the helper nor anyone else will be tempted to take 'worm' as an airplane or a gangster, to mention two possibilities less remote than Satan or a passionate lover. If we are given to image making, we may have a visual or aural response to 'flying,' but we cannot find any verbal hints of other related images. Certain types of multiple significance and design—imaginal, metaphorical, dramatic—are almost entirely wanting. There is of course little complexity in sound design.

We can now make a rough though critically useful distinction between degrees of imaginative organization. Note first that to call the gardener's statement less imaginative, is not to say that it is unimaginative. For the primary sense of imagination implied in my use of the adjective is any activity by which we make relationships among experiences. The gardener's statement represents as bold an imaginative leap as any single connection made by Blake. He recognizes and expresses the link between 'diseased' and 'eaten petals' and 'flying worm,' a jump involving perceptions, analogies, and inferences as difficult to explain as those by which Blake moved from 'worm' as rose-worm to 'worm' as evil, to a love that is destruction and death. But the gardener is interested in only one kind of connection because he is thinking and speaking in a certain situation, in what Valéry calls 'the practical universe of ends.' His statement is a direction to do something about this 'sick rose.' Relevant action for him is not multiple, but single: 'Reach for the flying-worm spray.' His talk, to give it a proper name, is technological.

Discourse of this type is less imaginative because in reading it we make fewer sorts of relationship than in reading the type of discourse of which Blake's poem is a fair sample. There are, to be sure, pieces of technological prose in which the reader may discover almost every design except metrical. A passage from a physics text describing the structure of the atom may present us with an exceedingly complex metaphor. But we rarely find—or we should be very disturbed if we did—statements that offer a blend of three or four metaphorical meanings at once. Still more rarely, if ever, do we encounter technological discourse in which a complex metaphor is combined with equally complex imaginal, dramatic, and rhythmic relationships. If we do—and accounts of exploration offer examples—we say, 'This is *literature.*'

For when we encounter such rich combinations of design, something remarkable takes place, something very nearly inexpressible. In any account of imaginative organization, we must finally stress the wonderful and mysterious experience of almost simultaneously perceiving many sets of relationships. The reader, at the center of the expanding web,

> Feels at each thread, and lives along the line.

Blake's poem *as read* is not the sum of my list of different designs. The vivid response to the total design they compose needs a special name: at the risk of being misunderstood, I am calling this response the 'total attitude' expressed by the poem.

As we read Blake's lyric from beginning to end, we experience the growing inter-relationship of designs which builds up the total design of the poem. Our qualitative registering of this order is the total attitude, or evaluation, or sense of life, which the poem communicates. For the reader of 'The Sick Rose' it is a finely structured sense of evil in created nature, of evil as passionate immediacy and dramatic discovery, of evil sensuously imaged and heard in spoken words. The total attitude in this or any poem is not the cream of emotion skimmed from the describable structure; and though it can be fully comprehended only at the end, it is not found waiting there like the pot of gold at the end of a poetic rainbow, a beatific reward for good reading. The total attitude has been growing all along as a constant overtone to the musical progression of the work; or, if it has not, we are left with vacancy or fragmentary echoes. Nor is the attitude to be confused with the set of adjectives by which we remind ourselves of its character before consigning it to some Proustian vase of memory. It is the complex feel of evolving, finally completed relationships and absolutely inseparable from our perception of them through the poet's language. Without this 'body' the attitude is 'some lovely glorious nothing,' unballasted because undefined.

The experience of poetry that goes by the name of attitude can never be adequately described to another person. In trying to define the sense of evil-in-created-beauty expressed by 'The Sick Rose,' I was limited to a few inept gestures. For the only complete description of the attitude conveyed by a poem is the poem itself. It is the prime function of poetry to communicate such complex evaluations.

What can the reader do if he wants to be more certain that he has grasped the attitude, or if he wants to lead someone else to discover what he has himself experienced? He can begin by looking for and pointing out the designs to which every reader of the poem must respond and through which alone the poet's peculiar sense of life can be registered. Design as experienced, as 'felt in the blood and felt along the heart,' cannot be directly communicated. (There is of course no direct communication of any experience.) But if users of the same language have some common responses to words and to things, a useful description of a design can be made.

We can never convey completely the felt quality of a design, but we can outline the configuration of relationships to which we respond. We can select words, name the items of experience they stand for, and by observing the infinitely subtle indications of grammatical inflection and word order, define the connections among the items. To explain exactly how we arrive at the description of a design lies beyond my aims as a practical critic, but the coming chapters will show, I believe, that we can describe designs with some success and lead others to share with us the sense of life conveyed by a work of literature.

I have referred indirectly to the two basic methods mentioned near the beginning of this chapter. To select words, to observe inflectional signs and the order of words, and to name the items of experience symbolized by words are all steps in defining by context. The second method, comparison of expressions, is implied in the remark about defining connections among items. The use of both methods was illustrated in the outline of designs in 'The Sick Rose,' though no definition of any word was summarized, and though no overt comparisons were necessary. In tracing various lines of relationship I was continually defining the word 'worm' by its context. The whole description of designs might be regarded as a full—I hope not fulsome—definition by context of a single word.

I began with the word as a printed symbol, noting its spelling and position in relation to the spelling and position of other printed words. I defined the word first as a sign within a grammatical and rhetorical unit, within its verbal context. 'Worm' was defined as the subject of 'has found'; it was also defined as part of an address to a Rose. All definition by context begins by observing the spellings and arrangements of words and the grammatical and rhetorical relationships so expressed. The word is always being defined in some limited verbal context; the limited context may be a phrase, a line, a sentence, a paragraph, any unit whatever, even the complete text of the work that is being read. In Jane Austen's *Mansfield Park* the word 'decorum' can be fully defined only from the whole novel.

But we did not read 'worm' merely as a grammatical and rhetorical sign. Once we thought of 'worm' as in a statement to a rose, we made a selection from one of the areas of remembered experience that 'worm' might represent. We may call such an area a 'non-verbal context'; and we may use the term 'meaning' for the selection made from such an area. In this instance the non-verbal context was rose gardening (as Wilde's Reverend Chasuble might say); and we gave 'worm' the meaning 'worm that has eaten into a rose.' But we gave it a meaning compatible with the arrangements of the verbal context. We could not think of the rose as attacking the worm, or of the worm as a screw in an automatic stoker!

As we took in other parts of the verbal context and attended to increasingly larger units, our definition became limited in various ways. Reading '*invisible* worm . . . has found,' we drew on another non-verbal context, one of phantasy and spiritual powers. Or reading 'invisible worm . . . has found out *thy bed,*' we adjusted our meaning to include human amorous connotations. Being resourceful readers, we drew in just as much as we dared from each of the additional areas subtended by the various word groups. But we were careful to regulate our selection precisely by all the subtle arrangements * of the verbal context. Full definition by context is a report of resourceful and

* We use such terms as 'grammatical,' 'rhetorical,' and 'metrical' to label these arrangements; but often we have no general term for the particular *compositio verborum* (!) that guides our choice of meaning.

accurate reading such as I have been describing. The chief novelty and value of the method lies in the completeness and the rigor exhibited in making particular definitions. Whether or not the method is novel and valuable as a critical tool can be judged from later chapters.

We traced designs in Blake's poem largely through defining a single key term. But the definition could not have been made, nor the designs brought out, without our also making some simple comparisons. We defined the sensuous meaning of 'worm' through grouping and comparing images of color and movement, and in this way we outlined the imaginal design of the poem. In later chapters I refer to this kind of comparison as tracing of continuities. In tracing a continuity we look for a series of expressions each of which evokes a similar response. The recurrent similarity, or continuity, may be of any sort that is definable, from a likeness of sound or word order to the most subtle analogies of meaning. In 'The Sick Rose,' a miniature continuity may be seen in the series, 'night . . . crimson . . . dark,' in which each expression conveys an impression of evil darkness. Although the repetition of a word produces a continuity of sound, such a continuity is of little importance unless the word also expresses some similar meaning in each of its recurrences. It is true that we often trace continuities of meaning in the repetition of a word or its etymological and inflectional cognates, but obviously the repetition of the same word does not entail the recurrence of a similar meaning.

We must always recall as vividly as possible the group of expressions to which a continuity refers and the analysis by which it was defined: a continuity has no life of its own, no spurious concreteness. To speak of the 'earth' continuity in *The Tempest* is to say that a series of expressions in the play ('earth,' 'earthy,' 'earthly,' 'filthy,' 'Caliban,' et cetera) share some similar meaning: each carries the connotation of primitive, non-human earthiness. But we find a similarity in the whole group only if we grasp a variant of the common meaning in each expression when taken within its local context. To grasp is to read with a lively awareness of what is being and has been said. When we read

What ho! slave! Caliban!
Thou earth, thou! speak . . .

we get the primitive sense of 'earth' only if we bear in mind that Caliban's mother was guilty of 'sorceries terrible / To enter human hearing,' that Miranda has just spoken of him as a 'villain,' that he is presently called a 'tortoise' and addressed as a 'poisonous slave, got by the devil himself.' It is easy to see that 'earthy' in 'earthy and abhorr'd commands' (as used of Sycorax) expresses like 'earth' a sense of less than human earthiness. Once this significance gets attached to 'earth' and 'Caliban,' it colors our reading of later occurrences of these words and their cognates, as for example 'earthly' in Caliban's 'the liquor is not earthly.' But there would be no carry-over unless, as here, later contexts prove that the earlier meaning has relevance. The continuity *cannot* be traced in

> this lord of weak remembrance, this
> Who shall be of as little memory
> When he is earth'd . . .

It is perhaps now painfully obvious that both of the basic methods are inseparable from the aims outlined earlier in the chapter. To be concerned with finding designs of imaginative organization is to be concerned primarily with defining the meaning * of words in literature and with showing their relationships with meanings of other words. For the interconnection, the variety and extensiveness of design that characterizes imaginative literature are experienced in response to words used with multiple significance. If we are trying to uncover lines of relation in our reading of literature, we must start with the single word in its local verbal context, fully define its meaning, and move on to look for and compare meanings that arise from other verbal contexts. So we may progress toward the discovery and description of the designs that mainly shape the growing evaluation, the total attitude which we want to enjoy more fully and make more easily accessible to other readers. As critics we descend to details of

* In defining a grammatical design we may temporarily regard the words solely as signs of grammatical connection; but in any complete interpretation we are concerned with grammatical relationships as a step toward fixing meanings and their relationships. In analysis of sound design, we are pointing out relationships among perceived sounds or between perceived sounds and meanings. (See chapter v.)

language in an effort to communicate our awareness of the full order of a work of literature.

The critic of literature like the critic of painting must direct us to the medium if he wishes us to share adequately his experience of a particular work. But while insisting on the necessity of descending to details, I am not overlooking the value of initial intuitions of connection or significance. They are both precious and deceptive. Hunches about how experience hangs together are necessary to any successful intellectual activity, whether in science or poetry, or in criticism, which lies somewhere between the other two. The Scylla and Charybdis for the literary critic are well represented by Caroline Spurgeon's catalogues of Shakespearean images and G. Wilson Knight's unerring insights into Shakespeare's integrity. Miss Spurgeon, by classifying images as though they were fixed units of meaning, finds on inspection certain patterns of emphasis. But the completely objective value she often assigns to the patterns is spurious, since the relation between the pattern and the dramatic sequence is not demonstrated or else not demonstrable. By contrast Professor Knight, who, as Miss Spurgeon sees, sometimes trusts intuitions where they are unreliable, bases much of his criticism on direct perceptions of the total dramatic effect or of metaphysical truths it projects. At his best, as in parts of *The Shakespearian Tempest,* he directs us to the variant expressions through which the metaphysical meaning is expressed.

The critic's visions may be as fantastic as 'black vesper's pageants'—and often they must seem so—but his mediation will often be simplicity itself. Like the cloud gazer, he must show others how he sees

> a pendant rock,
> A forked mountain, or blue promontory
> With trees upon't . . .

He must descend long enough to point out 'this long bar of cloud' and 'that darker mass' and to locate and relate them in space—that is, if he wants to share his visions and be regarded as sane. Although the literary critic has an enormous advantage over grammarians of clouds, who must rely on a meager language of forms and lights, his interpretation when most successful will often seem equally naïve.

For he is always translating the unfamiliar into the familiar and the complex into the simple. He may, for instance, quote a word and note its recurrence or its echo in a cognate. He may explain a grammatical relation, he may isolate the two halves of an analogy or group expressions which are scattered widely in the text. I believe that readers of the later chapters will see that such simple activities may lead to the discovery of imaginative patterns that are far from simple.

Part One

THE DISCOVERY OF DESIGN

Chapter I

THE SPEAKING VOICE

---

*Everything written is as good as it is dramatic. . . A dramatic necessity goes deep into the nature of the sentence. Sentences are not different enough to hold the attention unless they are dramatic. No ingenuity of varying structure will do. All that can save them is the speaking tone of voice somehow entangled in the words and fastened to the page for the ear of the imagination. That is all that can save poetry from sing-song, all that can save prose from itself.**

ROBERT FROST

I. The Speaker

Every poem is 'dramatic' in Frost's sense: someone is speaking to someone else. For a poem is a dramatic fiction no less than a play, and its speaker, like a character in a play, is no less a creation of the words on the printed page. The 'person spoken to' is also a fictional personage and never the actual audience of 'you and me,' and only in a special abstract sense is it the literary audience of a particular time and place in history. The voice we hear in a lyric, however piercingly real, is not Keats's or Shakespeare's; or, if it seems to be, as in

the fancy cannot cheat so well
As she is fam'd to do, deceiving elf

we are embarrassed and thrown off as if an actor had stopped and spoken to the audience in his own person. As Keats once remarked of men's lives, poems are 'continual allegories'; and if they have

* From the Introduction to 'A Way Out.'

biographical meaning it is at least one remove from the actual man who wrote. For the poet is always wrapping himself up in some guise, if only the guise of being a poet.

Shelley in the 'Ode to the West Wind' appears in his familiar character of priest-poet-prophet,' as his language everywhere reminds us. From the opening 'O' through the 'thous' and the 'oh, hears!' which follow, we are spectators of a religious drama, a rite that moves from prayerful incantation to a demand for mystic union and the gift of poetic prophecy. The priest prays in the language of litany, enumerating the powers of the wind spirit:

O thou,
Who chariotest to their dark wintry bed
The wingèd seeds . . .

Thou who didst waken from his summer dreams
The blue Mediterranean . . .

Thou
For whose path the Atlantic's level powers
Cleave themselves into chasms . . .

Be thou, Spirit fierce,
My spirit!

At one point,

I fall upon the thorns of life! I bleed!

the dramatic fiction slips disturbingly: the allegory refers us too directly to Shelley's biography. But it is only after the poem's high commotion is past that we feel the lapse, so compelling is the dramatic incantation of this verse. That Shelley takes us with him so completely, securing assent for what we may later reject, is largely due to this constant shaping of a role through the detail of his expression.

Shelley is of course creating not one character but two, and a whole set of relations between them—in short a complete dramatic situation. The situation, more closely regarded, is a series of swiftly changing situations, which gives the sense of dramatic movement already noted above. We must not confuse the full dramatic situation of this or any poem with the mere setting or scene, though one is always implied, if only the 'setting' of the poet's mind. The setting in Shelley's poem, for instance, is little more than the earth and sky. A comparable poem by Robert Frost will remind us even more forcibly that the dramatic situation is the relationship of fictional speaker and auditor 'entangled in the words' and not the physical scene, however vividly realized:

ONCE BY THE PACIFIC

The shattered water made a misty din.
Great waves looked over others coming in,
And thought of doing something to the shore
That water never did to land before.
The clouds were low and hairy in the skies,
Like locks blown forward in the gleam of eyes.
You could not tell, and yet it looked as if
The shore was lucky in being backed by cliff,
The cliff in being backed by continent;
It looked as if a night of dark intent
Was coming, and not only a night, an age.
Someone had better be prepared for rage.
There would be more than ocean-water broken
Before God's last *Put out the Light* was spoken.

The blend of crashing sounds and stormy lights, the felt counter-thrusts of land and water, the terror of the night of wrath are so present to us in reading 'Once by the Pacific' that we may easily over-look the dramatic artifice of the poem. But though unobtrusive it is not unimportant, for to experience such a vision through Frost's special 'voice' makes all the difference. Strictly speaking the situation is not that of the watcher by the sea, but (as indicated by the tenses) that of the reminiscent poet speaking after the event to no one in particular or to a receptive listening self. The speaker has a character of complete definiteness, which is why the poem is so *palpable* when read aloud. His character takes its distinctive form and pressure from the speculative way of talking, from the flow and arrest of American speech:

> You could not tell, and yet it looked as if

and again,

> It looked as if . . .

But this reckoning voice has other strains sounding through it—pronouncements of the Old Testament, talk about the end of the world, and echoes of older mythological styles. There may even be a reminiscence of Shelley's maenad in those clouds

> Like locks blown forward in the gleam of eyes.

II. Tone

As I have just been illustrating, to show exactly *who* is speaking in a poem it is necessary to consider *how* he speaks. In other words, it is necessary to define his tone. By tone I refer to: (1) the implied social relationship of the speaker to his auditor and (2) the manner he adopts in addressing his auditor. Whether we talk in terms of 'tone' or of 'dramatic situation' indicates that we are considering expressions for different purposes or considering different expressions. In 'Once by the Pacific,' the phrase 'you could not tell' may be regarded as defining both dramatic situation and tone; the past tenses, on the other hand, are primarily effective in fixing the situation.

It is important to remember that when we speak of the dramatic situation, we are thinking of all the relations implied between the fictional speaker and auditor in a poem, any connection one has with the other. In many poems, as in 'Once by the Pacific,' the main connection implied is that the second is listening to the first. In others, for example Browning's monologues, there are hints of a complicated history of loves and hates or of subtler attractions and aversions, the makings of a play or novel. Under the first aspect of tone I refer to a single relation within the whole dramatic complex, the *social* relation, where in the social hierarchy the fictional speaker and auditor stand. To take random examples, they may be lover and beloved, brother and sister, man and wife, servant and master. Under the second aspect of tone I refer to the *manner* the speaker adopts within this social relationship. The lover may speak in a manner more or less intimate, formal, casual, heroic, chivalric, et cetera.

Frost's control of this aspect of tone is where he shows his art most fully. He succeeds in maintaining a wonderful blend of manners, a poise between two voices, the high-poetic-apocalyptic and the down-to-earth, cautiously speculative. This nice duplicity appears in the word 'din' at the end of the first line, where we are almost ready for a grander word—almost, because the subtle exaggeration of 'shattered' points the way to a less simple form of expression. Those solemn 'great waves . . . thought of doing something to the shore' ('I'll do something to you'—a voice in a very human quarrel); and the Shelleyesque 'locks' were oddly enough 'low and hairy in the skies.' By these and similar touches Frost prepares us for the climactic last line with its stroke of parody across the solemnity of *Fiat lux*.

While describing the special blend of manners in 'Once by the Pacific,' we have introduced an important principle in the analysis of tone. We evaluated Frost's tone by making more or less overt comparisons with the high-poetic-apocalyptic style and everyday speech of reckoning. Our recognition of a manner always depends on a silent reference to a known way of speaking and on our perceiving variations from it. The poet—Frost notably in the poem we have been reading—relies on such norms and on our familiarity with them. The implied norm may be as vaguely definable as everyday speech or as relatively fixed as the idiom of eighteenth-century heroic poetry. Certainly our finest perception of a norm and of variations from it lies beyond our powers of expression. To define even one level of speech precisely would require an elaborate excursion in literary and social history. But without attempting so monstrous a task we can make helpful indications of a norm and so place the tonal level. We can point out an allusion or show how a phrase in the immediate context recalls some larger context and with it certain conventions of speech; we can quote comparable expressions from other pieces of literature or from any realm of discourse whatsoever. Once a norm has been indicated, the cruder variations are evident, but to define subtle variations from a literary manner is certainly a less simple assignment. Literary critics have the pleasant task of making such measurements.

I am hardly suggesting that the delineation of tone can be reduced to a single formula to be applied on any and all occasions. The application and choice of methods must be at least as flexible as the poet's manipulation of tone. In the two examples that follow I shall stress the usefulness of following certain grammatical and rhetorical cues in assaying the tone of a poem, but I shall also use other methods, including those just outlined.

The poems for analysis are two sonnets, John Donne's 'Show me deare Christ, thy spouse, so bright and clear' and Gerard Manley Hopkins' 'Thou art indeed just, Lord, if I contend.' Since the poems have similar situations, comparison will show more clearly what we mean by tonal pattern and how differences in tonal pattern are expressive of differences in attitude.

Both Donne and Hopkins appear as devout Christians addressing the Deity; both are puzzled by a religious problem; and both ask for a solution. But the relation in which each stands to God and the manner in which each addresses God are utterly different. Here is how Donne poses his problem:

> Show me deare Christ, thy spouse, so bright and clear.
> What! is it She, which on the other shore
> Goes richly painted? or which rob'd and tore
> Laments and mournes in Germany and here?
> Sleepes she a thousand, then peepes up one yeare?
> Is she selfe truth and errs? now new, now outwore?
> Doth she, and did she, and shall she evermore
> On one, on seaven, or on no hill appeare?
> Dwells she with us, or like adventuring knights
> First travaile we to seeke and then make Love?
> Betray kind husband thy spouse to our sights
> And let myne amorous soule court thy mild Dove,
> Who is most trew, and pleasing to thee, then
> When she'is embrac'd and open to most men.

Donne is speaking within the seventeenth-century religious situation, as one familiar with all the historic varieties of the Christian Church.

What is distinctive and surprising is the tone this theologian-controversialist assumes in talking with God. While approaching Christ in his consecrated role as the bridegroom of the Church, Donne talks as a man of the world in pursuit of a beautiful woman, and his manner combines worldly politeness with downright insolence. Let us see how his tone is defined through the language of the poem.

'Show me, deare Christ, thy spouse . . .' Donne begins with a bold command and an affectionate though polite address. (Verb forms, whether personal or impersonal, and forms of address are worth noting as cues to tone.) He uses 'thy,' which as Grierson observes is in Donne 'the pronoun of feeling and intimacy.' Both the intimacy and directness of the wooer appear again in the offhand, impatient 'What!' of the first of his questions. Although the tone now becomes less personal, the 'she's,' the unflattering adjectives, and above all 'peepes' recall the freedom of the opening command. But balance is maintained by the literary elegance and chivalrous sophistication of

> Dwells she with us, or like adventuring knights
> First travaile we to seeke and then make Love?

The lover is making just the right gesture of removal in view of his next request:

> Betray kind husband thy spouse to our sights
> And let myne amorous soule court thy mild Dove . . .

He has advanced from 'deare Christ' to 'husband' and 'kind husband,' at that! With the erotic pun of the final line of the sonnet, decency (in an eighteenth-century sense) is abandoned. But not quite, because of the knightly decorum of the immensely beautiful 'let myne amorous soule court thy mild Dove.' (Note the politeness indicated by using 'my soule' rather than the more personal 'me.') Though there is a progress in insolence, equilibrium is never quite lost throughout the whole poem.

If we consider similar cues in Hopkins' sonnet, especially forms of address and the persons of verbs, we shall find great differences in the tone assumed by each poet and in the over-all management of tone:

Justus quidem tu es, Domine, si disputem tecum:
verumtamen justa loquar ad te: Quare via impiorum
prosperatur? etc.

Thou art indeed just, Lord, if I contend
With thee; but, sir, so what I plead is just.
Why do sinners' ways prosper? and why must
Disappointment all I endeavour end?
  Wert thou my enemy, O thou my friend,
How wouldst thou worse, I wonder, than thou dost
Defeat, thwart me? Oh, the sots and thralls of lust
Do in spare hours more thrive than I that spend,
Sir, life upon thy cause. See, banks and brakes
Now, leavèd how thick! lacèd they are again
With fretty chervil, look, and fresh wind shakes
Them; birds build—but not I build; no, but strain,
Time's eunuch, and not breed one work that wakes.
Mine, O thou lord of life, send my roots rain.

The dramatic situation at the beginning of the poem, as indicated by the Latin quotation and by Hopkins' adaptation ('contends,' 'plead,' 'just') is a legal debate in which the plaintiff puts his case before the Lord (notice the capital letter). The value of the opening 'thou' as compared with Donne's use of the pronoun is changed completely. The seventeenth-century convention no longer holds because, among other reasons, the seventeenth-century 'amorous' relationship of worshipper and deity no longer holds. There are no loving graces to temper the dignity of 'thou' in Hopkins' line:

Thou art indeed just, Lord, if I contend . . .

Yet if judged by Victorian standards Hopkins has his insolence too: he 'sirs' the Lord, which is respectful though not quite worshipful. (His insolence may be further measured by comparing Auden's brash echo, 'Sir, no man's enemy.')

After the debate of the first four lines the tone moves with swift jumps and backward turnings to a conclusion which is as right as it is surprising. Asides break in with a poignant and unexpected intimacy:

> Wert thou my enemy, O thou my friend,
> How wouldst thou worse, I wonder, than thou dost
> Defeat, thwart me?

As the questions shift from impersonal forms to the accusing 'thous,' the pleader sacrifices dignity, though he recovers it for a moment in 'I that spend, / *Sir,* life upon thy *cause.*' A burst of springtime imagery marks a new situation and a completely new tone:

> See, banks and brakes
> Now, leavèd how thick! lacèd they are again
> With fretty chervil, look . . .

'See' is less to the Lord than to the poet's wondering self, while 'look' is only an inward noting of the puzzling fact. Hence the sudden force of the real imperative in 'send my roots rain.' For this demand the address, 'O thou lord of life,' is beautifully right. Debating decorum is forgotten, questionings and asides are dropped as Hopkins calls directly on God for help. He calls him 'lord,' not 'Lord,' yet with a new accent of awe perfectly in harmony with the metaphor which has been growing since early in the poem. The bitter and sweet contrast of his own straining barrenness and the thick, building liveliness of created things presses in our ears with 'O thou lord of life, send my roots rain.'

Both of these poems show that tone is fixed and so revealed at similar points in expression, and both show how pervasive the control of tone may be. But they differ enormously in the relationships implied, in the manner which each poet assumes, and in what may be called the total tonal pattern. Although Donne combines politeness and candor, throughout the sonnet he is shaping a voice of consistent, stable character. But Hopkins in his alternations of tone expresses a confusion of tongues: how is he to speak? He finds a way at last, but, as the sequence shows, the victory is hardly won and perhaps only temporary. We have in these contrasting patterns clear symbols of the religious attitudes being expressed by the two poets: Donne, for all his queries, certain of his close and passionate relation to Christ; Hopkins, tortured at the very center of his faith.

We shall next consider a religious poem that shows a further complexity of tonal pattern and another sort of relationship between this pattern and the attitude finally expressed:

LOVE

Love bade me welcome: yet my soul drew back,
Guiltie of dust and sinne.
But quick-ey'd Love, observing me grow slack
From my first entrance in,
Drew nearer to me, sweetly questioning,
If I lack'd any thing.

A guest, I answer'd, worthy to be here:
Love said, you shall be he.
I the unkinde, ungratefull? Ah my deare,
I cannot look on thee.
Love took my hand, and smiling did reply,
Who made the eyes but I?

Truth Lord, but I have marr'd them: let my shame
Go where it doth deserve.
And know you not, sayes Love, who bore the blame?
My deare, then I will serve.
You must sit down, sayes Love, and taste my meat:
So I did sit and eat.

GEORGE HERBERT

There are two situations here, the story-teller's and that of the drama he narrates; and within the drama there are the distinct and exactly complementary tones of the guest and of Love. In a tone of almost feminine intimacy the guest carries on sweet converse with the gently humorous host:

Ah my deare,
I cannot look on thee. . .
My deare, then I will serve.

He is the humblest of guests and sinners, not 'worthy to be here,' 'unkinde, ungratefull.' Love's accent is questioning, not accusing; her grammatical mood is imperative not in its brusque form, but softened with 'you' and 'shall' and 'must.' Hers is sweet questioning and sweet commanding.

The manner in which the guest-sinner tells the story needs a different description. The narrator does not speak to anyone; he merely tells what was said and done, rarely noting a look or a gesture and making hardly any comment on his own reactions. His statements, unobtrusively balanced in form, could be written as prose, with only one or two changes in order. As the story * goes on, it approaches the level of naïve colloquial narrative: 'I answer'd . . . Love said . . . sayes Love . . . sayes Love.'

We must consider now what is the effect in the complete poem of this trio of tones—the reserved decently colloquial manner of the narrator and within the story the intimate, deprecatory voice of the guest and the exquisite politeness and assurance of the host. Regarded as a whole the poem is a little drama of conversion. A sinner conscious of his guilt, feeling the pull of Christ's love ('Ah my deare') but unable to accept it, rediscovers the meaning of Christ's sacrifice and is redeemed. In relation to this sequence, the reserve of the telling becomes extreme: the full reversal of feelings at the climax is indicated only by a colon:

> You must sit down, sayes Love, and taste my meat:
> So I did sit and eat.

The restraint, the intimacy, and sweet politeness bring out by contrast the conflict and resolution which is so quietly presented. Hence the surprising tension and strength of a seemingly gentle poem.

When reading Herbert's lyric, we do not experience tension in the abstract; we hear the drama through the voice—or voices—which we have been describing. Our whole aim in analysis of tone is to delineate the exact speaking voice in every poem we read, but we can succeed only by attending to the special, often minute language signs by which the poet fixes the tone for us. The methods used in this chapter are intended to direct attention to a few of the com-

* I have not attempted here or later to treat story or narrative as a completely separate type of design, since I regard narrative as one of the patterns that make up dramatic design. As the example above shows, statements in a work of literature of what someone says or does (pure narrative statements) are always expressive of a dramatic relationship.

moner signs and to offer some questions that we may put to a poem in determining its tone. By answering questions such as 'What is the social relationship implied?' or 'What is the writer's manner?' we may clarify and express the set of relations which project the tone of the poet-speaker, and which taken together may be regarded as a tonal pattern.

As the tonal relations change—and they must in a living poem—they take their place in the sequence of relations we have called the dramatic movement, the succession of changing dramatic situations. All of these ordered relations together make up the dramatic design of a poem.

Chapter II

THE AURA AROUND A BRIGHT CLEAR CENTRE

. . . we are inclined to infer that the suggestiveness is the aura around a bright clear centre, that you cannot have the aura alone.

T. S. ELIOT

I. Toward the Analysis of Attitude

No poet creates a dramatic design as an end in itself: the dramatic design is expressive and has its main value in helping to shape the total attitude being communicated. Donne's 'courtship' with its controlled license of tone expresses his curiously passionate reverence, the combination perfectly symbolized in 'thy mild Dove,' the one striking metaphor in the poem. In Herbert's 'Love,' the gentle resolution of a deep conflict is expressed through a contrast between tones and the implied inner action of the drama.

In general a single word that seems primarily to fix a certain tone inevitably carries some shade of feeling. An expression that marks a shift in tone marks also a shift in attitude, as in the poignant contrast of 'O thou my friend' coming after 'Lord' and 'sir' in Hopkins' sonnet. Words in poetry, like social gestures, carry at once several kinds of significance, the interpretation varying with the attention of the observer. A bow in the street may be read as a bit of conventional politeness (a matter of tone) or a subtle insult (a matter of attitude). But attitude is being used here in a more limited sense than in the earlier references to total attitude and evaluation. It is clear from our talk about dramatic movement and changes of tone that the total attitude in a poem must be made up of many related attitudes. In every line and phrase the poet is conveying some sense of experience, and we are registering it. I shall frequently use the term for any single feeling that goes to build up the total attitude.

But we cannot truly experience attitudes or describe them with accuracy except through the discovery of design. We can get the main feeling from a cursory reading and hit it off in a sentence, but the result is not very satisfactory as an account of a complex poem. We might say that the main feeling communicated in 'Once by the Pacific' is obvious: we feel the threatening wrath of an oncoming storm. But if we are to suggest the quality of this particular storm vision, we must point to the gigantic half-human picture of waves peering over one another's heads; we must also add that the vision is not solemnly eschatological, since there is wit in the parody of *Fiat lux* and irony in the contrast between the sense of doom and the colloquial tone of the prophet. Unlike Shelley, Frost has taken one step backward from disaster, which he regards with something of a weather eye.

It would be just as unsatisfactory to sum up in one sentence the attitude expressed in 'Thou art indeed just, Lord, if I contend': The poet is conveying a sense of his own sterility as contrasted with the fruitfulness of sinners and natural creatures. But the attitudes expressed in the sonnet are as varied as the tones. In the final line,

> Mine, O thou lord of life, send my roots rain

the feeling like the tone is new. We can define the exact note of passionate desire in Hopkins' poem only by following the thread of image and metaphor that moves from the abstractness of

> Why do sinners' ways prosper?

to the morning freshness of

> See, banks and brakes
> Now, leavèd how thick!

As our experience with these two poems proves, the way to arrive at an adequate critical remark is the way of good reading. Instead of equating either poem with the first 'big emotion' we struck or with a paraphrase of the main idea, we looked rather closely at the poet's words and the relationships created through them. We moved on from our account of tonal patterns to the analysis of image, metaphor, and irony. Of course no one should miss the big emotion or the main idea in reading any poem. But if our reading ends at either of these way stations, we may be enjoying a stock experience instead of the one offered by the poem before us. We may be reading Frost's sonnet as though it were written by a second Shelley.

Some readers will feel that in insisting on the discovery of attitude through tracing design, I am overlooking the most poetic of all languages, the language of feeling. What about emotive adjectives and adverbs or abstracts of quality or names for emotions and feelings of every sort? Poets certainly use them to convey feeling, and only a very odd reader would overlook the fact that in some poems we learn through such expressions what we are to feel. But we need not conclude that they are mysteriously direct conveyors of emotion, much less that they will be effective in isolation. In one of the briefer lyrics of 'In Memoriam,' Tennyson uses the adjective 'calm' no less than eleven times; but to learn this curious fact apart from seeing the text is to understand nothing:

Calm is the morn without a sound,
  Calm as to suit a calmer grief,
  And only thro' the faded leaf
The chestnut pattering to the ground:

Calm and deep peace on this high wold,
  And on these dews that drench the furze,
  And all the silvery gossamers
That twinkle into green and gold:

Calm and still light on yon great plain
  That sweeps with all its autumn bowers,
  And crowded farms and lessening towers,
To mingle with the bounding main:

Calm and deep peace in this wide air,
  These leaves that redden to the fall;
  And in my heart, if calm at all,
If any calm, a calm despair:

Calm on the seas, and silver sleep,
    And waves that sway themselves in rest,
    And dead calm in that noble breast
Which heaves but with the heaving deep.

In the first four stanzas of the poem Tennyson succeeds completely in expressing the 'calm' of a morning that might 'suit a calmer grief.' The repetitions of 'calm,' taken by themselves, would induce only a ready-made attitude, the calm of grief appropriate to 'In Memoriam.' But Tennyson has exquisitely defined the quality of this morning by images of sound and light and color. This autumnal calm is fixed for us in the 'pattering' chestnut, in the jewel-like gossamers, in the leaf reddening *to* the fall (but not falling)—details suggesting the quiet of a morning in which such impressions stand out. In contrast with these minute and intimate particulars are the 'high wold,' the 'wide air,' and 'yon great plain' with its Turneresque blending of landscape and buildings and the sea. Tennyson gives us a sense of spaciousness and remoteness, an aesthetic removal from the object.

The precision with which Tennyson has defined this calm may be measured by the vagueness with which he expresses the calm despair. We respond powerfully with the stock calm-of-death, which we project too easily onto the sea and the 'noble breast.' The calm of the sea is convincingly expressed, but not the calm of despair. We have somehow been cheated: if we are to experience at all precisely this calm despair, dramatic detail is needed, some more specific way of representing what Hallam's death meant for the poet, a way such as Tennyson found in 'Ulysses.'

'Noble,' in 'that noble breast,' shows even more baldly than 'calm' the inadequacy of words of feeling apart from other language that evokes more particular, appropriate experience. As in communication outside poetry, we cannot express our feelings except by pointing to the objects and relationships by which they are occasioned. We respond vaguely to Tennyson's 'noble' because there is no defining detail of any sort. We do not find any more exact meaning for the adjective by referring to the dramatic situation; in fact the nobility Tennyson attributes to Hallam is not quite discoverable from the whole cycle. The adjective is sentimental, not because it is sentimental to call a friend 'noble,' but because of a failure in expression. Tennyson has given us no particular occasion and no analogy. We are just told to feel 'so.'

II. From Imagery to Metaphor

If we are to think of imagery as a way of defining particular attitudes we need to agree on a definition of 'image.' I am limiting my use of the term to two main meanings, one psychological and one rhetorical. The first is the replica in the nervous system of some past sensation, such as hearing a bell when the bell is not in fact ringing. The second is image in the sense of verbal image, that is, a word that for many readers produces a more or less vivid psychological image. As I. A. Richards has pointed out, the types of image (in the psychological sense) are manifold, and there are readers who have little or no experience of images of any kind. We need to remember also that when we speak of this or that image suggested by a word we are describing one of a large class of reactions. There is no inevitable, correct image. The red rose I see and the red rose you see in reading Burns's poem are almost certainly different. In referring to 'a red, red rose' as an image, we mean only that for a good many readers the words excite some visual sensation.

To avoid confusion I have rather heroically excluded image in the sense of metaphor; for an image need not be a metaphor, though it is certainly true that the images that interest us, that are significant in literary design, always have some metaphorical value. In citing any example of a verbal image I am not implying that the expression may not also be metaphorical; I am simply directing attention to one of its meanings, a meaning which may be salient for many readers.

Of poetic language that is limited to the recall of sights, sounds, and other sense impressions, we may well say what Keats once said of mere description: 'it is always bad.' We are liable to think of the variegated landscapes and beflowered gardens of eighteenth-century descriptive verse, in which 'pure description held the place of sense.' Pope's picture of the dying pheasant, from 'Windsor Forest,' is perhaps the most famous of all passages in this style:

See! from the brake the whirring pheasant springs,
And mounts exulting on triumphant wings:
Short is his joy; he feels the fiery wound,
Flutters in blood, and panting beats the ground.
Ah! what avail his glossy, varying dyes,
His purple crest, and scarlet-circled eyes,
The vivid green his shining plumes unfold,
His painted wings, and breast that flames with gold?

Though these exquisite lines are by no means limited to the recall of sights and sounds, they offer some clear examples of verbal images in my sense of the term. 'Whirring' will excite in most readers a distinct auditory image. 'Springs' and 'flutters' evoke primarily sensations of movement and muscular effort, so-called kinesthetic images. 'Purple,' 'scarlet-circled,' and 'green' are obvious examples of visual images. (In referring to these expressions as visual images, or to other expressions as auditory or kinesthetic images, we are of course using shorthand for: an expression that evokes such an image.)

While Pope wisely 'stooped to truth and moralized his song,' Thomson was writing 'The Seasons,' a poem in which passages of pure description alternate rather agreeably with some very solemn sense. The lines on spring flowers are sometimes quoted as an example of 'true' poetry in the eighteenth century:

Along the blushing Borders, bright with Dew,
And in yon mingled Wilderness of Flowers,
Fair-handed Spring unbosoms every Grace:
Throws out the Snow-drop, and the Crocus first;
The Daisy, Primrose, Violet darkly blue,
And Polyanthus of unnumber'd Dyes;
The yellow Wall-Flower, stain'd with iron Brown;
And lavish Stock that scents the Garden round:
From the soft Wing of vernal Breezes shed,
Anemonies: Auriculas, enrich'd
With shining Meal o'er all their velvet Leaves;
And full Renunculas, of glowing Red.
Then comes the Tulip-Race, where Beauty plays
Her idle Freaks: from Family diffus'd
To Family, as flies the Father-Dust,

The varied Colours run; and while they *break*
On the charm'd Eye, th' exulting Florist marks,
With secret Pride, the Wonders of his Hand.
No gradual Bloom is wanting; from the Bud,
First-born of Spring, to Summer's musky Tribes:
Nor Hyacinths, deep-purpled; nor Jonquils,
Of potent Fragrance; nor Narcissus fair,
As o'er the fabled Fountain hanging still;
Nor broad Carnations; nor gay-spotted Pinks;
Nor, shower'd from every Bush, the Damask-rose:
Infinite Numbers, Delicacies, Smells,
With Hues on Hues Expression cannot paint,
The Breath of Nature, and her endless Bloom.

The reader of these lines wanders in a pleasant, faintly amusing stream of almost pure delights of vision, smell, and touch. But they do loosely compose a metaphor—of Spring, and beyond that of the vaguely benign Thomsonian Nature. How loose it is we may see by examining the metaphorical gesture with which the passage opens,

Fair-handed Spring unbosoms every Grace . . .

'Fair-handed' and 'unbosoms' and 'Grace' ought to invite us to look for links in the lines that follow, but they most certainly do not. The lady Spring is overlooked like a piece of garden sculpture, while a lazy, hazy sense of springtime serves to connect almost anything. All of the flowers are of a 'springiness,' even to an American reader who ordinarily does not associate the daisy or wall-flower or stocks with spring. The failure of much eighteenth-century poetry, we might note in passing, is not due to over-generality but to the lack of a metaphorical sense which connects and gives meaning to detail. In this respect eighteenth-century poets and virtuoso scientists have much in common, as the work of the elder Darwin shows.

But once—as in Thomson's lines—we regard images as of something other than the sensations they recall, once, in Mr. Richards' handy definition, 'we perceive or think of or feel about one thing in terms of another,' we have metaphor. So Pope's pheasant images are metaphorical through personification; they are beauties of a dying hero. There is another metaphorical relation, important in much of

Pope's poetry, which is suggested by 'dyes' and 'painted' and even by the accumulation of color words: we are looking at a painting, something after the manner of Chardin. Pope's editors have pointed out that 'painted,' which the poet may have borrowed from Milton or Dryden, is not especially applicable to a pheasant's wings. We may suppose that Pope was not more concerned with biological accuracy than many painters, that he was in fact very much interested in producing a combination of colors which composed well to the eye.

Keats's ode 'To Autumn' may be regarded as the poem that the eighteenth-century describers were trying to write, a living union of their fondness for particulars with a sense of high powers in nature:

To Autumn

Season of mists and mellow fruitfulness,
  Close bosom-friend of the maturing sun;
Conspiring with him how to load and bless
  With fruit the vines that round the thatch-eves run;
To bend with apples the moss'd cottage-trees,
  And fill all fruit with ripeness to the core;
    To swell the gourd, and plump the hazel shells
  With a sweet kernel; to set budding more,
And still more, later flowers for the bees,
Until they think warm days will never cease,
    For summer has o'er-brimm'd their clammy cells.

Who hath not seen thee oft amid thy store?
  Sometimes whoever seeks abroad may find
Thee sitting careless on a granary floor,
  Thy hair soft-lifted by the winnowing wind;
Or on a half-reap'd furrow sound asleep,
  Drows'd with the fume of poppies, while thy hook
    Spares the next swath and all its twined flowers;
And sometimes like a gleaner thou dost keep
  Steady thy laden head across a brook;
  Or by a cyder-press, with patient look,
    Thou watchest the last oozings hours by hours.

Where are the songs of Spring? Ay, where are they?
  Think not of them, thou hast thy music too,—

While barred clouds bloom the soft-dying day,
 And touch the stubble-plains with rosy hue;
Then in a wailful choir the small gnats mourn
 Among the river sallows, borne aloft
  Or sinking as the light wind lives or dies;
And full-grown lambs loud bleat from hilly bourn;
 Hedge-crickets sing; and now with treble soft
 The red-breast whistles from a garden-croft;
  And gathering swallows twitter in the skies.

Study of the imagery of Keats's ode will show how a succession of images, becoming something more than mere succession, imperceptibly blends into metaphor. We shall also discover how groups of images are linked and how imagery works as design. (The method of analysis used is a good example of tracing continuities.)* We may begin by merely noting what Keats gives in the way of images. In the first stanza: we have 'to load and bless,' 'round the thatch-eves run,' 'to bend,' '[to] fill . . . the core,' 'to swell the gourd,' '[to] plump the hazel shells,' 'to set budding,' and 'o'er-brimm'd their clammy cells.' As in his other odes Keats tends to group together images from a single sense; here almost all are tactile-muscular, though there is no good name for the weighing, cupping sensations which we feel distinctly in hand and lips as we read these expressions. Because the sensations are closely related, almost any one image draws in the rest by attraction. 'To fill' becomes also 'to round' and 'to load'; and even words that properly should not have such meanings absorb them. So 'round' in 'round the thatch-eves run' trembles on the brink of meanings with which it has no logical connection. Together all the images of the stanza give rise to an over-meaning, a tactile awareness of fruitioning. In this evocation of a common, though hardly nameable meaning we have the first step from succession of images to metaphor.

The over-meaning in the first stanza of the ode leads insensibly to the central metaphor of the poem, the figure of Autumn. Since we have already lived its powers in our senses, we quite easily accept Autumn as person and divinity. We have also been prepared by the

* See Introduction, pp. 13, 14.

direct address in the opening lines of the poem and by the expressions joining Autumn with the sun, the natural object we most readily deify. Keats has made us feel that they are in the closest possible relationship, that they work together, almost breathe together as a single life-force: in the slow-paced rhythm of the ode we realize the full etymological force of 'conspiring.'

The being so unobtrusively and yet so warmly realized appears in a series of exquisite plastic poses. The images are now mainly visual; they are most often glimpses of arrested movement. Where there is motion, as in 'the winnowing wind,' it is a kind of motion-in-repose, the hair remains 'soft-lifted' as in sculpture. Surely nothing could be nearer complete rest than 'the last oozings hours by hours.' The single image from another sense comes with a slight though muted shock:

> Drows'd with the fume of poppies,

but here too the final effect is of slow motion to sleep. The Autumn metaphor as a whole conveys the sense of tremendous leisure, the great pause, the slowing down of autumnal life.

There is again a slight jar in the shift to another area of sensation—

> Where are the songs of Spring? Ay, where are they?

Against images that recall the mellow richness and the repose of the preceding stanzas (so Keats alludes to what he has been saying), the sounds of autumn arise. They have a peculiar character, which accounts in part for their metaphorical power. Look closely at the language of the autumnal sound images: 'in a wailful choir the *small* gnats *mourn,*' 'aloft or *sinking,*' '*light* wind lives or *dies,*' 'loud bleat *from hilly bourn,*' '*hedge*-crickets sing,' 'treble *soft* . . . whistles *from a garden-croft,*' '*gathering* swallows *twitter in the skies.*' The italics indicate the curious way in which the sounds are qualified. They are to be felt as withdrawing, diminished things. They are soft, mournful, small, or undulating and uncertain (the point of 'aloft or sinking' as colored by 'lives or dies'); or they come from a distance, or they are connected with confined places and with shutting in. This is the linking that counts most as metaphor in the last phase of the poem. To the autumn richness and slowing down Keats adds a sense of closing in and withdrawal, a poignant autumnal note.

Such, very roughly outlined, are the attitudes Keats conveys through his images and especially through the metaphorical patterns in which they merge.

In our reading of Keats's ode we have begun to see how connection through imagery is made. The behavior of these images, the way in which they compose metaphors is quite typical. We note, for example, that the images in the opening stanza of the poem give rise to an over-meaning, a special sense of fruitioning. In the last stanza a similar meaning, one of diminution and withdrawal, grows out of the sound images. These groupings are potent not merely as sets of observed facts, of actual autumn phenomena—which we suppose they are. No, that is the grouping of classifiers for use, of Thomsonian versifiers, and quite different from the fuller alliances of analogy experienced in reading Keats's stanzas. How can we express this difference? A list of flowers with the heading, 'spring-blooming,' implies a crude analogy and composes a metaphor. But the only likeness implied, the only connection we need make in reading the list, is one of time: we recall that the flowers indeed do 'bloom in the spring.' Even Thomson's catalogue—which has its Miltonic complexity of rhythm and allusion—requires little more of us. But though we connect the images in Keats's lines through simple analogies of time and space, we also link them by another sort of analogy, the analogy of sensation. If we respond to Keats's words at all, we must be conscious of qualitative likeness in each of the sense experiences they evoke. Our consciousness of similarity is qualitative in a primitive physiological meaning of the term; it consists, for instance, in felt similarities of muscular tension or release. And we must pass through these special qualifications of sensation if we are to reach the over-meaning. Thomson's grouping, which has its random charm, does not force us to take any such intermediate step. If we look for signs in the language of any peculiar felt character in the successive images, we cannot find them. Keats, and all poets who compose at his level of intensity, connect images for us by this special type of analogy while also expressing other simpler likenesses. They create those fuller alliances of analogy which are the surest sign of imaginative power.

Chapter III

SAYING ONE THING AND MEANING ANOTHER

*Poetry provides the one permissible way of saying one thing and meaning another.**

ROBERT FROST

I. Metaphor

We begin our search for design from a desire to realize and describe the total attitude communicated by a poem. Crudely speaking, we cannot 'get' the attitude except by fully exploring the relationships through which it is expressed. In reading the ode 'To Autumn,' the arrest of growing things at their moment of richest growth, the peculiarly Keatsian sense of this pause, comes to us through the poet's biased linkage of images into a metaphorical design. The analysis of imagery leads to the analysis of metaphor.†

I. A. Richards' definition of metaphor, which we have had in mind during much of our discussion, is in type psychological: thinking of one thing in terms of another, a thing being shorthand for an experience of any object or situation whatsoever. A rhetorical definition might run: any verbal expression which stands for such thinking. To take the most obvious example from Keats's poem, the reader thinks of or experiences the autumn season as a vaguely humanized being. Rhetorically, Keats expresses this analogy in a number of ways, notably through grouping related images of fruitioning, of arrested movement, and of diminishing sounds.

* From 'Education by Poetry.'

† The brief account of metaphor and symbol in this chapter is supplemented by the analysis in chapter v, The Sinewie Thread (on key designs).

Our task in interpreting metaphor is always the same, to isolate and describe the two levels of experience connected through the writer's language. Having done this, we must put them together again and characterize the new experience resulting from the combination, which *is* the metaphor. How we name the two levels does not seem to me very important, providing the names do not get in our way. Certainly most terms in use do. I. A. Richards' 'tenor' and 'vehicle,' though excellent in their freedom from past associations, involve metaphors of carrying and transferring which often prove inappropriate and misleading. Whatever names we invent for the two halves of a metaphor, at times we are sure to want to exchange them: 'tenor' becomes 'vehicle,' and vice versa. I suggest, with not too much confidence, the terms 'subject' * and 'icon.' † I can indicate their application to the two levels by a fairly simple example from the ode 'To Autumn': 'close bosom-friend of the sun.' In the opening line Keats addresses the 'season' (the subject). The subject is not the word, but an awareness of autumn qualified only as a time of 'mists and mellow fruitfulness.' Keats then asks us to think of this 'season' in a peculiar way, as a 'close bosom-friend of the sun' (the icon), that is, as an intimate friend of the sun, so like the sun as to be almost indistinguishable in its working. But it is a 'bosom' friend, which implies sensuous intimacy and fertility; the 'season' becomes a half-feminine sensuously active sun-power. In more general terms, the subject may be defined as the experience which the writer wishes us to think of in terms of a given icon; the icon is that other experience, whatever it may be. Often, but not necessarily, the iconic experience takes the form of an image. I should suppose that 'bosom-friend' has for most readers only a slight image value, if any.

The rhetorical means through which subject and icon are expressed are almost unlimited; there are no consecrated metaphorical

* I owe the term 'subject' to Mr. James I. Merrill, who made use of it in his unpublished honors thesis on Proust, *A la Recherche du temps perdu: Impressionism in Literature* (Amherst College, 1947).

† I have borrowed the term 'icon' from Charles Morris: *Signs, Language, and Behavior* (New York, 1946), pp. 191, 192. My definition of the term has little in common with that of Mr. Morris. I have chosen the term 'icon' in order to avoid the ambiguities of 'image' and, more positively, to denote any experience that might bear some likeness to the subject-experience.

forms. We may have the 'A is B' type of statement, or its equivalent, as in 'season . . . close bosom-friend' or as in the Anglo-Saxon 'sea-road.' Or we may have a simile with 'as,' or 'as' and 'so.' I sometimes refer to these common types as conventional, or explicit, metaphor. Note that in conventional metaphor there is always a brief grammatical unit (compound word, phrase, or sentence) which contains distinct expressions, one naming the icon and the other naming the subject. In the more implicit types of metaphor there is no similar grammatical unit including distinct iconic and subject expressions, and often there is nowhere in the text a brief grammatical unit that names the subject. Nashe's '*brightness* falls from the air' is an excellent example of implicit metaphor. It is impossible to cite a distinct expression for icon and for subject: 'brightness' does duty for both; and there is nowhere in the whole song any brief grammatical unit that names the subject:

Beauty is but a flower
Which wrinkles will devour:
Brightness falls from the air,
Queens have died young and fair,
Dust hath closed Helen's eye.
I am sick, I must die.
    Lord, have mercy on us!

In longer works, especially, the subject may be expressed through a dramatic situation, a whole dramatic sequence, or a logical argument, to name three possibilities at random. The degree of explicitness varies enormously from poet to poet, from the extreme indirection of T. S. Eliot in 'Gerontion' to the all but bald directness of George Herbert in 'The Windows,' the poem which we shall consider next. There is a similar variation among poets in the closeness of correspondence between the two experiences they are comparing. We must of course not assign any special value either to explicitness in expression or to exactness of correspondence.

We may describe the more implicit types of metaphorical expressions as symbolic, there being no absolute division between symbolic and nonsymbolic metaphor. Any iconic expression or experience regarded as standing for the subject experience, or any conventional metaphor taken as an icon for a further unnamed subject, may be called a symbol. In practice I usually restrict the term 'symbol' to implicit metaphors, especially to cases where there is little or no explicit statement of the subject. For examples of interpretation of literature that is quite purely symbolic, the reader may turn to the discussion of Yeats's 'Two Songs from a Play' in chapter v and to the analysis of symbols in *A Passage to India* (chapter x).

To illustrate the basic method of interpreting metaphors, it will be helpful to examine one that is relatively explicit and extraordinarily clear in structure. From reading 'The Windows' we can also learn how a poem may be ordered through a single metaphor, and we can see in particular that the success of Herbert's poem depends directly on the nicety of its metaphorical design:

THE WINDOWS

Lord, how can man preach thy eternall word?
He is a brittle crazie glasse:
Yet in thy temple thou dost him afford
This glorious and transcendent place,
To be a window, through thy grace.

But when thou dost anneal in glasse thy storie,
Making thy life to shine within
The holy Preachers; then the light and glorie
More rev'rend grows, & more doth win;
Which else shows watrish, bleak, & thin.

Doctrine and life, colours and light, in one
When they combine and mingle, bring
A strong regard and aw: but speech alone
Doth vanish like a flaring thing,
And in the eare, not conscience ring.

Again as in the dialogue of 'Love,' the mildness of the drama is deceptive; it is admittedly remarkable that Herbert can carry us so far from such an opening line. The poem brings us finally to a sense of a life transformed by Christ, a life which becomes at once more beautiful and more effective, a change felt not as a proposition but as a blend of experience in the eye and in the ear. This fusion is fully realized in the last stanza only because of the nice preparation in the two earlier stanzas.

The diagram below, which I regard less solemnly than the reader perhaps supposes, shows at a glance how curiously clear and complete the metaphorical design is.

A Diagram of the Metaphor in 'The Windows'

SUBJECT	ICON
A_1 LIFE	A_2 LIGHT
man preach	brittle, crazie glasse
less rev'rend, less win	watrish, bleak, thin
B_1 DOCTRINE	B_2 COLOURS
anneal (Christ's action in Preacher)	anneal (colored figures of Christ)
making shine (making Preacher's life Christlike)	making shine
within the holy Preachers	in glasse
thy life	thy story (figures of Christ in color)
C_1 DOCTRINE AND LIFE	C_2 COLOURS AND LIGHT
life	light
glorie (beauty of transformed life)	glorie (glow of windows; of halo)
more rev'rend	more rev'rend (increase religious quality of light)
in one combine and mingle	in one combine and mingle
a strong regard (of listener's attention)	a strong regard (of viewer)
aw	aw (overpowering effect of blended light and color)
more doth win (influence on lives)	more doth win (effect of light on viewers)
CONTRAST	
D_1 speech alone	D_2 a flaring thing
not ring in conscience	ring in the eare

Notice how the summing up at the beginning of the third stanza,

> Doctrine and life, colours and light, in one
> When they combine and mingle . . .

outlines the whole pattern. Notice, too, the closeness of correspondence between the two levels of the metaphor. In much of the poem (see A, B, D) different expressions can be quoted for each point in the analogy, and elsewhere the meaning that corresponds can be defined with remarkable exactness.

If we return to the poem and read the second half (the poem divides with 'then' at the exact middle by line measurement), we can appreciate what Herbert has achieved by the explicitness of his design. 'Then the light and glorie' grow, for every expression is now doubled or tripled in force through meanings that have been anticipated. The 'glorie' is the beauty of the transformed life and of persuasive eloquence felt as the glow of the annealed coloring, as the pictured aureole, the 'glory' about Christ's figure in the window.

The contrast that follows in the closing lines of the poem proves to be no contrast but a fulfilment of the earlier promise of transcendent change:

> . . . but speech alone
> Doth vanish like a flaring thing,
> And in the eare, not conscience ring.

For the paradox of the sound that 'flares' and 'rings' is thoroughly logical, since Herbert has brought forward an image and a metaphor which have been moving under the surface all along. In 'like a flaring thing' he reminds us by the internal rhyme that preaching *is* sound, that we have been comparing sound and light since the second line of the poem. The final 'ring,' which might be commonplace in another poem, contains both a visual and an aural echo of the light metaphor in 'flaring.' After the affirmations in the first half of the closing stanza, the negative, 'not in the conscience ring,' accentuates its opposite: at the end of the poem we hear preaching which is the glorified light of Christ's life and doctrine acting through the life and speech of the 'holy Preacher.'

Herbert's way of spreading the whole metaphor before us, with clearly outlined resemblances and with frequently explicit statement of iconic and subject meanings, has no merit in itself, though it is the perfect vehicle for his balancing and reconciliation of values. To exorcise the heresy that there must be distinct statements for each level of meaning or that we can always surely label icon and subject, let us consider a poem by Marianne Moore:

ROSES ONLY

You do not seem to realize that beauty is a liability rather
than an asset—that in view of the fact that spirit creates
form we are justified in supposing
that you must have brains. For you, a symbol of the
unit, stiff and sharp,
conscious of surpassing by dint of native superiority
and liking for everything
self-dependent, anything an

ambitious civilization might produce: for you, unaided,
to attempt through sheer
reserve, to confuse presumptions resulting from obser-
vation, is idle. You cannot make us
think you a delightful happen-so. But rose, if you
are brilliant, it
is not because your petals are the without-which-noth-
ing of pre-eminence. Would you not, minus
thorns, be a what-is-this, a mere

peculiarity? They are not proof against a worm, the elements, or mildew;
but what about the predatory hand? What is brilliance
without co-ordination? Guarding the
infinitesimal pieces of your mind, compelling audience to
the remark that it is better to be forgotten than to be
remembered too violently,
your thorns are the best part of you.

This poem offers amusing possibilities for students of metaphor. Marianne Moore is an exceedingly coy author; obliquity is her particular forte; and she defies searchers for summaries, in spite of the fact that her poems are full of seeming pronouncements. 'Roses Only' gives very reluctant answers to the questions we have just been putting to Herbert's poem. What is the subject? And what is the icon? What indeed is being compared to what? The title, as often in Miss Moore's poems, is a quiet joke, perhaps two or three at once. These roses are certainly not roses only, a reading made impossible by the tone, with its calculated pomposity ('we are justified in supposing,' 'to confuse presumptions') and social cattiness ('if you are brilliant,' 'to attempt through sheer reserve,' 'the best part of you').

Suppose we say, however, that the poem is mainly about roses (flowers), that we are to think of a rose as a brainless, snobbish though beautiful female who supposes her superiority is due to birth and beauty, when in fact her distinction lies in her least pleasant characteristic:

> . . . it is better to be forgotten than to be
> remembered too violently.

We are to amuse ourselves with thinking of a rose as having brains or at least 'infinitesimal' ones, as being reserved, as a possible victim of 'the predatory hand' (The Rape of the Rose), and so on. We can support our choice of subject by pointing out certain expressions that seem to fit 'roses only': the creature of the poem is said to have thorns and petals, and only a rose could have thorns that 'are not proof against a worm, the elements, or mildew.'

But the botanical expressions, except the last one, are involved in a context which makes them double-valued. The speaker says: 'Would *you* not, minus thorns,' '*your* petals,' and 'Guarding the / infinitesimal pieces of *your* mind . . . *your* thorns are the best part of *you*.' The use of personification and direct address, the tone, and the substance of nearly every statement to the rose may well make us conclude that the poem is really about a recognizable type of woman, or at least a recognizable type of personality, which is symbolized by a rose. We find ourselves reversing our original choice of subject and icon.

Certainly either choice may be defended almost equally well. But when we come to cite statements in support of our choice, we find (with the one possible exception already noted) that any expression may be read as referring either to a rose or a beauty. In other words, the poem is a triumph of calculated ambiguity. The solution to our pedagogical questions lies in accepting the ambiguity and in reading the metaphor in a poise between 'roses only' and 'not only roses.' The metaphors are subordinated to a controlling irony.

II. Irony

Irony and metaphor both belong to the literary art of saying one thing and meaning another. Both present two levels of meaning which the reader must entertain at once if he is to respond imaginatively to either of these forms of expression. The difference between the two lies particularly in the nature of the contrasting levels and in their relation to each other. In irony one level of meaning always negates the other in some degree however slight, the context alone telling us what the opposed meanings are and whether they are relevant. It is true that in a metaphor relevant meanings may also be in conflict, and in so far as they are, some tang of irony enters. As Cleanth Brooks and other critics have observed, the blend of irony and metaphor is characteristic of both Metaphysical and modern poetry:

> My vegetable Love should grow
> Vaster than Empires, and more slow.
>
> * * * * *
>
> An aged man is but a paltry thing,
> A tattered cloak upon a stick, unless
> Soul clap its hands and sing, and louder sing
> For every tatter in its mortal dress.

But when we speak of irony in its purest form, we are thinking only of opposition of meaning and only of meaning as narrowed to opposition. For a clear example of ironic negation we might take the word 'fine' in Marvell's

> The Grave's a fine and private place.

Yes, it's fine, it's built of marble and convenient for love because it is so very private. But the cunningly active worms and the dust and the ashes make it something less than fine. The context indicates the two ways in which we are to take the lover's remark. The impatient reader is perhaps saying that the irony is obvious, which means simply that he has supplied conventional contexts for 'grave' and 'fine.' But the exact edge of Marvell's irony is to be felt only in the particular oppositions he expresses, for example, in the contrast between the grandiose tone of

> Thy Beauty shall no more be found;
> Nor, in thy marble Vault, shall sound
> My echoing Song . . .

and the macabre image in

> worms shall try
> That long preserv'd Virginity.

To experience the irony of 'fine and private place' we must entertain both of the clashing possibilities: therein lies the irony of it.

So obvious a point needs stressing, I believe, because some definitions of irony imply that the reader finds the intended or true meaning beneath the apparent, a view that tends to destroy irony both as a literary experience and as a vision of life. When so interpreted the lover's remark in Marvell's poem becomes a gross platitude, and its blend of insolence and persuasiveness disappears. (Relatively few persons, we might note in passing, are willing to bear the strain of the ironic vision: it is more comforting to rest in certainties. Socrates and Swift exemplify in diverse ways the inconvenience of being a thoroughgoing ironist.) To interpret irony, as to interpret metaphor, is something more than to decode it, and though as critics our first task is to bring the reader to see the more and less apparent, or more and less pleasant, meanings of an ironic expression, we must not let him rest content with either alone.

In both poetry and prose ironic meaning like ironic emphasis in speech tends to focus in a single word or two, where the lines of opposition seem to meet. Though it is easy enough to spot an expression of this sort, it is much more difficult to define the relevant opposed meanings, and since irony is by tradition an art of concealment, the cues to the less apparent meaning may be slight or even misleading. For the first condition of communication, that reader and writer must share some areas of experience, applies with especial force to ironic discourse. In a classical satire, such as Dryden's 'Absalom and Achitophel,' the reader is often expected to possess all sorts of special information about personalities and events and to be familiar also with the author's prejudices and principles. Certainly there must be some slight allusion in the text to each of these special kinds of knowledge; otherwise the reader would never discover their relevance. But it is the general rule in the purer forms of irony that infinitely more is assumed than is stated.

There is one type of assumption in particular that the reader must grasp and define if he is to enjoy the special amusement of irony and if he is to describe and discover the design in any longer piece of sustained irony. He must understand and accept (at least temporarily) the positive allegiances, the values through which the individual ironies gain their exact meaning and their force, 'the strength of applied irony being,' as Henry James has said, 'in the sincerities, the lucidities, the utilities that stand behind it.' Dryden's irony in 'Absalom and Achitophel' will not work for the reader unless he perceives and acknowledges Dryden's aristocratic principles. If he is interested in irony as design he will try to define the relation between the utilities and the irony, he will want to explain in what sense they stand behind it. In Dryden, as I shall show in a moment, this relationship is fairly easy to describe; but in the more subtle satire of Pope or of Jane Austen, it is considerably more difficult to define; and in Swift and in James himself the relationship is so subtle as to defy satisfactory analysis.

'The irony' that 'the lucidities stand behind' is expressed in local ironies, through those expressions in which the conflict of meanings is most surely and clearly perceived. Before we can show the connection between assumption and irony in any work, we need to define the opposed meanings through which the irony is experienced. On a first reading, continuously ironic poetry often seems to explode in all directions at once; but by looking for expressions that exhibit similar uses of language and similar oppositions, we may discover continuities not wholly unlike those to be found through studying recurrent images and metaphors. Tracing such continuities is the first and most important step in the discovery of ironic design. The second step is to ask how the continuities are related to the implied assumptions.

To trace a complete design in irony as in metaphor, it is necessary to consider a complete poem. In analyzing a fairly brief passage from Dryden's 'Absalom and Achitophel,' I shall indicate how to trace different sorts of continuity in a longer work and how to describe the design of a whole satire. (The reader who wishes to see an analysis of a complete poem may turn to chapter VIII, The Groves of Eden: Design in a Satire by Pope.)

There is nothing veiled or Jamesian about the assumptions behind the satire of Dryden. In 'Absalom and Achitophel' he exhibits the rare happiness of a satirist who is completely clear about his allegiances and serenely at one with the members of his audience. He and they are—almost by royal command—pro-King, anti-Commonwealth, pro-Established Church, anti-Presbyterian, pro-aristocratic, and anti-democratic. Listen to the note of sublime assurance in his lines on the miserable Titus Oates (Corah), the Presbyterian (Levite) 'weaver's issue' who testified that the Jesuits were plotting to murder Charles II: (The lines must be read aloud if their high heartiness and oratorical thump are to be thoroughly appreciated.)

To speak the rest, who better are forgot,
Would tire a well-breath'd witness of the Plot.
Yet Corah, thou shalt from oblivion pass:
Erect thyself, thou monumental brass,
High as the serpent of thy metal made,
While nations stand secure beneath thy shade.
What tho' his birth were base, yet comets rise
From earthy vapours, ere they shine in skies.
Prodigious actions may as well be done
By weaver's issue, as by prince's son.
This arch-attestor for the public good
By that one deed ennobles all his blood.
Who ever ask'd the witnesses' high race,
Whose oath with martyrdom did Stephen grace?
Ours was a Levite, and as times went then,
His tribe were God Almighty's gentlemen.
Sunk were his eyes, his voice was harsh and loud,
Sure signs he neither choleric was nor proud:

His long chin prov'd his wit; his saintlike grace,
A church vermilion, and a Moses' face.
His memory, miraculously great,
Could plots, exceeding man's belief, repeat;
Which therefore cannot be accounted lies,
For human wit could never such devise.
Some future truths are mingled in his book;
But where the witness fail'd, the prophet spoke:
Some things like visionary flights appear;
The spirit caught him up, the Lord knows where;
And gave him his rabbinical degree,
Unknown to foreign university.

Many of the ironies in the passage are simple 'yes-no' oppositions such as:

This arch-attestor for the public *good*
By that one deed ennobles all his blood.

Prodigious actions may *as well* be done
By weaver's issue, as by prince's son.

While nations stand *secure* beneath thy shade.

Sure signs he neither choleric was nor proud.

These outright ironies of negation together compose one of the more obvious continuities in the passage. They exemplify also one of the simplest and most common relationships between local ironies and a writer's allegiances. Each statement, and especially the italicized words, includes by implication a denial of some principle or prejudice shared by Dryden and his audience.

But it is Dryden's intonation that sets his mark on the lines and gives them life and their peculiar singleness of design. His note is clearly heard in 'arch-attestor,' with its upper level of churchly associations, and in 'prodigious,' which nicely combines Latinate solemnity with the common Latin meaning of monstrous. The irony of tone overlying the logical oppositions is characteristic and unifying. At the beginning of the passage Dryden fixes the august level of his commemoration of Oates by suggesting that it belongs to a Homeric catalogue of heroes ('To speak the rest . . .'). He then addresses Oates in a line so nobly reminiscent of Virgil that it is hardly recognizable as parody (the 'near-parody' of which T. S. Eliot speaks):

> Yet Corah, thou shalt from oblivion pass . . .

The occasional Latinisms are also vaguely allusive in effect, suggesting the style of classical epic. As we should expect, Dryden's language is at many points more or less Biblical, ranging from near-quotation to expressions with religious or churchly associations, such as 'martyrdom,' 'vermilion,' 'witness,' and 'prophet.' Working within a fairly narrow range of allusion Dryden maintains a high declamatory tone that is both ecclesiastical and Roman. It is hardly mock-heroic; indeed allusive irony is a more adequate label for Dryden's satirical mode throughout 'Absalom and Achitophel' and most of 'Mac Flecknoe.'

By occasionally slapping down an expression from a much lower level, Dryden produces an obvious joke which underlines the incongruity of his august manner and also indicates the tone really appropriate to Oates and his kind:

> His tribe were God Almighty's gentlemen

or

> The spirit caught him up, the Lord knows where.

But these and all sorts of incongruities are successfully masked through the dominant tone. They are also linked by a kind of metaphor of elevation, for rather curiously the high tone is matched by high expressions of another sort: 'high as a serpent . . . yet comets rise . . . ere they shine in skies . . . high race . . . visionary flights . . . the spirit caught him up . . .'

The variety and concentration of Dryden's irony is at its peak in the wonderful address that introduces the portrait of Oates:

> Yet Corah, thou shalt from oblivion pass:
> Erect thyself, thou monumental brass,
> High as the serpent of thy metal made,
> While nations stand secure beneath thy shade.

A whole battery of incongruities centers in the single resonant phrase, 'thou monumental brass.' This beneficent hero—or base faker—is monumental (tremendous) in his greatness and in his despicable action; his 'brass' (effrontery) is monumental, or he is worthy of a monumental brass (as in an English church); and finally, this monument, contrary to decent custom, is to be erected by the hero, and contrary to the laws of gravity it is to rise of its own accord. Contemporary readers may have also recognized in the line a preposterous parody of Horace's

> Exegi monumentum aere perennius . . .

They would certainly have appreciated the splendid inapppropriateness of comparing Oates to 'the serpent of brass' in the Bible. In this compound the doublings of irony and of metaphor are inseparable, for each time the reader detects an incongruity, he is also uncovering a fresh point of analogy.

It is hardly surprising that the lines of greatest ironic intensity should show traces of all the characteristic continuities we have noted. As these four lines illustrate, there is a most active relation between the continuities and Dryden's political and religious beliefs. The august ecclesiastical and Roman tone and the ironic metaphors of elevation, like the logical inversions, are more than literary modes adopted to secure uniformity of style. Indulgence in allusions to classical epic and the use of a Latinate and churchly vocabulary are especially appropriate to the aristocratic supporters of Church and King. The metaphors are symbolic of the disdain they felt for 'low fellows' and for 'enthusiastic' religion. There is also a special insolence in the lavish use of scriptural language and allusion in a satire directed in part against 'Bible readers.' This passage—and the whole poem—owes much of its impact and totality of effect to the vigorous pressure of beliefs confidently held by writer and public. And the pressure is perceptible in individual uses of language, in the local ironies that make up the continuities we have been briefly tracing.

Even if we leave the rather special poetic worlds of Dryden and Pope we find that irony is always breaking in, lending another relation, and sending its arrowy light through our reading. Some glimmer of an ironic meaning appears in nearly every poem we have been discussing in these chapters, and the various instances show that irony may be expressed through any one of the main designs we are describing. In 'Once by the Pacific,' irony is conveyed through contrasting tones, as it is also in Donne's sonnet, especially in the insolent and paradoxical wooing of Christ's 'mild dove':

> Who is most trew, and pleasing to thee, then
> When she'is embrac'd and open to most men.

Herbert's 'quick-ey'd Love' chides her guest in a serious pun, which is one of the most compact forms of ironic expression:

> Who made the eyes but I?

In Hopkins' sonnet there is absurdity as well as pathos in the metaphor of 'time's eunuch' coming after 'birds build—but not I build.' And the images at the close of the ode 'To Autumn' have their irony, too, since the songs of Autumn are scarcely songs at all. We should feel this contrast less keenly if the broken movement of the closing lines were not counterpointed against the rich leisurely pace of the first and especially the second stanzas, an opposition that suggests the possibility of an irony of rhythm.

Chapter IV

THE FIGURE OF SOUND

*. . . that subtle monotony of voice which runs through the nerves like fire.**

The purpose of rhythm . . . is to keep us in that state of perhaps real trance, in which the mind liberated from the pressure of the will is unfolded in symbols.†

W. B. YEATS

I. The Sound Matters

Most critics since Coleridge, whom Yeats may be unconsciously echoing, would probably agree that one important function of sound in poetry is to maintain 'that subtle monotony' which induces something like a hypnotic state. They might also agree that in this state the reader responds more fully to the manifold suggestions of poetic language. Analogies unfold, more varied and more excited feelings are released, an intonation is imposed that sets the reading of verse apart from all but the most verse-like prose. Beyond general agreements of this sort chaos begins, especially when critics try to demonstrate more particular relations between sound and sense, or between what is heard and the kinds of design we have been considering up to this point.

Whatever relationship we hold for, most of us will agree that the reader cannot know how a poem 'sounds' or make any valid remark about what he hears unless as he reads he enacts the dramatic situa-

* From 'Speaking to the Psaltery.'

† From 'The Symbolism of Poetry.'

tion, unless he senses the value of the images and the bindings of metaphor, and unless he is constantly responding with the feelings that are ordered through all the possible organizing modes. Let us suppose that such a reader—or one enough like him to be of this world—having read the first two stanzas of 'The Windows' reads the third in the following form:

> When doctrine and life, colours and light, combine and mingle in one, they bring a strong regard and aw: but speech alone doth vanish like a flaring thing and doth ring in the eare, not conscience.

This miserable change results from rearranging the words as prose, with only a single 'doth' added. If we now reread the poem with the stanza restored, all that we expected and more takes place:

> Doctrine and life, colours and light, in one
> When they combine and mingle, bring
> A strong regard and aw: but speech alone
> Doth vanish like a flaring thing,
> And in the eare, not conscience ring.

Certainly what we now hear is determined by more than the mere ordering of words and syllables. For example, we are much affected by the major change in tone from the preceding stanza. As so often at the close of a Metaphysical poem, the poet, rising to a pronouncement of truth freshly and dramatically discovered, becomes grandly general and impersonal in tone. We read his words with a voice that suits his change of role and now release with full confidence the feeling anticipated in

> Yet in thy temple thou dost him afford
> This glorious and transcendent place,
> To be a window, through thy grace.

As we feel the possibilities of the metaphor opening up, we slow down the tempo, we give a fresh warmth of stress and a new resonance to nearly every word in the stanza. In the inner ear we record all those nameless but wonderful modelings of the spoken word that take place under the pressure of feeling and that express its quality better than any words can do.

Since the sounds we make and hear depend so largely on tone and feeling, we might suppose that much of the sound experience would survive in reading the hacked prose version. It is surprising and to me gratifying to see how far this is from being the case. The essential grammar, the metaphor, the thought remain, but dramatically nothing happens. We find ourselves saying, bathetically, 'How true!' The voice rings in the conscience but not in the ear. Only when Herbert's stanza is restored is dramatic tone vividly actualized and the full tide of feeling released.

It is absurd to suppose that we can explain why and how this happens, although most readers of poetry will agree that it does. But without attempting to explain the mystery—for it is one—we can describe how in particular cases our experience is enriched by reading Herbert's words in the original stanzaic pattern. We can show how at some points word, syllable, and stress orders induce us to make certain sounds and how these sounds are appropriate to dramatic and metaphorical structure. For example, when we read in the verse form

> Doctrine and life, colours and light

we note an exact matching of stresses in the two phrases, and peculiar stresses, at that. By this time in the poem we have come to expect an iambic swing, but now in two successive phrases we start with a trochee only to reverse the rhythm at once:

/ ⏑ ⏑ / / ⏑ ⏑ /

Phrasing and punctuation also accentuate the balance of sounds and pauses; but observe that in the prose form these devices are not nearly so effective as in the verse form. When the line is read in the stanza, the resultant increase of stress, the balancing of stresses, the evening up of the length of pauses, and the syllabic flow of sound are all demonstrably right. For we hear in isolation the two phrases that sum up the two phases of the central metaphor, we hear in matched sounds the words that embrace most generally the abstract meanings and images that are opposed and yet harmonized throughout the poem.

For a second example, listen to how we say 'one,' at the turn of the first and second lines:

Doctrine and life, colours and light, in one
When they combine and mingle . . .

We give 'one' increased stress because of meter; we increase both stress and resonance because of the coming rhyme; and we make ever so slight a break for the line-end, a pause we must balance by keeping the voice up, since the sense runs over into the next verse. The extended sonority, the prominence to the ear of 'one' direct us to the extraordinary union Herbert is here expressing.

In the next line, 'bring' (which gets a somewhat similar emphasis because of position) belongs to an odd chain of rhymes and assonances: 'mingle . . . bring . . . flaring thing . . . ring.' We must—with considerable tact—slightly lengthen each of the -ing-ring syllables, 'entuning it through the nose.' (Herbert would be expert at this, we suppose.) By this chain of recurrent sounds we make up a kind of 'poetic morpheme': * we feel the sense of 'ring' in words of very different meaning. So we are kept close to the physical fact, the heard voice of the holy Preacher. When we hear 'ring' in the word which is also an image of light we experience, in little, the fusion of light and sound which is central in the poem. The force with which we come down on the final 'ring,'

And in the eare, not conscience ring

suggests by analogy the eloquence that resounds in the inner life. But the prose version, by removing metrical and rhyme stresses and so diminishing the salience of the '-ings,' does not allow or encourage us to make the sounds through which we more fully experience the images, the metaphor, and the triumphant assurance of tone.

II. Definitions and Method

In discussing Herbert's stanza so relentlessly I have tried to show the importance of sound in poetry and to give some examples of practical analysis of sound design. I have limited myself quite strictly to features that can surely be analyzed, keeping in mind the basic critical rule that it is wiser to discuss what we can discuss. The total

* See Appendix B, The Echo of Sound, pp. 72, 73.

sound experience of a poem is beyond analysis for many reasons, the most obvious being that it embraces too many experiences and experiences for which we have no language whatsoever. The richness and variety of sounds and rhythms heard in reading a poem of the highest order—the 'Ode on a Grecian Urn' or 'Sailing to Byzantium' —is and always will remain indescribable.

Under the total sound experience of a poem, we must include first the perception of all the sounds and pauses that might be recorded on a machine if we read the poem aloud and if we were successful in making the sounds that the words seem to demand. For silent readers such perception is replaced by images* of the sounds. Indeed it may be argued that the best readers of poetry try in reading aloud to render the sounds they first 'hear' as images, that any actual sounds they make are only helpful as reminders of those heard in the inner ear. We must also include under sound experience all the sound images evoked by words, all the heard groupings of pronunciation images, in short all the auditory experience of words which no one can reproduce with his voice. Even among sounds we can render, the variety to be included in the total is enormous: vowel and consonant sounds in all their combinations, variations of pitch, variations in tempo, in loudness or softness, and so on. In brief we must include in the total sound experience any sounds heard or imaged whether there is or is not any observable pattern to be found in them.

Within this total there are rhythms. There are 'rhythms' that may be of immense significance in our reading, which we cannot describe and which are beyond analysis, for instance, the modulations of voice expressive of changes in tone and feeling. For the analysis of sound design I shall use the term rhythm to mean only a perceptible and demonstrable pattern of sounds (or pauses) in sequence: any pattern of stresses,† rhymes, phrases, sentence and line units, pitch variations, pauses for punctuation or sense or pauses due to omission of metrical stress, assonances, alliterated consonants or vowels, et cetera. Ac-

* These pronunciation images are replicas of the sounds made in pronouncing the words of the poem. They must not be confused with auditory images evoked by meanings of the words, which are referred to as sound images in the next sentence but one.

† See Appendix A, A Note on Scansion, pp. 70, 71.

curate sound analysis must be limited mainly to pointing out such patterns, as I have already illustrated in the discussion of Herbert's stanza.

There is another and important meaning for rhythm, for which I shall ordinarily use the term 'movement.' By movement I mean the total heard rhythm, the composite of all the separate rhythms. Although movement is not completely demonstrable apart from reading aloud, and though our ability to describe individual examples is quite limited, some characterization of the total rhythmic pattern is indispensable for the analysis of imaginative design. This meaning of rhythm is not to be confused with I. A. Richards's 'total rhythm,' a term that describes the progress of the whole poem-experience. Note that the term 'movement' embraces only perceptible and demonstrable patterns of sound, that the definition excludes whole areas of sound experience that are beyond analysis. In insisting that some analysis of total rhythmic pattern may be made, I am not overlooking the fact that the total of what is heard, the full sound experience, is very largely dependent on meaning, that the character of the heard pattern is shaped by other designs. There are, for example, subtle shadings of stress and of phrasing almost certainly traceable to the dramatic role which the poet imposes on the reader. But it is impossible to define such qualitative aspects of rhythm or to demonstrate their relationship to another design.

It can easily be inferred that sound design, like dramatic or metaphorical design, includes several sorts of pattern, the various kinds of rhythm that I have been describing. But though all of these configurations of sound are recognizable in reading experience, they cannot all be described with equal success. As practical critics interested in analyzing the sound design of a poem, what can we do? Or rather, where shall we begin? We begin, as I emphasized at the beginning of the chapter, with alert reading, with the fullest possible response to the words and the relationships they express. Where we have been uncertain or confused in our response, or simply numb, we may find that some systematic analysis of tone or metaphor or irony will help us to enjoy a more orderly and more complete experience of the poem. But such analysis is no substitute for the response, any more than beating time is equivalent to hearing a rhythm in the playing of a symphony orchestra. If we are to analyze any aspect of the sound design of a poem, we must hear the words with all the vocal colorings demanded by their meanings and by their arrangements in English sentences and in lines of verse on the printed page. We should be quite sure that we know how the poem goes, and how it sounds, whether we read aloud or silently. Again, analysis of some of these arrangements may be helpful. We may find through scansion, or through noting a rhyme scheme or a peculiarity of punctuation or a series of assonances, that we should alter our emphasis or add a stress somewhere or group words differently from what we had supposed. Most of us will of course make these and similar adjustments quite automatically and only discover on reflection why our voices behaved as they did.

Assuming that we have read a poem with some success, how can we describe the sound design we have been experiencing? We begin, probably, with making some gestures which may express to others our sense of the whole design; we make any tentative formulation we are capable of making. But as in analyzing other sorts of design, if we wish to define and communicate our discoveries, we must descend to details, in this instance to the details of word and syllable arrangement in sentences and in lines of verse on the printed page. We must, of course, immediately translate these arrangements into their heard equivalents; that is we must say, given this grouping of letters and words, how are they to be rendered in speech? We must be continually asking ourselves how the orderings affect our utterance; we need to try them out by reading aloud. For we are not aiming to describe printed syllable and word patterns, but sequences of sounds. There are two kinds of analysis—one, fairly crude; one, fairly refined—that we can make by such study of the orderings of words and syllables. We can roughly define the movement of a poem and indicate its relation to the rest of the imaginative structure; and we can show with some accuracy the appropriateness of a particular sound pattern (or of a detail within a pattern) to one or more of the other designs in a poem.

In defining the movement of a group of lines or of a whole poem, we are trying to describe the character common to the rhythms. We may begin by listening to the lines and seizing on the first adjective that comes to mind. But to test the accuracy of our label and to define its meaning, we need to make at least a rapid survey of the word and syllable arrangements. We note, for example, recurrent irregularities of meter, pauses due to punctuation, typical sentence patterns, recurrence of balanced phrasing. We make some rough statistical guesses about which arrangements are more frequent, and which are therefore typical. As we review the sounds made as a result of these arrangements, we ask if there is any common quality perceptible in the more typical patterns. We test our original label and perhaps reject it for a new one. Or we decide that no single expression will do, that the best way to describe the movement of this poem or group of lines is to point out two or three of the dominant rhythmic patterns.

The final step is to ask whether there is any definable relationship of likeness or unlikeness between the movement and some other design or designs in the poem. There is no simple method for proving such relationships and no assurance that all readers will accept our demonstration of any particular one. Agreement on any statement concerning movement or its relation to meaning will always depend largely on whether the reader has followed the whole interpretation of the poem in question. For this reason and also because analysis of movement apart from interpretation is of merely technical interest and hardly of critical value, I am offering no sample analysis at this point. An example is given in the complete interpretation of a poem with which this chapter concludes, and other examples may be found in chapters v and viii.

While any definition of movement is necessarily rough, necessarily incomplete, and often unconvincing, it is possible to demonstrate with some refinement and fair completeness the appropriateness of a single pattern (or of a detail within a pattern) to one or more designs of another sort. As this variety of analysis has been already illustrated in the discussion of sound in Herbert's 'The Windows,' only a brief summary of the general method is necessary here. As a rule we start from some point in our reading where we have felt some felicity or infelicity in the sounds we have been making; we have perhaps half-perceived an irregularity of some kind, a variation from a conventional norm or from the norm established by the poem itself. In every instance selected for analysis, we take two distinct steps: (1) we point out a particular arrangement of words, syllables, or stresses; and (2) we describe exactly the sounds uttered and heard as a result of the arrangement. Then we attempt to show how those sounds are related to some other design in the poem's organization. In many cases we can show a relation between the sounds heard (or imaged in silent reading) and the meanings of particular words. (The meanings will in turn presumably belong to a set of meanings that compose a design.) When we cannot show any appropriateness (or significant inappropriateness), we don't. It is certainly not my intention to argue that there always is or must be a demonstrable appropriateness of sound to sense.

But I have been arguing (rather mildly) that occasionally in reading poetry we do discover analogies of sound that can be successfully described to others. The '-ings' and 'rings' of Herbert's stanza have various metaphorical values in relation to the central design of his poem. Clearly these sounds are not meaningful in themselves apart from the context in which they are heard; clearly, too, the reader co-operates in making them expressive. But take away Herbert's curious arrangement of rhyming syllables and of accents, and it becomes quite unlikely that the most enthusiastic of readers will create any such analogies as I suggested. The reader does make sounds expressive, but not any chance collocation of sounds.*

For the 'figure of sound,' like all other figures in poetry, is a game which must be played by both writer and reader. No one who has glanced at Keats's revisions of the prologue to 'Hyperion' or of 'Bright Star' can confidently deny that some poets, though not necessarily all, are aware of this figure in composing. The good reader is a composer too, and as he reads he uses everything he can lay his voice on. If he creates values the poet never dreamed of, he need not be concerned. He is merely discovering what he learns every time he reads a line of poetry, that the essence of imaginative literature is offered potentiality of making more and more various relations.

III. Sound in the Whole Poem

As I have hinted more than once in this chapter, analysis of sound must always be kept in its place. Clearly, talk of sound in itself has

* For a full and I believe convincing statement of this argument, see appendix B to this chapter, The Echo of Sense, an account of onomatopoeia.

little importance or meaning; and though tone in itself and metaphor in itself are abstractions of equally limited value, most readers will nevertheless regard a complete analysis of sound in a poem as a more violent distortion of their experience than a complete analysis of tone or metaphor. By choosing a well-known poem and by making a fairly complete interpretation of it, I hope to keep analysis of sound in its place and to balance the evils of overemphasis on any one design.

> At the round earths imagin'd corners, blow
> Your trumpets, Angells, and arise, arise
> From death, you numberlesse infinities
> Of soules, and to your scattred bodies goe,
> All whom the flood did, and fire shall o'erthrow,
> All whom warre, dearth, age, agues, tyrannies,
> Despaire, law, chance, hath slaine, and you whose eyes,
> Shall behold God, and never tast deaths woe.
> But let them sleepe, Lord, and mee mourne a space,
> For, if above all these, my sinnes abound,
> 'Tis late to aske abundance of thy grace,
> When wee are there; here on this lowly ground,
> Teach mee how to repent; for that's as good
> As if thou'hadst seal'd my pardon, with thy blood.
>
> JOHN DONNE

Donne's poem is conceived in two sharply contrasted situations and tones: the imagined judgment day in which the poet all but assumes the voice of God, and the meditation in which he speaks to his Lord in humble intimacy. The two dramatic lines and all they imply are brought to sharp focus in two words, 'there' and 'here.' 'There' is before God, at the Judgment, and recapitulates the vision of that tremendous day which Donne has so terribly pictured. The controlling metaphor, the key to Donne's attitude in the first eight lines of the sonnet, lies in his insistence on the numberlessness of the dead:

> I had not thought death had undone so many.

Characteristically, Donne goes over and over this impression: 'numberlesse infinities . . . all . . . all . . . all these.' The Lucretian clash of images in the opening line, 'at the round earths imagin'd corners,' sets a vast geographic stage for the enumeration. The angels must blow, and the poet must call twice on the souls to 'arise.' To the vastness of space and the vastness of numbers is added the horrible inclusiveness of kinds:

> All whom the flood did, and fire shall o'erthrow,
> All whom warre, dearth, age, agues, tyrannies,
> Despaire, law, chance, hath slaine . . .

The gentleness of 'let them sleep' marks the shift in tone and feeling to Donne's sense of his own sinfulness, which he measures in immediate relation to his vision:

> But let them sleepe, Lord, and mee mourne a space,
> For, if above all these, my sinnes abound,
> 'Tis late to aske abundance of thy grace,
> When wee are there . . .

The terrible recollection of 'there' moves him to learn repentance 'here.' In the promise of atonement to those who repent he finds some assurance, and he speaks to his Lord (now Christ) in a tone that is everyday and even a little offhand, touched by the irreverence that is the sign of assured faith.

The continuity between the two dramatic situations and the contrasting attitudes lies mainly in our remembered sense of the grand and awful scene of the opening lines. But this continuity is in part rhythmic, for the bigness of movement which marks the octet is not wholly lost in the sestet. Both are single long sentences. In each there is a good deal of rather elaborate balancing of phrases and clauses, and in each the balancings are broken in ways that are perfectly harmonious with the dominant tone and feeling. In the octet, as the sense of all-inclusiveness increases, the balance is broken, the meter disintegrates in a series of continuous stresses and sharp pauses:

> All whom warre, dearth, age, agues, tyrannies,
> Despaire, law, chance, hath slaine, and you whose eyes . . .

The assonance and vowel alliteration in the first of these lines help us to keep a measured swing in reading, while the tumbling sounds, the confusion of meter to the ear fit exactly the helter-skelter gathering which Donne is describing. It is all mere accumulation. The sestet has breaks of another sort, the freely distributed pauses of reflective conversation, a movement thoroughly appropriate to the intimacy of Donne's prayer.

Nearly everywhere we can point out wonderfully nice adjustment of particular sound patterns to meaning. As the first of a number of instances of different types, note 'blow' at the end of line one,

> At the round earths imagin'd corners, blow . . .

The break, the rhyme and metrical stress, and the run-over of line and sense have curious effects on our reading. We must stress rather loudly for accent and rhyme and pause slightly for the break and for the coming rhyme. Yet because of the continuing sense, because the command is incomplete, we must extend the sound by keeping the voice steady and up. And the long 'o' gives a fine chance for 'trumpeting.' All of these 'soundings' which the word arrangement demands or allows * are what we want for this

> Tuba mirum spargens sonum
> Per sepulchra regionum . . .

This memorable sound serves as one of the links through which we feel the immediacy of the opening scene in the second half of the poem.

The key to Donne's attitude, as we have seen, is first clearly revealed in 'all,' a word which the reader comes down on with full force:

> arise
> From death, you numberlesse infinities
> Of soules, and to your scattred bodies goe,
> *All* whom the flood did, and . . .

We must of course emphasize the word for sense, but a shift in meter forces us to give an even greater stress and to mark a change in rhythm at the moment of a change in intensity of feeling. Up until this point Donne has begun each line in conventional iambic fashion, the ˘ ˘ / of the first line being an accepted variation. The reversal of

* See Appendix B, The Echo of Sound, pp. 71-4.

meter in 'all' occurs at the first critical moment in the poem's progress, just as the meaning of 'numberlesse infinities' begins to unfold. We have already noticed the irruption of stresses in the lines that follow; we should observe also the increase in number to seven in each. The resultant increase in time as we make each stress and pause gives a spaciousness of measure to the ear just as the enumeration reaches its climax in immensity.

Perhaps the most wonderful variation of all comes at the point where the main dramatic lines and the main attitudes of the poem are most sharply opposed:

> When wee are there; here on this lowly ground . . .

The reversal of accent increases the stress and makes us put in a pause for the unaccented syllable we have lost; while 'here' gets a further stress due to the chiasmus and the lack of a connective corresponding to 'when.' The extraordinary stress, the two blows of sound with a sharp break, is the sound equivalent for this crucial contrast in tone and feeling.

As we return to the lower key of the conclusion Donne gives us one of his pieces of coalescing sound,

> for that's as good
> As if thou'hadst seal'd my pardon, with thy blood.

He contracts, he elides, he brings consonants together of very similar sound, and accordingly we must telescope sounds in reading. The devices force and encourage us to relax our utterance as we do in casual speech. This is what we want to do, in order to move into the new tone and the new mood of assurance which we have at long length reached. The movement of drama in Donne's sonnet, from cosmic vision to private confession, is accompanied throughout by a movement of sound that is exquisitely adjusted to the moments of most significant change.

APPENDIX A: A Note on Scansion

The rhythm that is easiest to detect, though hardly the most important, is that of stress—any sequence of stressed and unstressed syllables. Meter is a single type of stress-rhythm. Defined, it is the systematic, conventional ordering of stressed and unstressed syllables within a line. Scansion is a technique of notation, of showing the stresses we make in reading a line of verse and where that order of stresses agrees with or varies from the conventional sequence of meter. Analysis of stress-rhythm by means of scansion is dangerous only if we forget how tiny a sector of the sound experience we are discussing, but scansion is indispensable if we want to point out fine relationships. If, as Voltaire said, 'Poetry is made up of exquisite details,' the reader may be expected to note variations of stress in a line of verse. Scansion may tell us little, but what it tells is often precious.

The *meter* of the long and of the short lines in a stanza of 'The Windows' is:

(long) ⏑ / ⏑ / ⏑ / ⏑ / ⏑ / (short) ⏑ / ⏑ / ⏑ / ⏑ /

The *scansion* of two particular lines is:

Dóctrĭne ănd lífe, cólŏurs ănd líght, ĭn óne

(´)
Ănd ín thĕ eáre, nŏt cónsciĕnce ríng.

The three most common peculiarities of stress in English verse are shown in these two lines: in 'doctrine' there is a change in order of stress resulting from normal pronunciation of a polysyllable; in 'And in' a stress is given to a monosyllable in order to conform to the meter; and 'not' receives a secondary stress, that is, a stress added for sense emphasis *in addition* to the conventional number of stresses in the line. 'Secondary' carries no implications of importance or relative loudness. In the example, 'not' probably receives the loudest stress of any word in the line. It should be clear that stress-rhythm and meter are the same only when a verse is completely regular.

APPENDIX B: The Echo of Sound

Onomatopoeia is the *bête noire* or perhaps more properly the red herring of all discussions of sound in poetry. If we mean by onomatopoeia that the sounds of a word as pronounced are like the heard sound of whatever the word names, and that the sounds have this character independently of the sense, we must agree that onomatopoeia is almost nonexistent. We may possibly except a handful of words such as buzz and cuckoo, but even these cases are suspect. Who would surely recognize the sound of a cuckoo on hearing the word, if he did not already know that it referred to a cuckoo? There are other groups of words, such as glare, flare, blare or spatter, shatter, tatter, scatter, where it is also tempting to suppose that certain sounds have imitative value. I. A. Richards, in *The Philosophy of Rhetoric,* has given the proper explanation of this false supposition. Such groups of words share morphemes, or an element which has both a common sound and a common meaning. It is 'the existence of a group of words with a common sound and meaning' which 'is the explanation of our belief in a correspondence' between certain sounds and a meaning, for example that *-atter* by itself means 'noise of explosion.' We ought to note, however, that morphemes are a positive resource in poetry. In reading any single word from a morpheme group, we are influenced by our awareness of the other members. Our response to the common element may thus be intensified, and we may draw in meanings that belong properly to some of the other words having similar sounds. So Herbert's 'flaring' owes part of its effect to a happy confusion with blaring.

But what shall we say of more dubious cases, where readers and critics insist that somehow the sounds of certain letters resemble or illustrate the meaning of the words? Let us answer the question by taking an example for analysis. I believe we shall find a kind of illustration, though not of the sort ordinarily assumed.

It will be a very hardened reader who feels no appropriateness of sound in the wonderful opening line of 'Once by the Pacific':

> The shattered water made a misty din.

How can we fairly account for this feeling beyond saying that we tend to attribute representative value to any words that name sounds? Perhaps we are beguiled by a simple ambiguity. We may mean by appropriateness of sound that the auditory images evoked by 'din' or 'shattered' are appropriate, or we may mean—as I do—that the speech sounds seem in some way fitting. Certainly the sounds heard in saying these words do not resemble what we hear when ocean waves fall against a cliff. These same words might form the first line of a poem about a waterfall, a geyser (English or American), a waterspout, or a hurricane. In all of these cases we can be sure that there would be some readers who would insist that the speech sounds actually were like those made by the particular phenomenon.

But let us leave the mazes of fancy and turn to the prosaic business of describing the sounds we make in reading the line:

> The shattered water made a misty din.

We note that in every word (except the two articles) there is either a t-sound or a d-sound, that two have also an s-sound, and that 'shattered' combines all three plus belonging to the morpheme group mentioned above. There is also the alliteration in 'made' and 'misty.' The t's and d's being stops (or mutes) are consonants with which we can easily make a considerable noise in pronunciation: we stop the sound and let it out with a slight explosion. (They are sometimes called plosives.) The st and sh combination are also usable for the same purpose. More important than the selection of a particular type of consonant is the heaping up of similar sounds, since in poetry as in most other arts, one or two occurrences of an element often convey an impression that a much larger number of repetitions has been made. Thanks to this law of repetition, we are in the present instance made extremely conscious of the consonant sounds; we are, so to speak, distracted *to* the sounds we are making. Because of the companion words in -atter, the sense of violent going apart in 'shattered' is reinforced, and the word is enunciated with a corresponding increase of stress. Finally there is the alliteration, which forces us to accentuate the initial m's and to give both 'made' and 'misty' more than ordinary emphasis. For whenever words are alliterated—whatever their sense—we have a tendency to exaggerate emphasis, even against our will, as everyone knows from reading slogans.

How, without falling into any of the ancient traps, can we explain the appropriateness we certainly feel when we read the line containing the sounds we have been describing? We can say that the poet has given us sounds and especially a collocation of sounds with which we can make a big noise if we want to. And the meanings—'din,' 'shattered,' and the later references to waves and storm—give us a very good excuse. The reader makes a metaphor of sound, but he makes it from resources given by the poet. Frost heaped up the t's and d's and wrote in the alliteration and by various devices directed our attention to the sounds of the words we were pronouncing.

We make sounds expressive, but not any chance collocation of sounds, a fact that translation proves most painfully. How often we try to summon to a translation the sound values of the original, and with how little success! 'Translation' of Frost's line into other English may serve as a crude device to show that we cannot create a metaphor of sound or feel any appropriateness in what we hear unless we are given the proper resources. Suppose we read:

> The broken water made a hazy roar.

This bald line must not be read as having the same meaning as Frost's, but as if it were a new first line to the poem. Let us read it for all that is in it and try to discover, as in reading the original, a striking appropriateness in the sounds uttered. Read in the context of the poem, 'broken' and 'roar' invite some noise and vehemence in enunciation, but the line as a whole does not thrust its sound on our attention. The most elocutionary of readers could not force a very satisfactory noise from this set of sounds. Why? Not merely because there are no noisy consonants in the new line. There are in fact single examples of the various types noted above. But the accumulation of like sounds, the devices by which the sound was made a bit obvious, are gone, and with their loss goes the possibility of making particularly expressive sounds. We cannot make or feel any relationship of appropriateness.

Chapter V

THE SINEWIE THREAD

. . . the sinewie thread my braine lets fall
Through every part,
Can tye those parts, and make mee one of all . . .

JOHN DONNE

Surprised by joy—impatient as the Wind
I turned to share the transport—Oh! with whom
But Thee, deep buried in the silent tomb,
That spot which no vicissitude can find?
Love, faithful love, recalled thee to my mind—
But how could I forget thee? Through what power,
Even for the least division of an hour,
Have I been so beguiled as to be blind
To my most grievous loss!—That thought's return
Was the worst pang that sorrow ever bore,
Save one, one only, when I stood forlorn,
Knowing my heart's best treasure was no more;
That neither present time, nor years unborn
Could to my sight that heavenly face restore.

WILLIAM WORDSWORTH

Wordsworth's sonnet, as he might himself say, carries us so quickly into the heart of passion that in discussing it we may forget that we have been reading a poem. Which is another way of saying that it is the purest poetry. The words reach fulfilment in holding up a moment of experience for full appreciation, and that is all * they do. It is

* A biographical reading, which the usual footnote to the poem invites, is altogether misleading and singularly unprofitable.

a poem we can memorize while being oddly unaware of the words of which it is made, a beguiling example for those who talk about direct communication of emotion in poetry.

We may well hesitate to ask how such a poem is composed. For while our sense of its wholeness is immediate, the success of the sonnet is precarious enough (characteristically so, as F. R. Leavis has remarked) to make us doubt whether it will bear close scrutiny. It may be asked whether the poem will not put an embarrassing strain on the critical method of this book, or whether analysis of such simple and passionate poetry is at all possible. The reader can decide later how both the poem and the method have fared; for the moment the sonnet may stand as a reminder of the questions to be raised in this chapter: what do we mean by a key design and how do we find one in a particular poem; and how can we show that it *is* a key design?

When we made a full interpretation of a poem, we saw the most complete coalescence of all designs—dramatic, metaphorical, and rhythmic. At the turning point of Donne's judgment day sonnet, we felt at once the contrast between the cosmic and personal situations, between the all-ness of the first and the alone-ness of the second, between the grand movement of godlike commands and the variability of human meditation. If we reread the poem with a sense of these interweaving patterns, we can see also that there is a key design, which, as compared with any of the other designs, connects more phases of the poem and so has more to do with determining the total attitude. The key design of Donne's sonnet lies in the contrast of situations and tones; it is primarily dramatic rather than metaphorical. (From the discussion of sound patterns it is fairly certain that the possibility of a key design in sound can be excluded.)

Throughout the rest of the book I shall be discussing works in which the key design is primarily of a single type, either metaphorical or dramatic or ironic. Though this happens to be true of many works of literature, blends of every sort are as frequent, and a flexible reader will be ready for them. It is important also to keep our questions in the right order: we ask first if there is a key design, and next, if at all, what is its type. There is not necessarily a single dominant design, or one easily discernible. Poets must write as they write, and readers are not to rewrite for them. The balance of power among patterns in some poems is extremely even; in others, notably those in the Symbolist tradition, it is easy enough to see that the unifying design is metaphorical, but because of the deliberately broken movement of images it is almost impossible to trace the connecting links. In looking for a key design,* we are putting a question to a piece of literature, not setting up an inflexible requirement.

I shall try to show how the question may be answered by analyzing three poems, each of them very differently organized, though the key design of each is metaphorical. Finding a key design, it will appear, is largely a business of showing someone else that we have already found one.

I

The Extasie

I Where, like a pillow on a bed,
  A Pregnant banke swel'd up, to rest
The violets reclining head,
  Sat we two, one anothers best.
Our hands were firmely cimented
  With a fast balme, which thence did spring,
Our eye-beames twisted, and did thred
  Our eyes, upon one double string;
So to'entergraft our hands, as yet
  Was all the meanes to make us one,
And pictures in our eyes to get
  Was all our propagation.
II As 'twixt two equall Armies, Fate
  Suspends uncertaine victorie,

* Though on occasion I refer to *the* key design, it will not matter seriously if the reader does not agree with my choice. If he can admit that the design is important, he can follow with profit the analyses in this and the following chapters. If he can see something of what I do in finding a major design and if he glimpses the possibility of making similar discoveries for himself, we need not quarrel over terms and particular judgments. Complete agreement may be left to angelic intelligences who dwell in a less imperfect environment than any inhabited by readers and writers of literary criticism.

Our soules, (which to advance their state,
  Were gone out,) hung 'twixt her, and mee.
And whil'st our soules negotiate there,
  Wee like sepulchrall statues lay;
All day, the same our postures were,
  And wee said nothing, all the day.
If any, so by love refin'd,
  That he soules language understood,
And by good love were growen all minde,
  Within convenient distance stood,
He (though he knew not which soule spake,
  Because both meant, both spake the same)
Might thence a new concoction take,
  And part farre purer then he came.

III This Extasie doth unperplex
  (We said) and tell us what we love,
Wee see by this, it was not sexe,
  Wee see, we saw not what did move:
But as all severall soules containe
  Mixture of things, they know not what,
Love, these mixt soules, doth mixe againe,
  And makes both one, each this and that.
A single violet transplant,
  The strength, the colour, and the size,
(All which before was poore, and scant,)
  Redoubles still, and multiplies.
When love, with one another so
  Interinanimates two soules,
That abler soule, which thence doth flow,
  Defects of lonelinesse controules.
Wee then, who are this new soule, know,
  Of what we are compos'd, and made,
For, th'Atomies of which we grow,
  Are soules, whom no change can invade.

IV But O alas, so long, so farre
  Our bodies why doe wee forbeare?
They are ours, though they are not wee, Wee are
  The intelligences, they the spheare.

We owe them thankes, because they thus,
Did us, to us, at first convay,
Yeelded their forces, sense, to us,
Nor are drosse to us, but allay.
On man heavens influence workes not so,
But that it first imprints the ayre,
Soe soule into the soule may flow,
Though it to body first repaire.
As our blood labours to beget
Spirits, as like soules as it can,
Because such fingers need to knit
That subtile knot, which makes us man:
So must pure lovers soules descend
T'affections, and to faculties,
Which sense may reach and apprehend,
Else a great Prince in prison lies.
To'our bodies turne wee then, that so
Weake men on love reveal'd may looke;
Loves mysteries in soules doe grow,
But yet the body is his booke.
v And if some lover, such as wee,
Have heard this dialogue of one,
Let him still marke us, he shall see
Small change, when we'are to bodies gone.

JOHN DONNE

The 'day' of 'The Extasie' is a compact and surprising biography of love in which two lovers go from sensual intimacy to a marriage of minds to a union that is both sensuous and beyond the senses. Though the main outlines are clear enough, full understanding of the poem demands some familiarity with certain ideas about love, the soul, and the relation of the soul and body * that are important in other poems by Donne, notably 'Aire and Angels'; and like 'Aire and Angels,' 'The Extasie' has a salient metaphor which is worked out in a strictly logical order. The progress of love is compared to

* For the relation between 'The Extasie' and the Neoplatonic concept of 'ecstasy,' see the notes in *The Poems of John Donne,* ed. H. J. C. Grierson (Oxford, 1912), vol. II, pp. 51, 52.

the achievement of a mystical union between the individual soul and God. But the analogy with religious ecstasy, though apparently the key metaphor, does not control the whole poem. Donne is writing of human lovers, and their drama reaches a conclusion quite different from that of the mystic union to which certain stages of their love are compared:

> But O alas, so long, so farre
>   Our bodies why doe wee forbeare?

The poem moves in five act-like phases (marked in the text by Roman numerals): (I) a fairly objective view of the lovers; (II) the two preparatory stages of 'ecstasy': the flight of the soul from the body and the trance; (III) the ecstatic vision; (IV) the 'descent' of the souls to the body; (V) the complete union (again a more objective view). As the outline rather baldly indicates, the different phases of the poem are clearly related both as steps in an analogical argument and as stages in a changing relationship between the two lovers. Donne makes us feel that every step is logically right and humanly true. And certainly our sense of a finely ordered experience owes much to the clarity of this logical and dramatic design and to the fine tact with which it is expressed. But we should not feel so fully the connection between the stages or a sensuous unity in the whole poem apart from the peculiar sequence of metaphors that make up its key design. Let me go through the different phases of the poem, pointing out the salient metaphors in each and indicating what they express and how they connect the steps in the drama-argument. In the process the key metaphor * will appear almost of itself.

(I) The opening section, through both the setting and the voice of the speaker, anticipates the last phase of the poem, the new and more complete union of the lovers. The 'banke' is a bed and a symbol of propagation. The voice is 'we' and also 'one,' a curious 'dialogue of one,' as we discover at the end of the poem. The language of this section is filled with metaphors of sensuous closeness and of a physical union not yet realized: 'cimented,' 'twisted,' 'upon one double string,' 'entergraft,' 'meanes to make us one.'

* See footnote p. 91 for a general account of a key metaphor.

(II) In the first stage of religious-like ecstasy the souls seem to move out of the body; they are not merely 'out,' but hanging ' 'twixt' the two and in communication with one another. (Note the emphasis on between-ness.) In the moment of ecstatic calm the lovers' souls are curiously confused:

> (though he knew not which soule spake,
> Because both meant, both spake the same) . . .

The extreme purity of a love become all soul is expressed by a chemical metaphor which includes in passing still another metaphor of uniting ('concoction').

(III) In the moment of revelation the lovers have a rare understanding of the fusion that has taken place:

> This Extasie doth unperplex . . .

'Unperplex' (paradoxically a metaphor of disuniting) by its derivation harks back to 'twisted.' But the paradox is not superficial, because the union of souls is an undoing of the earlier sensuous union. Their present relation, like all mystical experiences, can be suggested only by reaching for analogies, and Donne pushes language out in all directions, even coining a word ('interinanimates') in his effort to express this ineffable closeness. But he does not forget the human situation and the physical setting of his drama:

> A single violet transplant,
> The strength, the colour, and the size,
> (All which before was poore, and scant,)
> Redoubles still, and multiplies.

The symbol of the violet comes both as a recollection and a surprise; for while 'violet' recalls the scene, 'transplant' anticipates a meaning we cannot exactly define before reading

> That abler soule, which thence doth flow,
> Defects of lonelinesse controules.

As so often in Donne, one metaphor is completed only by introducing a second, for the transplantation of souls symbolized by the violet is expressed by a shift to the wholly new metaphor of 'interinanimation,' the most intricate and intense expression of mutuality in the whole poem. The stress at this point is on the miraculous 'com-posing' of souls to produce a new one, or—in other terms—to reach a oneness of mind.

(IV) But the lovers reach for a still richer and more complex relation, one, in Yeats's phrase, of 'blood, intellect, and soul all running together.' To express this relation Donne builds up a whole new chain of metaphors of union. There is novelty but no break in continuity, since the same body of belief allows for the union of souls and the connection between divine intelligence and physical manifestation, whether an astronomical sphere, or air, or the human body. The sequence of metaphors has its supporting logic while giving ever subtler impressions of the meeting of the lovers' souls through their senses. The sequence runs: 'intelligence' through its 'sphere'; divine 'influence' through 'ayre'; 'soule flowing into soule'; the likeness of 'spirits' (sensations, et cetera) to 'soules'; the knitting of the 'subtile knot'; and the 'revelation' of love through the body's 'booke.'

(V) Finally it appears that this completed union is so like the 'ecstatic' one that 'small change' ('so little disparitie') can be seen:

> And if some lover, such as wee,
> Have heard this dialogue of one,
> Let him still marke us, he shall see
> Small change, when we'are to bodies gone.

We have been brought with the lovers through various stages, from sensuous closeness to 'abstraction' from the body and the purest union of souls to a new union of souls within the senses. And we have been brought successfully, we feel the drama as an unbroken curve of experience, because of the connection achieved through Donne's metaphors. Looking back over the poem, we note a remarkable series of expressions, many of which have already been pointed out: 'two one anothers best . . . dialogue of one . . . meanes to make us one . . . knew not which soule spake . . . mixt soules . . . interinanimates . . . soule into soule . . . ' Each metaphor, from 'two one anothers best' to 'small change' expresses some form of extraordinarily close union, each shares in some degree the meaning of 'subtle interfusion,' the key metaphor of 'The Extasie.'

We are made to experience every stage of the drama in terms of this single basic metaphor.

The metaphorical design of the poem is thus of an 'over-and-over' sort, being built up by a series of explicit metaphors each of which is a variation on a central analogy. Within this large continuity there are minor continuities, each expressing some peculiar analogy of union. There is, for instance, the odd chain of metaphors of wound-togetherness: 'twisted . . . entergraft . . . one double string . . . unperplex . . . knit that subtile knot.' Or there are the metaphors of physical-chemical combination: 'refin'd . . . concoction . . . mixture . . . mixt . . . mixe . . . Atomies.' Though certainly minor in our consciousness, they are there, and they contribute immensely to that Donnesque sense of 'all throughtherness'—to borrow a phrase of Hopkins'—which, incidentally, Hopkins understood as a technical as well as an imaginative fact. Or rather, he saw what we are demonstrating over and over, the inseparability of imaginative power from technical control.

II

The building up of a key design through a number of variants of a single metaphor is probably more common in works of a certain length. But it is often important in unifying short as well as long poems. My next example, Yeats's 'Two Songs from a Play,' shows some recurrent metaphors and images in a key design that is altogether different from that of 'The Extasie':

Two Songs from a Play

I

I saw a staring virgin stand
Where holy Dionysus died,
And tear the heart out of his side,
And lay the heart upon her hand
And bear that beating heart away;
And then did all the Muses sing
Of Magnus Annus at the spring,
As though God's death were but a play.

Another Troy must rise and set,
Another lineage feed the crow,
Another Argo's painted prow
Drive to a flashier bauble yet.
The Roman Empire stood appalled:
It dropped the reins of peace and war
When that fierce virgin and her Star
Out of the fabulous darkness called.

II

In pity for man's darkening thought
He walked that room and issued thence
In Galilean turbulence;
The Babylonian starlight brought
A fabulous, formless darkness in;
Odour of blood when Christ was slain
Made all Platonic tolerance vain
And vain all Doric discipline.

Everything that man esteems
Endures a moment or a day.
Love's pleasure drives his love away,
The painter's brush consumes his dreams;
The herald's cry, the soldier's tread
Exhaust his glory and his might:
Whatever flames upon the night
Man's own resinous heart has fed.

Although each song has its completeness, the two may be regarded as a single poem, since they have in common a group of related symbols—a metaphorical design that is fairly typical of more purely symbolic * composition in literature. What is important for the present discussion is that there is a real and effective key symbol in the 'Songs' and that its connecting power is realized throughout

* The term is used here in the sense defined in chapter III, and not in any restricted historical 'Symboliste' sense. I am not, for example, thinking of Yeats's symbols as representing mystic realities or primitive, though unrecognized, desires.

both. One need not read 'A Vision' or be a Yeatsian to recognize most of the expressions that are symbolic and to get their more obvious meanings, for they are familiar in literary or historical tradition. It is necessary to have some notion of the Magnus Annus, the great astronomical cycle of the ancients, the end of which marked the beginning of a new era, as in Virgil's

> magnus ab integro saeclorum nascitur ordo.

A memory of Shelley's 'world's great age' is convenient, too, and a minimum knowledge of the Dionysiac cult and its connection with Greek tragedy is assumed. Yeats apparently alludes to the rather curious myth in which Athena, the virgin goddess, carries the heart of the dead Dionysus to Zeus.

The best way to grasp the pattern of the poem is not to collect allusions, but to feel how it goes as we read:

> I saw a staring virgin stand . . .

we are hearing a visionary song that moves in glimpses of revelation. The poem proceeds with 'lyric inconsequence,' in rhythms having marked rhymes and striking repetitions. Under the influence of these turning and returning sounds, along with even a vague notion of the Magnus Annus, we soon feel the cycle metaphor as dominant, certainly in the first and possibly in the second song.

The historical meaning of the cycle is expressed through a series of allusive symbols. First comes a compressed picture of the Dionysiac cult and the spring festivals in which the god's death was in a real sense enacted in 'a play,' the cult and art being symbolic of the Greek city-state at its height. The more familiar symbols of the next two stanzas present later stages in the cycle: the decline of Greece, followed by the Roman achievement ('another Troy'), which was in turn followed by Rome's decline and the beginning of Christian civilization. 'Another Troy' also points back to the rise and fall of a pre-Greek civilization.

So much for 'cycle' as a symbol of historical evolution. Now to see how the connecting power of the symbol as a key metaphor is realized and how an imaginative unity in the poem is created. In my outline of the historical cycle the symbols are connected primarily in a chronological scheme; in the poem, they are linked—

and wonderfully—by the 'play' of a similar ambiguity in the expression of each symbolic allusion and image. The 'virgin' who 'stares' in ecstasy as she rends the 'holy Dionysus' is also the Virgin, since the spring festival anticipates Easter and Christian rites. This sense of Christianity as a rebirth of barbarism permeates the following vision of Christ's birth, life, and death. The Virgin is 'fierce,' and 'her Star' comes not as light but as darkness. 'The Babylonian starlight' suggests the astrological superstitions of Babylon, 'the fabulous formless darkness' expressing the chaos of strange religions (the cults of Mithras, of the Great Mother, et cetera) which came into the Empire from the East. In attaching these overtones to 'the ceremony of innocence' Yeats is expressing a profound historic irony and in particular the irony of Christianity or of any similar religion:

> The uncontrollable mystery on the bestial floor.

His awareness of opposing values is so subtly poised that we can feel it in the shifting meanings of single words, for instance, 'darkening' and 'turbulence' in the following lines:

> In pity for man's darkening thought
> He walked that room and issued thence
> In Galilean turbulence . . .

Christ became flesh in pity for man as living in ignorance of true salvation, as living in a world of gradual intellectual decay. 'Darkening' anticipates the irony of the next two lines: by being born and by entering the world, Christ (the Word) submitted to the confusion of human life and the violence of Calvary and so loosed another 'turbulence,' the chaos of superstitious beliefs that brought the end of civilized order in mind and state ('Platonic tolerance' and 'Doric discipline').

The light that plays on the pagan symbols is equally blended. There is an ambiguity in the happy song that symbolizes the Greek achievement, 'God's death' reminding us of a latent barbarism which would triumph in the future. There is irony too in the expressions used of the Roman conquest:

> Another Troy must rise and set,
> Another lineage feed the crow,

Another Argo's painted prow
Drive to a flashier bauble yet.

The peace of Augustus was both a moment of high civilization and the moment of a fatal relaxation of control, a 'dropping of the reins of peace and war.' In his attitude to Graeco-Roman civilization as in his attitude to Christianity, Yeats is expressing an inherent and universal irony: the achievement of a value is the loss of a value. The universality is apparent in the lines just quoted, which apply equally well to Roman or Greek or modern Christian or any civilization.

The final stanza comes as a fulfilment of this larger meaning of the key symbol; it expresses with similar ambiguities the equivalent in the individual life of the cyclical movement of history:

Everything that man esteems
Endures a moment or a day.
Love's pleasure drives his love away,
The painter's brush consumes his dreams;
The herald's cry, the soldier's tread
Exhaust his glory and his might:
Whatever flames upon the night
Man's own resinous heart has fed.

The first two lines are slightly inadequate, perilously near to a mere *sic transit,* but the metaphors that follow are expressive of the central paradox: all achievement is self-destructive. In the last of these symbols the paradox is expressed in images that recall the earlier symbols and so imply the identity of the individual and historical cycles:

Whatever flames upon the night
Man's own resinous heart has fed.

The 'flame' of man's accomplishment in its 'night' (the surrounding ignorance, difficulty, disorder) reminds us of the ambiguous brightness of Graeco-Roman glory and of Christ's revealing Star. The 'formed' is from the 'formless.' The 'resinous heart' is perhaps the most brilliant imaginative link in the poem, for 'resinous' takes us back via 'flame' to the pine torch, the *taeda* of the ancients, which was brandished by the worshipping Maenads. The 'heart' recalls the Dionysiac element which is in human life the source of both creation and destruction.

The cycle metaphor is thus the key to a large imaginative unity. The ambiguities we have noted are not merely mechanical uniformities used to connect symbols; they are the expression of what 'cycle' means for Yeats. We feel its meaning and its unifying power through the constant glow of irony and through recurrent images of darkness and light which are the sensuous equivalent of the ironic implications.

The result is a poem (regarding the two songs as a unit) remarkable in concentration and scope. It is large in its view of history, in the awareness of human potentiality of every sort, and large in the balance of its awareness. There is the most direct relation between this success and the economy of Yeats's symbolic design.

III

What happens now if we put our questions about key design to the Wordsworth sonnet that stands at the head of this chapter? (See page 75.) In rhetorical surface it seems very different from the other poems we have been discussing, no salient metaphor or image or any sequence of images being immediately apparent. But on rereading, the poem occupies us fully and continuously, from the initial surprise through the puzzled questionings to the recognition of a final loss. Can we describe any special ordering of language that accounts for our sense of wholeness and power?

We may start with what seems to be a key expression, 'vicissitude' ('That spot which no vicissitude can find'), a clue to be followed with tact, or the poem may be turned into a parable. The suggested design is a vicissitude-no-vicissitude movement which throughout the poem barely breaks the surface of attention. 'Vicissitude,' taken in the immediate context, is experiencing a shock of sudden personal emotion:

> Surprised by joy—impatient as the Wind . . .

'No vicissitude' is the negative and more; with the surrounding images ('deep,' 'buried,' 'silent'), its meaning widens out into a remote and spacious silence free from all change. The poem holds together through the tension between change-of-sudden-emotion and no-change-whatever.

But in all poetry the continuous realization of the key design is everything; in 'Surprised by Joy' the metaphorical connection works largely through dramatic and rhythmic analogies. Considered dramatically, the opening is extraordinary: we are dropped without warning into the midst of another person's experience. The almost incoherent phrases and the sentence-breaks express the impact of a feeling out of the blue, which belongs only to an absorbed self. The second shock (and change) in the poem comes with the mere implication that someone else may be concerned:

> I turned to share the transport—Oh! with whom
> But Thee, deep buried in the silent tomb . . .

The run-over lines, the relief of an expected pause, bring us down on 'Thee' with extreme force. But the intensely personal tone with its warmth of relation is at once brought up against images of remoteness and isolation in

> That spot which no vicissitude can find . . .

The personal tone is recovered in the next line, however, and is maintained through the following five or six lines. But fluctuations in attitude and movement continue. No sooner has a feeling and a rhythm been set (as in the lyric swing of 'Love, faithful love,') than it is broken by a contrasting feeling and rhythm:

> Love, faithful love, recalled thee to my mind—
> But how could I forget thee?

Then comes the passage in which Wordsworth gives us the fullest sense of his odd 'vicissitude,' of being 'possessed' by emotion. The accentuation of rhyme in 'power-hour,' the reiteration of -e's and -be's produce a round-and-round hypnotic rhythm that serves as still another figure of beguiled consciousness:

> Through what power,
> Even for the least division of an hour,
> Have I been so beguiled as to be blind
> To my most grievous loss!

'My most grievous loss'—the generalized and conventional phrase coming after the earlier 'thees'—marks the completion of a beautifully graded shift in tone, a shift that introduces the last major break in the poem's progress:

> —That thought's return
> Was the worst pang that sorrow ever bore . . .

The puzzlings are now dropped without an answer; the turn in the sonnet comes at this unexpected place; the stress falls heavily and abnormally on 'that'; and the rhyme for 'return' is imperfect:

> —That thought's return . . .

The three words arrive out of the course that the poem has been following dramatically, rhetorically, and rhythmically. There is no escaping their finality.

After so many shocks and fluctuations the poem concludes with the fullest possible emphasis on the unchanging fact of loss:

> . . . the worst pang that sorrow ever bore,
> Save one, one only, when I stood forlorn,
> Knowing my heart's best treasure was no more;
> That neither present time, nor years unborn
> Could to my sight that heavenly face restore.

The contrast with the situation at the opening of the poem is portrayed dramatically by the shift in memory to the moment when the loss was first fully realized. There is an even sharper contrast in the difference between the movement of the two divisions of the sonnet. In the octet we felt the sentence patterns pushing against the regularity of the meter and rhyme, riding across them or surprising us with coincidences. (The meter is astonishingly regular.) But in the last five lines of the poem this rivalry tends to disappear. Line-ends and pauses for sense fall together; there are no complete stops within the lines; there is more balance in phrasing; the rhymes are true and ring in the ear. We have reached the most stable sense of changelessness: the intimations of the key line have been (rather unexpectedly) fulfilled.

It is now clear that 'Surprised by Joy' does have a key design and that its design is as certainly metaphorical as that of Yeats's

'Songs' or Donne's 'The Extasie.' Wordsworth's poem, for all its seeming directness, is equally a triumph of literary art, of creating rich analogies through language. But its key metaphor is almost completely hidden, since the analogies are expressed only through dramatic and rhythmic means. Yeats's central metaphor is hardly less implicit, but his design is of a different type. He presents a group of symbolic metaphors related in a curious way to the key symbol: each is similarly ambiguous and so expressive of the double meaning of 'cycle.' Although Donne expresses his central metaphor by indirection, his design is immediately manifest.

The initial choice of a key metaphor presented quite a different problem in each poem. In no one of the three was there a direct statement comparable to Herbert's

> Doctrine and life, colours and light, in one
> When they combine and mingle. . .

Donne's key metaphor was the least common denominator of a whole series. Yeats, by referring to the Magnus Annus, gave a broad hint of his main analogy. In 'Surprised by Joy' the hint of the key relationship was even more oblique.

But we were not certain that we had found the key metaphor * of Wordsworth's sonnet or of the other two poems until we had tried out our initial guess and proved that it was sound. When it came to showing that the key metaphor *was* a key metaphor, our procedure was very nearly the same. We were always tracing continuities in ironies, or in recurrent metaphors and images, or in tonal and rhythmic patterns. We were always looking for evidence that the central analogy was being renewed as the poem progressed.

The interrelation of designs being so close, it is not strange that we cannot always be sure whether this or that design is the key one. The choice between calling the key design of 'Surprised by Joy'

* Note the two requirements for a key metaphor: (1) The key metaphor is the analogy common to most of the other metaphors that make up the key design; it is the basic analogy of which they are variants. (The 'other metaphors' may be expressed through explicit metaphors, symbols, rhythmic and tonal patterns, et cetera.) (2) The key metaphor names the relationship that connects most phases of the poem-experience. This connection will be traceable through all or most of the other designs.

metaphorical or dramatic is close and not worth arguing. But the difficulty of choosing is a reminder that we are dealing with whole structures and that a dominant relationship (whatever its type) is being actively realized through all the sets of relationships in the poem.

Before setting out to find key designs in larger and often more complex works we need to recall why we look for designs at all. Our purpose has some limited likeness to that of earlier seekers for design. Like them we are concerned with evidences only for the experiences that are guaranteed and made accessible by the search. To return more certainly to much smaller universes, we are concerned with designs as they give us access to the attitudes expressed through them. By grasping the figure of 'Surprised by Joy' we catch Wordsworth's peculiarly sharp yet stable vibration to the rediscovery of loss. By perceiving the central analogy of 'The Extasie' and seeing how it extends through nearly every detail of the poem, we experience the closeness and refinement of relationship which is the principal subject of Donne's poetry. By discovering the link between ambiguity and symbol in Yeats's 'Songs' we participate in the balance and integrity of his imaginative vision.

If we acquire a habit of always 'sounding' for a large relation in our reading experience and have some notion of how we find one, we need not worry about naming the type of the design. And since we are always asking basically the same question of every work, we can use, with intelligent variation, the same modes of analysis. In describing designs primarily dramatic or ironic, it is equally useful to look for key words or phrases, for recurrent expressions, or for a recurrent similarity in a series of expressions. So labeled, these methods sound crude and mechanical, but their definition in practice is more subtle, and there are other more flexible and more refined techniques which the reader may observe in the various analyses.

Part Two

IN LARGE LETTERS

. . . suppose that a short-sighted person had been asked by some one to read small letters from a distance; and it occurred to some one else that they might be found in another place which was larger and in which the letters were larger . . .

PLATO

Chapter VI

THE MIRROR OF ANALOGY: 'THE TEMPEST'

The Mind, that Ocean where each kind
Does streight its own resemblance find;
Yet it creates, transcending these,
Far other Worlds, and other Seas . . .

ANDREW MARVELL

Of *The Tempest,* we may say what Ferdinand said of the masque,

> This is a most majestic vision, and
> Harmonious charmingly.

The harmony of the play lies in its metaphorical design, in the closeness and completeness with which its rich and varied elements are linked through almost inexhaustible analogies. It is hard to pick a speech at random without coming on an expression that brings us by analogy into direct contact with elements that seem remote because of their place in the action or because of the type of experience they symbolize. Opening the play at the second act we read,

> Four legs and two voices; a most delicate monster!

The last phrase is comic enough as used of Caliban and as issuing from the lips of Stephano, a 'most foul' speaker. But 'delicate' evokes a more subtle incongruity by recalling characters and a world we might suppose were forgotten. Stephano is parodying Prospero when he rebukes Ariel as 'a spirit too delicate / To act her [Sycorax's] earthy and abhorr'd commands' and when he says,

> delicate Ariel,
> I'll set thee free for this!

We have in Stephano's words not only the familiar Shakespearean balancing of comic and serious, but a counterpointing of analogies that run throughout the play. 'Delicate' as the antithesis of 'earth' points to the opposition of Ariel and Caliban and to the often recurring earth-air symbolism of *The Tempest*. 'Delicate' used of this remarkable island creature echoes also the 'delicate temperance' of which the courtiers spoke and 'the air' that 'breathes . . . here most sweetly.' 'Monster'—almost another name for Caliban—balances these airy suggestions with an allusion to 'the people of the island . . . of monstrous shape' and thereby to the strain of fantastic sea lore in *The Tempest,* which is being parodied in this scene.

So viewed, Shakespeare's analogies may perhaps seem too much like exploding nebulae in an expanding though hardly ordered universe. But Shakespeare does not 'multiply variety in a wilderness of mirrors'; he makes use of a few fairly constant analogies that can be traced through expressions sometimes the same and sometimes extraordinarily varied. And the recurrent analogies (or continuities) are linked through a key metaphor into a single metaphorical design. Shakespeare is continually prodding us—often in ways of which we are barely conscious—to relate the passing dialogue with other dialogues into and through a super-design of metaphor.

In concentrating on how the design is built up, I am not forgetting that it is a metaphorical design in a *drama,* that we are interested in how Shakespeare has linked stages in a presentation of changing human relationships. Toward the end of the chapter I hope to show how wonderfully the metaphorical design is related to the main dramatic sequence of *The Tempest,* especially in the climactic speeches of Acts IV and V.

The play moves forward, we should remember, from a scene of tempest to a final promise of 'calm seas, auspicious gales,' and through a series of punishments or trials to a series of reconciliations and restorations. Although, as Dr. Johnson might say, there is a 'concatenation of events' running through Prospero's 'project' and though the play has a curiously exact time schedule, there is often little chronological or logical connection between successive dialogues or bits of action. To be sure Shakespeare has the Elizabethan conventions on his side, but the freedom of his dramatic composition in

The Tempest never seems merely conventional or capricious because the linkage of analogy is so varied and so pervasive.

The surest proof of the pervasiveness of Shakespeare's design lies in the mere number of continuities that can be discovered in the play. But some are more important than others because they can be traced through more expressions or in more scenes and because they express analogies more closely related to the key metaphor. The six main continuities, roughly labelled to indicate their character, are: 'strange-wondrous,' 'sleep-and-dream,' 'sea-tempest,' 'music-and-noise,' 'earth-air,' 'slavery-freedom,' and 'sovereignty-conspiracy.'

All of these continuities appear during the second scene of Act I, which is an exposition of Shakespeare's metaphorical and dramatic designs for the entire play. Near the close of the scene, Ariel's two songs offer wonderfully concentrated expressions of both designs. 'Come unto these yellow sands' calms the 'fury' of the waves and Ferdinand's 'passion,' thus charting in brief the course of the action. 'Full fathom five' is anticipatory in a very different fashion. It presents in miniature the main lines of the metaphorical design and sounds the key note of 'sea-change,' Shakespeare's most direct expression of the key metaphor of *The Tempest.*

The central portion of the scene follows:

ACT I, *scene* ii

Enter Prospero and Miranda

Miranda. If by your art, my dearest father, you have
Put the wild waters in this roar, allay them.
The sky, it seems, would pour down stinking pitch,
But that the sea, mounting to th' welkin's cheek,
Dashes the fire out. O! I have suffer'd
With those that I saw suffer: a brave vessel,
Who had, no doubt, some noble creatures in her,
Dash'd all to pieces. O! the cry did knock
Against my very heart. Poor souls, they perish'd.
Had I been any god of power, I would
Have sunk the sea within the earth, or e'er
It should the good ship so have swallow'd and
The fraughting souls within her.

Prospero. Be collected:
No more amazement. Tell your piteous heart
There 's no harm done.
Miranda. O, woe the day!
Prospero. No harm.
I have done nothing but in care of thee,—
Of thee, my dear one! thee, my daughter!—who
Art ignorant of what thou art, nought knowing
Of whence I am: nor that I am more better
Than Prospero, master of a full poor cell,
And thy no greater father.
Miranda. More to know
Did never meddle with my thoughts.
Prospero. 'Tis time
I should inform thee further. Lend thy hand,
And pluck my magic garment from me.—So:
[*Lays down his mantle.*
Lie there, my art.—Wipe thou thine eyes; have comfort.
The direful spectacle of the wrack, which touch'd
The very virtue of compassion in thee,
I have with such provision in mine art
So safely order'd, that there is no soul—
No, not so much perdition as an hair,
Betid to any creature in the vessel
Which thou heard'st cry, which thou saw'st sink. Sit down;
For thou must now know further.
Miranda. You have often
Begun to tell me what I am, but stopp'd,
And left me to a bootless inquisition,
Concluding, 'Stay; not yet.'
Prospero. The hour's now come,
The very minute bids thee ope thine ear;
Obey and be attentive. Canst thou remember
A time before we came unto this cell?
I do not think thou canst, for then thou wast not
Out three years old.
Miranda. Certainly, sir, I can.

Prospero. By what? by any other house or person?
Of anything the image tell me, that
Hath kept with thy remembrance.
Miranda. 'Tis far off;
And rather like a dream than an assurance
That my remembrance warrants. Had I not
Four or five women once that tended me?
Prospero. Thou hadst, and more, Miranda. But how is it
That this lives in thy mind? What seest thou else
In the dark backward and abysm of time?
If thou remember'st aught ere thou cam'st here,
How thou cam'st here, thou may'st.
Miranda. But that I do not.
Prospero. Twelve year since, Miranda, twelve year since,
Thy father was the Duke of Milan and
A prince of power.
Miranda. Sir, are not you my father?
Prospero. Thy mother was a piece of virtue, and
She said thou wast my daughter; and thy father
Was Duke of Milan, and his only heir
A princess,—no worse issued.
Miranda. O, the heavens!
What foul play had we that we came from thence?
Or blessed was 't we did?
Prospero. Both, both, my girl:
By foul play, as thou say'st, were we heav'd thence;
But blessedly holp hither.
Miranda. O! my heart bleeds
To think o' the teen that I have turn'd you to,
Which is from my remembrance. Please you, further.
Prospero. My brother and thy uncle, call'd Antonio,—
I pray thee, mark me,—that a brother should
Be so perfidious!—he whom next thyself,
Of all the world I lov'd, and to him put
The manage of my state; as at that time
Through all the signiories it was the first,
And Prospero the prime duke; being so reputed
In dignity, and for the liberal arts,

Without a parallel: those being all my study,
The government I cast upon my brother,
And to my state grew stranger, being transported
And rapt in secret studies. Thy false uncle—
Dost thou attend me?
Miranda. Sir, most heedfully.
Prospero. Being once perfected how to grant suits,
How to deny them, who t' advance, and who
To trash for over-topping; new created
The creatures that were mine, I say, or chang'd 'em,
Or else new form'd 'em: having both the key
Of officer and office, set all hearts i' the state
To what tune pleas'd his ear; that now he was
The ivy which had hid my princely trunk,
And suck'd my verdure out on't.—Thou attend'st not.
Miranda. O, good sir! I do.
Prospero. I pray thee, mark me.
I, thus neglecting worldly ends, all dedicated
To closeness and the bettering of my mind
With that, which, but by being so retir'd,
O'erpriz'd all popular rate, in my false brother
Awak'd an evil nature; and my trust,
Like a good parent, did beget of him
A falsehood in its contrary as great
As my trust was; which had, indeed no limit,
A confidence sans bound. He being thus lorded,
Not only with what my revenue yielded,
But what my power might else exact,—like one,
Who having, into truth, by telling of it,
Made such a sinner of his memory,
To credit his own lie,—he did believe
He was indeed the duke; out o' the substitution,
And executing th' outward face of royalty,
With all prerogative:—Hence his ambition growing,—
Dost thou hear?
Miranda. Your tale, sir, would cure deafness.
Prospero. To have no screen between this part he play'd
And him he play'd it for, he needs will be

Absolute Milan. Me, poor man,—my library
Was dukedom large enough: of temporal royalties
He thinks me now incapable; confederates,—
So dry he was for sway,—wi' the king of Naples
To give him annual tribute, do him homage;
Subject his coronet to his crown, and bend
The dukedom, yet unbow'd,—alas, poor Milan!—
To most ignoble stooping.
Miranda. O the heavens!
Prospero. Mark his condition and the event; then tell me
If this might be a brother.
Miranda. I should sin
To think but nobly of my grandmother:
Good wombs have borne bad sons.
Prospero. Now the condition.
This King of Naples, being an enemy
To me inveterate, hearkens my brother's suit;
Which was, that he, in lieu o' the premises
Of homage and I know not how much tribute,
Should presently extirpate me and mine
Out of the dukedom, and confer fair Milan,
With all the honours on my brother: whereon,
A treacherous army levied, one midnight
Fated to the purpose did Antonio open
The gates of Milan; and, i' the dead of darkness,
The ministers for the purpose hurried thence
Me and thy crying self.
Miranda. Alack, for pity!
I, not rememb'ring how I cried out then,
Will cry it o'er again: it is a hint,
That wrings mine eyes to 't.
Prospero. Hear a little further,
And then I'll bring thee to the present business
Which now 's upon us; without the which this story
Were most impertinent.
Miranda. Wherefore did they not
That hour destroy us?

Prospero. Well demanded, wench:
My tale provokes that question. Dear, they durst not,
So dear the love my people bore me, nor set
A mark so bloody on the business; but
With colours fairer painted their foul ends.
In few, they hurried us aboard a bark,
Bore us some leagues to sea; where they prepar'd
A rotten carcass of a boat, not rigg'd,
Nor tackle, sail, nor mast; the very rats
Instinctively have quit it: there they hoist us,
To cry to the sea that roar'd to us; to sigh
To the winds whose pity, sighing back again,
Did us but loving wrong.
Miranda. Alack! what trouble
Was I then to you!
Prospero. O, a cherubin
Thou wast, that did preserve me! Thou didst smile,
Infused with a fortitude from heaven,
When I have deck'd the sea with drops full salt,
Under my burden groan'd; which rais'd in me
An undergoing stomach, to bear up
Against what should ensue.
Miranda. How came we ashore?
Prospero. By Providence divine.
Some food we had and some fresh water that
A noble Neapolitan, Gonzalo,
Out of his charity,—who being then appointed
Master of this design,—did give us; with
Rich garments, linens, stuffs, and necessaries,
Which since have steaded much; so, of his gentleness,
Knowing I lov'd my books, he furnish'd me,
From mine own library with volumes that
I prize above my dukedom.
Miranda. Would I might
But ever see that man!
Prospero. Now I arise:— [*Resumes his mantle.*
Sit still, and hear the last of our sea-sorrow.
Here in this island we arriv'd; and here

Have I, thy schoolmaster, made thee more profit
Than other princes can, that have more time
For vainer hours and tutors not so careful.
Miranda. Heavens thank you for 't! And now, I pray you, sir,—
For still 'tis beating in my mind,—your reason
For raising this sea-storm?
Prospero. Know thus far forth.
By accident most strange, bountiful Fortune,
Now my dear lady, hath mine enemies
Brought to this shore; and by my prescience
I find my zenith doth depend upon
A most auspicious star, whose influence
If now I court not but omit, my fortunes
Will ever after droop. Here cease more questions;
Thou art inclin'd to sleep; 'tis a good dulness,
And give it way;—I know thou canst not choose.

As we trace the first two continuities ('strange-wondrous,' 'sleep-and-dream'), the reader can appreciate how unobtrusively they emerge from the developing dramatic pattern. Prospero's narrative, with which the scene opens, tells us of the past and describes the present situation while symbolizing the quality of *The Tempest* world. Prospero explains that his enemies have come to this shore 'by accident most strange,' and Miranda, who falls to sleep at the end of his tale, accounts for her lapse by saying,

The strangeness of your story put
Heaviness in me.

Prospero's tale was strange indeed: it included a ruler 'rapt in secret studies,' a 'false uncle' who 'new created / The creatures' of the state, the miraculous voyage of Prospero and Miranda (who was 'a cherubin') and their safe arrival 'by Providence divine.' This 'strangeness' is best defined by Alonso's remarks near the end of the play:

These are not natural events; they strengthen
From strange to stranger . . .

This is as strange a maze as e'er men trod;
And there is in this business more than nature
Was ever conduct of . . .

They are 'unnatural' in a broad seventeenth-century sense of the term; that is, outside the order which includes all created things. The theme is almost constantly being played on: 'strange,' 'strangely,' or 'strangeness' occur altogether some seventeen times, and similar meanings are echoed in 'wondrous,' 'monstrous,' 'divine.'

Of all the analogies of the play this is probably the vaguest, the nearest in effect to the atmospheric unity of nineteenth-century Romantic poetry. But a more precise metaphor of strangeness appears, the 'strangeness' of 'new created creatures.' From the 'accident most strange' of the shipwreck we come to Alonso's ponderous woe:

> O thou, mine heir
> Of Naples and of Milan! what strange fish
> Hath made his meal on thee?

and then to Trinculo's discovery of Caliban—'A strange fish!' With a similar comic antiphony, Miranda finds Ferdinand 'a thing divine,' and Ferdinand replies, 'O you wonder'; while a little later Caliban hails Trinculo as his god and cries, 'Thou wondrous man.' The full significance of these strange births will appear later.

The vague 'strangeness' of the island world is closely allied to a state of sleep, both continuities appearing in Miranda's remark about the 'heaviness' that came over her while listening to Prospero's story. The feeling that we are entering on an experience of sleep-and-dream arises beautifully out of the dramatic and rhythmic texture of the opening dialogue between father and daughter. The movement of these speeches with their oddly rocking repetitions is in key with the sleepy incredibility of the events about to be described: 'Canst thou remember . . . thou canst . . . I can . . . thy remembrance . . . my remembrance . . . thou remember'st . . . Twelve year since, Miranda, twelve year since . . .' Throughout the story Prospero is continually reminding Miranda to 'attend' to the telling, and it seems perfectly natural that at the end she should be 'inclin'd to sleep.' (Note in passing how neatly Shakespeare has broken a long narrative into dialogue and also given a distinct impression of Prospero's firmness and of Miranda's innocent dependence.) Miranda's images of the past come back to her 'rather like a dream,' and Prospero seems to be drawing their story from a world of sleep, 'the dark backward and abysm of time.'

With the next scene (the mourning King and his courtiers) we meet one of Shakespeare's typical analogical progressions. The sleep which affects the courtiers is, like Miranda's, a strange 'heaviness.' Their dialogue runs down, psychologically and rhythmically, through three echoes of Miranda's words:

Gonzalo. Will you laugh me asleep, for I am very heavy? . . .
Sebastian. Do not omit the heavy offer of it . . .
Alonso. Thank you. Wondrous heavy.
Sebastian. What a strange drowsiness possesses them!

The conversation that follows between the conspirators shows how Shakespeare uses an analogy to move to a new level of action and experience and to make them harmonious with what precedes and follows. Sebastian and Antonio begin by talking about actual sleep and waking: why are they not drowsy like the others? Then Antonio shifts to talking of sleepiness and alertness of mind, and from that to imagining that he sees 'a crown dropping' upon Sebastian's head. The wit becomes more complex as Sebastian describes Antonio's talk as 'sleepy language'—without meaning—though indicating that it does have meaning, 'There's meaning in thy snores.' This dialogue, which readers are liable to dismiss as so much Elizabethan wit, has its place within the play's metaphorical pattern. The plotting takes on a preposterous dreamy-sleepy character like that of Prospero's narrative and Miranda's recollections. Through such verbal trifling Shakespeare maintains the continuous quality of his imagined world.

References to similar wakings and sleepings, to dreams and dreamlike states, abound from here to the end of the play, where the sailors are 'brought moping . . . even in a dream,' and the grand awakening of all the characters is completed. But up to that point confusion between waking and sleep is the rule, being awake is never far from sleep or dream. In *The Tempest* sleep is always imminent, and more than once action ends in sleep or trance.

The witty talk of the conspirators glides from conceits of 'sleep' to conceits of 'the sea,' to talk of 'standing water' and 'flowing' and 'ebbing.' The 'good Gonzalo,' in consoling the King, speaks in similar figures:

It is foul weather in us all, good sir,
When you are cloudy.

Recurrent expressions of 'sea and tempest,' like those of 'sleep and dream,' are numerous and have a similar atmospheric value of not letting us forget the special quality of life on Prospero's island. But they also have far more important effects, for many of them become metaphors which are more precisely and more variously symbolic and which link more kinds of experience together.

By tracing two groups of 'tempest' expressions, metaphors of 'sea-swallowing' and images of 'clouds,' we may understand how these more complex analogies are built up. We may also see how Shakespeare moves from narrative fact to metaphor, from image or metaphor referring only to narrative fact to metaphor rich in moral and psychological implications. As in creating the analogies of 'strangeness' and 'sleep,' Shakespeare starts from a dramatic necessity: the audience must be told what the situation was in the storm scene with which the play opens, and they must learn through an actor (Miranda) how they are to take it. (See the speech on page 97.) Although there is a hint of magic in Miranda's vision of the tempest, she pictures it as a violent actuality:

Had I been any god of power, I would
Have sunk the sea within the earth, or e'er
It should the good ship so have swallow'd and
The fraughting souls within her.

As if there were an inner rhythm in these responses, this metaphor, like others we have been tracing, recurs in the plotting episode. Antonio is speaking of his sister Claribel, left behind in Tunis:

she that from whom
We all were sea-swallow'd, though some cast again,
And by that destiny to perform an act
Whereof what 's past is prologue, what to come
In yours and my discharge.

In this new context 'sea-swallowed' does several things at once. It brings back Miranda's horrified impression; but the magical nature of the storm now being known, the phrase reminds us that there was no 'sea-swallowing,' no actual sinking of 'fraughting souls.' Next, with a curiously Shakespearean 'glide and a jump' via the pun on 'cast,' 'sea-swallowed' merges into another metaphor (they are now 'cast' as actors in destiny's drama). 'Sea-swallowing' has become a metaphor that expresses destiny's extraordinary way of bringing Sebastian to the throne.

The irony of Antonio's words, which is clear to the audience, is made explicit later in the solemn speech in which Ariel explains the purpose of the tempest:

> You are three men of sin, whom Destiny—
> That hath to instrument this lower world
> And what is in 't,—the never-surfeited sea
> Hath caused to belch up you . . .

Few passages could show better how Shakespeare carries his analogies along and at the same time completely renews them. The 'belching up' recalls the wreck and the casting ashore and the earlier connection with destiny. But the sea's action is now described in much grosser terms and with grim sarcasm, while the oddly compact grammar makes 'the never-surfeited sea' very nearly a synonym for 'Destiny.' The violence though increased is now religious and moral; the imagery has become expressive of the strenuous punishment and purification of 'three men of sin.' * So by the continuity of his varying metaphor Shakespeare has expressed an unbroken transition from actual storm to the storm of the soul. This sequence, which expresses both physical and metaphysical transformations, points very clearly to the key metaphor of *The Tempest.*

The recurrent cloud images present a similar sequence as they take on various symbolic meanings in the course of the play. 'Cloud' does not actually occur in the opening storm scene, but when Trinculo sees 'another storm brewing' and speaks of a 'black cloud,' we are reminded of the original tempest. The cloud undergoes an appropriate change in Trinculo's speech; it 'looks like a foul bombard that would shed his liquor.' This comic cloud is very different from 'the curl'd clouds' on which Ariel rides, though they too are

* Alonso, Antonio, Sebastian.

associated with storms. The clouds of Caliban's exquisite speech are those of Ariel and the deities of the masque:

and then, in dreaming,
The clouds methought would open and show riches
Ready to drop upon me . . .

Clouds—here linked with magical riches—become in Prospero's 'cloud-capp'd towers' speech a symbol for the unsubstantial splendor of the world. One of the subordinate metaphors there, the 'melting into air' and the 'dissolving' of the clouds, is picked up in Prospero's later words about the courtiers:

The charm dissolves apace;
And as the morning steals upon the night,
Melting the darkness, so their rising senses
Begin to chase the ignorant fumes that mantle
Their clearer reason.

This dissolution of night clouds (suggested also by 'fumes') is a figure for the change from madness to sanity, from evil ignorance to the clear perceptions of reason. Although the cloud images of the play are so varied, they have a common symbolic value, for whether they are clouds of tempest or of visionary riches or of the soul, they are always magically unsubstantial. The reader is led to feel some touch of likeness among experiences as different as a storm at sea, a bit of drunken whimsy, a vision of heavenly and earthly beauty, and a spiritual regeneration. The cloud sequence, as an arc of metaphor, is in perfect relation to the gradual dramatic movement from tempest and punishment to fair weather and reconciliation, the images having meanings more and more remote from any actual storm.

The 'cloud-like' change in the distracted souls of the guilty nobles was induced (as if in reminiscence of Plato) by *Solemn music*—

A solemn air and the best comforter
To an unsettled fancy.

Many of the expressions referring to music, like the stage direction above, are not explicitly metaphorical, but along with the continuities of 'sleep' and 'strangeness' they help maintain the magical character of the action. The music is always the music of spirits and always a sign of more than natural events.

The one fairly constant musical metaphor * in *The Tempest* is the symbolic opposition of confused noises, especially storm sounds, and harmonious music. The key word and the central impression of the opening scene is certainly 'noise' † in the modern sense. The impression is carried over in the first words of the next scene:

> If by your art, my dearest father, you have
> Put the wild waters in this roar, allay them.

Miranda's request is soon answered by Ariel's first song, 'the wild waves' are 'whist.' The *solemn and strange music* heard when the *strange Shapes* bring a banquet to the courtiers makes Alonso say, 'What harmony is this? my good friends, hark!' Gonzalo replies: 'Marvellous sweet music!' By contrast, when Ariel enters shortly after, in order to inform the 'three men of sin' of their punishment by the storm, there is an off-stage sound of *Thunder and lightning.* The masque vision which Ferdinand finds 'harmonious charmingly' is rudely interrupted by *a strange, hollow, and confused noise* which symbolizes the stormy anger expressed by Prospero in the speeches that follow. When in the next scene he prepares to forgive his enemies, he abjures the 'rough magic' by which he

> call'd forth the mutinous winds,
> And 'twixt the green sea and the azur'd vault
> Set roaring war . . .

As the *solemn music* is played the clouds of ignorance 'dissolve,'

* The music and tempest metaphors have been traced in a very different fashion and with quite different aims by G. Wilson Knight in *The Shakespearian Tempest.* My analysis (which I had worked out before reading Professor Knight's essay) has a more limited purpose: to show a continuity of analogy and a development of metaphor parallel to that of the other continuities I have traced.

† The scene is full of expressions such as: *A tempestuous noise of thunder and lightning heard,* 'roarers,' 'command these elements to silence,' *A cry within,* 'A plague upon this howling! they are louder than the weather, or our office,' 'insolent noisemaker,' *'A confused noise within,'* et cetera.

and so the musical metaphor, like the sea metaphor, has moved from outer to inner weather.

The music analogy has some close links with the earth-air continuity which we glanced at in the introductory chapter* of the book. Ferdinand, following Ariel's 'yellow sands' song, asks, 'Where should this music be? i' th' air, or th' earth?' And a little later:

> This is no mortal business, nor no sound
> That the earth owes: I hear it now above me.

The connection of air and music can never be long forgotten: Ariel and his spirits of 'thin air' are the musicians of the island.

The earth-air, Caliban-Ariel antithesis coincides at points with what we might call a slavery-freedom continuity, for Caliban is in Prospero's words both 'slave' and 'earth.' Ariel too is called a 'slave'† by Prospero, and for the time of the play he is as much a slave as Caliban. He is always asking for his freedom, which is at last granted, his release being symbolically expressed in the airy rovings of his final song. He flies into perpetual summer and, like air, becomes merged with the elements. By contrast, the 'high-day, freedom!' of which Caliban sings is ironically enough simply a change of masters.

The 'slaves' and 'servants' of the play suffer various kinds of imprisonment, from Ariel in his 'cloven pine' to Ferdinand's mild confinement, and before the end of Act IV everyone except Prospero and Miranda has been imprisoned in one way or another. During the course of Act V all the prisoners except Ferdinand (who has already been released) are set free, each of them by Prospero's special command.

A sovereignty-conspiracy analogy parallels very closely the slavery-freedom analogy, some of the same persons, e.g. Ferdinand and Caliban, appearing as both slaves and conspirators. 'That foul conspiracy / Of the beast Caliban, and his confederates' is of course a parody version of the 'Open-ey'd Çonspiracy' of Sebastian and Antonio. Ferdinand, too, is charged fantastically by Prospero with

* See pp. 13, 14.

† Both are called 'slaves' in Act I: ii, the scene of metaphorical exposition.

plotting against his island rule. Talk of kings and royalty turns up in many scenes, being connected usually with the denial of kingship, as in 'good Gonzalo's' speech on his golden age commonwealth where 'he would be king' and yet have 'no sovereignty.' Though no single explicit metaphor for conspiracy or usurpation is often repeated, Shakespeare rings many changes on the theme as he moves from plot to plot. Prospero's brother, we recall, is said to have 'new created the creatures' of state. Alonso's seizure of power is called a 'substitution': 'crediting his own lies,' he began to believe 'he was indeed the duke,' and from merely playing a part he went on to become 'absolute Milan.' The figure is picked up in the somnolent dialogue of Sebastian and Antonio:

I remember
You did supplant your brother Prospero.

In the second of the scenes in which Caliban and his fellows plot to overthrow the island 'tyrant,' Sebastian's 'supplant' is recalled with a difference:

Caliban. I would my valiant master would destroy thee; I do not lie.

Stephano. Trinculo, if you trouble him any more in his tale, by this hand, I will supplant some of your teeth.

The figure recurs a little later in a more serious context:

. . . you three
From Milan did supplant good Prospero.

In Act v after various supplantings, serious and comic, accomplished or merely projected, all true kings are restored and all false ones dethroned.

The two continuities, sovereignty-conspiracy and slavery-freedom, are also alike in the fact that their metaphorical force is expressed through scenes that are just one step removed from allegory. The more serious of the restorations and releases convey similar kinds of moral meaning. Ferdinand's release from 'wooden slavery' signifies that he is a true lover and a true prince. In being freed from madness Alonso has escaped from 'heart-sorrow' and regained his rightful rank and a 'clear life ensuing.' Both continuities convey an impression of topsy-turvydom in the order of things, an unnatural interchange of status among creatures of every kind. Both express a return to stability after a disturbance of degree.

What then is the key metaphor through which the various continuities are linked, and how are they connected through it? Shakespeare's most direct expression of his key metaphor is 'sea-change,' the key phrase of Ariel's song. But what does Shakespeare mean by 'sea-change'? Ariel sings of 'bones' being made into 'coral' and of 'eyes' becoming 'pearls.' 'A change into something rich and strange,' we now understand, is a change 'out of nature.' 'Sea-change' is a metaphor for 'magical transformation,' for metamorphosis. The key metaphor of the play is 'change' in this special sense, and 'change' is the analogy common to all of the continuities we have been tracing. (I am not forgetting that they are also expressive of many other relationships, or that Shakespeare is often playing with two or three metaphors at once, as in the various figures of 'sea-swallowing.' But all are at least expressive of change, or changeableness.)

Through the first rather vague analogies we traced, of 'strangeness' and 'sleep-and-dream,' numerous events and persons in the play are qualified as belonging to a realm where anything may happen. Expressions of 'strangeness' and 'sleep,' like many of the references to sea and music, suggest 'far other Worlds and other Seas,' where magical change is to be expected. A more particular metaphor of change is expressed through the stress on the 'strangeness' of 'new creations' and on the confusion between sleep and dream and waking. The island is a world of fluid, merging states of being and forms of life. This lack of dependable boundaries between states is also expressed by the many instances of confusion between natural and divine. Miranda says that she might call Ferdinand

> A thing divine; for nothing natural
> I ever saw so noble.

Ferdinand cannot be sure whether she is a goddess or a maid, and Caliban takes Trinculo for a 'brave god.' There is a further comic variation on this theme in Trinculo's difficulty in deciding whether to classify Caliban as fish or man, monster or devil.

But 'change' is most clearly and richly expressed through the sequence of tempest images (especially 'cloud' and 'sea-swallowed') and through the noise-music antithesis. All kinds of sounds, harmonious and ugly, like the manifestations of sea and storm, are expressive of magical transformation. 'The fire and cracks / Of sulphurous roaring' (imagery in which both storm and sound analogies are blended) 'infects' the courtiers' 'reason,' and *solemn music* induces the 'clearing' of their understanding. The 'music' and the 'tempest' continuities, taken together as metaphors of 'sea-change,' are perhaps the most extensive of all the analogies in their organizing power. They recur often, they connect a wide diversity of experiences, and they express in symbolic form some of the main steps in the drama, in particular, the climactic moments of inner change: Ariel's revelation to the courtiers of their guilt, Alonso's first show of remorse, and the final purification.

The earth-air or Caliban-Ariel antithesis may seem to have very little to do with metamorphosis. But the relation of this theme to the key metaphor is clear and important. Air, Ariel, and his music are a blended symbol of change as against the unchanging Caliban, 'the thing of darkness.' He can be punished, but hardly humanized; he is, says Prospero,

> A devil, a born devil, on whose nature
> Nurture can never stick; on whom my pains,
> Humanely taken, are all lost, quite lost.

The other continuities parallel to earth-air, of slavery-freedom and conspiracy-sovereignty, are frequently expressive of major and minor changes of status among the inhabitants and temporary visitors on Prospero's island.

But the interconnection of Shakespeare's analogies through the key metaphor cannot be adequately described, since we are able to speak of only one point of relationship at a time. We can get a better sense of the felt union of various lines of analogy in *The Tempest* by looking at the two passages where Shakespeare expresses his key metaphor most completely, the 'Full fathom five' song and Prospero's 'cloud-capp'd towers' speech.

Rereading Ariel's song at this point we can see how many of the main continuities are alluded to and related in the description of 'sea-change' and how the song anticipates the metaphorical design that emerges through the dialogue of the whole play. The total metaphorical pattern is to an amazing degree an efflorescence from this single crystal:

Full fathom five thy father lies;
Of his bones are coral made:
Those are pearls that were his eyes:
Nothing of him that doth fade,
But doth suffer a sea-change
Into something rich and strange.
Sea-nymphs hourly ring his knell:
Burthen: 'Ding-dong!'
Hark! now I hear them,—Ding-dong, bell.

In addition to the more obvious references to the deep sea and its powers and to the 'strangeness' of this drowning, there are indirect anticipations of other analogies. 'Fade' prefigures the 'dissolving cloud' metaphor and the theme of tempest changes, outer and inner. 'Rich,' along with 'coral' and 'pearls,' anticipates the opulent imagery of the dream-world passages and scenes, the 'riches ready to drop' on Caliban and the expressions of wealth * and plenty in the masque. The song closes with the nymphs tolling the bell, the transformation and the 'sea sorrow' are expressed through sea-music. Ferdinand's comment reminds us that the song has connections with two other lines of analogy:

The ditty does remember my drown'd father.
This is no mortal business, nor no sound
That the earth owes:—I hear it now above me.

The song convinces Ferdinand that he is now King of Naples (the first of the interchanges of sovereignty), and it is a 'ditty' belonging not to the 'earth,' but to the 'air.'

The sense of relationship between the many continuities is still more vividly felt in the lines of Prospero's most memorable speech:

You do look, my son, in a mov'd sort,
As if you were dismay'd: be cheerful, sir:

* 'Rich' and 'riches' occur no less than five times in the masque.

Our revels now are ended. These our actors,
As I foretold you, were all spirits and
Are melted into air, into thin air:
And, like the baseless fabric of this vision,
The cloud-capp'd towers, the gorgeous palaces,
The solemn temples, the great globe itself,
Yea, all which it inherit, shall dissolve
And, like this insubstantial pageant faded,
Leave not a rack behind. We are such stuff
As dreams are made on, and our little life
Is rounded with a sleep.

In Prospero's words Shakespeare has gathered all the lights of analogy into a single metaphor which sums up the metaphorical design and the essential meaning of *The Tempest.* The language evokes nearly every continuity that we have traced. 'Melted into air,' 'dissolve,' 'cloud,' and 'rack' bring us immediately to Ariel and tempest changes, while 'vision,' 'dream' and 'sleep' recall other familiar continuities. 'Revels,' 'gorgeous palaces,' and 'pageant' (for Elizabethans closely associated with royalty) are echoes of the kingly theme; and 'solemn' is associated particularly with the soft music of change. The 'stuff' of dreams is at once cloud-stuff (air) and cloth, both images being finely compressed in 'baseless fabric.' Taken with 'faded' these images refer obliquely to the garments so miraculously 'new-dyed . . . with salt water,' one of the first signs of 'sea-change' noted by Gonzalo. Within the metaphor of tempest-clearing and of cloud-like transformation, Shakespeare has included allusions to every important analogy of change in the play.

But it is through the twofold progress of the whole figure that the change metaphor is experienced and its most general meaning fully understood. We read first: that like the actors and scenery of the vision, earth's glories and man shall vanish into nothingness. Through a happy mistake we also read otherwise. By the time we have passed through 'dissolve,' 'insubstantial,' and 'faded,' and reached 'leave not a rack behind,' we are reading 'cloud-capped towers' in reverse as a metaphor for tower-like clouds. 'Towers,' 'palaces,' 'temples,' 'the great globe,' 'all which it inherit' are now taken for cloud forms. Through a sort of Proustian * merging of icon and subject, we experience the blending of states of being, of substantial and unsubstantial, or real and unreal, which is the essence of *The Tempest* metamorphosis.

Similar meanings are expressed through the closing dream figure, which grows equally out of the metaphorical context of the speech and the play. 'Rounded,' we should take with Kittredge as 'surrounded,' but without losing the force of round, as in Donne's 'surrounded with tears.' 'Our little life' is more than sentimental, it is our little life (microcosm) in contrast with 'the great globe' (macrocosm). There may also be an over-image in 'surrounded' of the world in classical myth and geography with its encircling ocean, sleep being the stream that 'rounds' the lesser world. In relation to the metaphorical design of the play, 'rounded with a sleep' and the notion of life ending in dreams express again the sense of confusion between sleep and dream and waking. This metaphor which completes the figure of cloud-change is Shakespeare's most perfect symbol for the closeness of states that to our daylight sense are easily separable. Although the vision here expressed goes far beyond the play, it is still a natural extension of the dramatic moment and a fulfilment of the metaphor that has been implicit since the noisy opening lines of *The Tempest.*

But if Shakespeare's total metaphor is in a sense present everywhere, it is also a design that develops in close relation to the main dramatic movement of the play. As we have noted more than once, a particular metaphor will be varied to fit a new dramatic situation and so serve to express the situation more fully and to anticipate the next step in the development of the drama. The best example of this adaptation of metaphor comes in a speech in which Shakespeare seems to be playing capriciously with his noise-music theme. At first sight the passage seems inconsistent with the symbolic contrast between storm noise and music:

> *Alonso.* O, it is monstrous! monstrous!
> Methought the billows spoke and told me of it;
> The winds did sing it to me; and the thunder,

* This merging in Proust was brought to my attention by J. I. Merrill in the thesis already referred to, chapter III, p. 43.

> That deep and dreadful organ-pipe, pronounc'd
> The name of Prosper: it did bass my trespass.

It is admittedly odd that the confused noise of the tempest should, in Alonso's soul, compose a harmony—however gloomy—but the paradox fits in perfectly with the developing structure of the play. Alonso has just been told by Ariel that the storm had a purpose as an instrument of Destiny. Since at this moment remorse first appears in the play and the inner clearing begins, it is exactly right that the storm sounds should seem harmonious and so point forward to the events of the fourth and fifth acts. No use of metaphor in *The Tempest* reveals more clearly Shakespeare's exact sense of the movement of his drama, of the changing human relations and feelings he is presenting.

In building up his metaphorical design, Shakespeare prepares us for the moment in *The Tempest* when the major shift in dramatic relationships takes place. The moment comes in the speech in which Prospero describes the behavior of the King and the courtiers as they slowly return from madness to sanity. The first important step toward this climax, Alonso's acknowledgment of his guilt, was expressed through a metaphor combining both sea and musical changes. The next step, Ferdinand's release from his tempest-trials and from dream-like enchantment, is expressed through the masque, which is an elaborate dramatization of metamorphosis, Ariel's 'meaner fellows,' 'the rabble,' being now transformed into majestic Olympian goddesses. Once again, familiar continuities appear, and again they are transformed to fit a new occasion. 'Earth,' for example, is no longer 'barren place and fertile,' but the earth enriched by human cultivation and symbolized now by Ceres—not by Caliban, who is 'nature resisting nurture.' Iris summons this new Earth in the gorgeous speech beginning 'Ceres, most bounteous lady, thy rich leas . . . ,' lines in which we hear a quite new majesty of tone and movement. The couplet form sets the dialogue apart from human speech, while the longer periods, the added stresses, the phrasal balancings are especially appropriate to 'that large utterance of the early gods.' (Here is one of many instances of how Shakespeare adapts his sound patterns to his metaphorical and dramatic designs.) Prospero's visionary speech that ends 'the revels' is not simply a concentration of metaphor without reference to the dramatic development. It announces the changes to come, it gives a rich expression of their meaning, and it anticipates the dream-like flux of the psychological events of the last act.

If we now read Prospero's words in Act v, in which he describes the great changes as they take place, we see many references back to Shakespeare's metaphorical preparation for this moment. We also realize that various lines of action and various lines of analogy are converging almost simultaneously. The speech opens with Prospero's farewell to his art, after which he turns his thoughts to 'restoring the senses' of the courtiers, whom Ariel has just gone to release:

> A solemn air and the best comforter
> To an unsettled fancy, cure thy brains,
> Now useless, boil'd within thy skull! There stand,
> For you are spell-stopp'd.
> Holy Gonzalo, honourable man,
> Mine eyes, even sociable to the show of thine,
> Fall fellowly drops. The charm dissolves apace;
> And as the morning steals upon the night,
> Melting the darkness, so their rising senses
> Begin to chase the ignorant fumes that mantle
> Their clearer reason.—O good Gonzalo!
> My true preserver, and a loyal sir
> To him thou follow'st, I will pay thy graces
> Home, both in word and deed.—Most cruelly
> Didst thou, Alonso, use me and my daughter:
> Thy brother was a furtherer in the act;—
> Thou'rt pinch'd for 't now, Sebastian.—Flesh and blood,
> You, brother mine, that entertain'd ambition,
> Expell'd remorse and nature; who, with Sebastian,—
> Whose inward pinches therefore are most strong,—
> Would here have kill'd your king; I do forgive thee,
> Unnatural though thou art!—Their understanding
> Begins to swell, and the approaching tide
> Will shortly fill the reasonable shores
> That now lie foul and muddy. Not one of them
> That yet looks on me, or would know me.—Ariel,

Fetch me the hat and rapier in my cell:—[*Exit Ariel.*
I will discase me, and myself present,
As I was sometime Milan.—Quickly, spirit;
Thou shalt ere long be free.

If this is a climactic moment, what changes in dramatic relationships are taking place, what is happening dramatically? The 'men of sin,' like Ferdinand, have come to the end of the trials which began with the storm and continued through various 'distractions.' Now, as Prospero explains, they are undergoing a moral as well as a mental regeneration, they are 'pinch'd' with remorse and are being forgiven. The twofold regeneration is further dramatized in the speeches that follow: 'th' affliction of Alonso's mind amends,' he resigns Prospero's dukedom and 'entreats' him to pardon his 'wrongs.'

But these are the prose facts, the bare bones of the changes in dramatic relationships. We cannot feel the peculiar quality of what is taking place or grasp its meaning apart from the metaphorical language through which it is being expressed. And the expressions acquire their force and precision from the whole metaphorical preparation we have been tracing. The courtiers' senses are restored by 'an airy charm,' by magic similar to that which was worked by Ariel and his spirits. The allusions to 'heavenly music' and 'a solemn air,' in contrast to the 'rough magic' that Prospero has abjured, remind us that these changes will be musically harmonious, like the songs of Ariel, and not noisy and confused like the storm sent to punish these men and reveal their 'monstrous' guilt. Toward the end of the speech, the imagery recalls the tempest metaphor, but it is altered so as to express the mental and moral change that is taking place. The return of understanding is like an approaching tide that covers the evidence of a storm (both 'foul' and 'muddy' have storm associations from earlier occurrences).

But the metaphor that best expresses this clearing is the one for which the preparation has been most complete:

The charm dissolves apace;
And as the morning steals upon the night,
Melting the darkness, so their rising senses
Begin to chase the ignorant fumes that mantle
Their clearer reason.

'Dissolving' and 'melting' and 'fumes' take us back at once to the grand transformations of the masque speech, to the earlier cloud transformations both serious and comic; and they take us back further to the association of clouds with magical tempests, inner storms, and clearing weather. We read of the moral and psychological transformations with a present sense of these analogies. They are qualified for us as a dream-like dissolution of tempest clouds, as events in the 'insubstantial' region where reality and unreality merge.

It is through such links that Shakespeare concentrates at this climactic moment the fullest meaning of his key metaphor. There is of course no separation in the reader's experience between the dramatic fact and the metaphorical qualification. The images that recur in Prospero's speech take us back to felt qualities, but to felt qualities embedded in particular dramatic contexts. 'Melting,' for example, carries us to the spirit-like dissolution of 'spirits . . . melted into air, into thin air'; but it also reminds us of the masque pageantry and of Prospero's calming of Ferdinand's fears. We hear Prospero's soothing and mysterious tone in both the earlier and later uses of the word. The dramatic links and the analogical links are experienced at once, which is to say that metaphorical design and dramatic design are perfectly integrated.

We can now realize that metamorphosis is truly the key metaphor to the *drama,* and not the key metaphor to a detachable design of decorative analogies. Through the echoes in Prospero's speech of various lines of analogy, Shakespeare makes us feel each shift in dramatic relationships as a magical transformation, whether it is the courtiers' return to sanity, or Prospero's restoration to his dukedom, or Ariel's flight into perpetual summer. While all of the 'slaves' and 'prisoners' are being freed, and while all of the 'sovereigns' are being restored, the sense of magical change is never wholly lost. The union of drama and metaphor in *The Tempest* is nowhere more complete than in the last act of the play.

The larger meaning of Shakespeare's total design, which was anticipated in the cloud and dream metaphor of Prospero's visionary speech, is most clearly and fully expressed in these final transformations. In a world where everything may become something else, doubts naturally arise, and in the swift flow of change the confusion about what is and what is not becomes fairly acute. When

Prospero 'discases' himself and appears as Duke of Milan, Gonzalo says with understandable caution:

Whether this be,
Or be not, I'll not swear.

And Prospero answers:

You do yet taste
Some subtilties o' the isle, that will not let you
Believe things certain.

Whereas in the earlier acts the characters had often accepted the unreal as real (spirits, shipwrecks, drownings, visions), they now find it difficult to accept the real as truly real. The play concludes with their acceptance of the unexpected change to reality. But for the spectator there remains the heightened sense of the 'thin partitions' that 'do divide' these states. The world that common sense regards as real, of order in nature and society and of sanity in the individual, is a shimmering transformation of disorder. 'We shall all be changed, in a moment, in the twinkling of an eye.' (This or something like it is as near as we can come to describing the total attitude conveyed by *The Tempest.*)

Thus *The Tempest* is, like Marvell's 'Garden,' a Metaphysical poem of metamorphosis,* though the meaning of change is quite different for the two writers. It is worth noting too that Shakespeare 'had Ovid in his eye,' a fact that is obvious from the echoes of Golding's famous translation. There could be no better proof of Shakespeare's maturity than the contrast between the 'sweet witty' Ovidianism of 'Venus and Adonis' and the metaphorical design of *The Tempest,* which gives philosophic meaning to a drama of Ovidian metamorphosis. We remember 'a lily prison'd in a gaol of snow' as an isolated 'beauty,' but hardly as an apt symbol of the amorous relations of Venus and Adonis, or as symbolic of some larger meaning in their story. (Indeed a 'gaol of snow' is rather inept for the fervid goddess of the poem.) 'Those were pearls that were his eyes' revives Ariel's sea-music, Ferdinand's melancholy, and a world of fantasy and transshifting states of being. The increased concentration

* See the excellent analysis of the poem in M. C. Bradbrook and M. G. Lloyd Thomas: *Andrew Marvell* (Cambridge, 1940), pp. 59-64.

in meaning of the image from *The Tempest* is a sign of a growth in the command of language which is command of life for a poet. As Arnold said of Wordsworth, Shakespeare now 'deals with more of *life*' and 'he deals with *life*, as a whole, more powerfully.' His maturity and power appear in the variety of experience so perfectly harmonized through the imaginative design of *The Tempest*.

Chapter VII

SOMETHING CENTRAL WHICH PERMEATED: VIRGINIA WOOLF AND 'MRS. DALLOWAY'

It was something central which permeated . . .
Mrs. Dalloway

The best preparation for understanding *Mrs. Dalloway* is to read *The Tempest,* or *Cymbeline,* or, better still, *A Winter's Tale.* One might go further and say that in her singleness of vision and in her handling of words, Virginia Woolf has a Shakespearean imagination. If that sounds like nonsense—and it may—perhaps by the end of this chapter the reader will agree that it sounds 'so like sense, that it will do as well.'

Mrs. Dalloway has a story and some characters—by conventional standards, a fragmentary dramatic design—but the fragments of which the novel is composed would not seem related or particularly significant without another sort of connection. The dramatic sequences are connected through a single metaphorical nucleus, and the key metaphors are projected and sustained by a continuous web of subtly related minor metaphors and harmonizing imagery.

Once we have seen this design and the vision of experience it implies, we shall understand why *Mrs. Dalloway* takes the form it does, why as a story it has properly no beginning or ending. It opens one morning with Clarissa Dalloway in the midst of preparing for a party; it closes in the early hours of the next morning with Clarissa very much involved in giving the party. The major event of her day is the return of Peter Walsh, the man she had almost married instead of Richard Dalloway, a successful M.P.

Clarissa and Richard have a daughter, Elizabeth, who is temporarily attached to a religious fanatic, a woman with the Dickensian name of Miss Kilman. There is also in the novel another set of characters who at first seem to have no connection with Clarissa and her world: Septimus Smith, a veteran of the First World War, and his Italian wife, Rezia, a hatmaker by trade. Septimus, who is suffering from shell shock, is being treated—somewhat brutally—by a hearty M.D., Dr. Holmes. During the day of Clarissa's preparations, Septimus visits Sir William Bradshaw, an eminent psychiatrist, who recommends rather too firmly that Septimus should be taken to a sanatorium. In the late afternoon, as Dr. Holmes comes to take him away, Septimus jumps from the balcony of his room and kills himself. That evening, Sir William Bradshaw reports the story of his death at Clarissa's party.

Readers of the novel will recognize this outline as more or less accurate, but they will want to add that the impression it gives is very remote from their remembered experience of *Mrs. Dalloway*. For the peculiar texture of Virginia Woolf's fiction has been lost. The ebb and flow of her phrasing and the frequent repetition of the same or similar expressions, through which her characteristic rhythmic and metaphorical designs are built up, have completely disappeared.

No one needs to be shown that the novel is full of odd echoes. The Shakespearean tag, 'Fear no more,' occurs some six or seven times; certain words turn up with surprising frequency in the various interior monologues: 'life,' 'feel,' 'suffer,' 'solemn,' 'moment,' and 'enjoy.' Less obvious, and more peculiar to Virginia Woolf is the recurrence in the individual monologues of expressions for similar visual or aural images. Some of these images—the aeroplane and the stopped motorcar are examples—connect separate dramatic sequences in a rather artificial way; but others, such as Big Ben's striking and the marine images, often connect similar qualities of experience and so function as symbolic metaphors. There are many repeated words, phrases, and sentences in the novel, besides those already quoted, which gradually become metaphorical: 'party,' 'Holmes and Bradshaw,' 'there she was,' 'plunge,' 'wave' and 'sea,' 'sewing,' 'building' and 'making it up,' 'Bourton,' et cetera. Almost innumerable continuities, major and minor, may be traced through the various recurrent expressions; but as compared with Shakespeare's practice in *The Tempest,* the continuities are less often built up through the use of explicit metaphors. The repeated word does not occur in a conventional metaphorical expression, and its metaphorical value is felt only after it has been met in a number of contexts. Virginia Woolf's most characteristic metaphors are purely symbolic.

I can indicate from the adjective 'solemn' how a recurrent expression acquires its special weight of meaning. By seeing how metaphor links with metaphor, the reader will also get a notion of the interconnectedness of the entire novel. The word appears on the first page of *Mrs. Dalloway:*

> How fresh, how calm, stiller than this of course, the air was in the early morning; like the flap of a wave; the kiss of a wave; chill and sharp and yet (for a girl of eighteen as she then was) solemn, feeling as she did, standing there at the open window, that something awful was about to happen . . .

It is echoed at once, on the next page, in the first account of Big Ben's striking (an important passage in relation to the whole novel):

> For having lived in Westminster—how many years now? over twenty,—one feels even in the midst of the traffic, or waking at night, Clarissa was positive, a particular hush, or solemnity; an indescribable pause; a suspense (but that might be her heart, affected, they said, by influenza) before Big Ben strikes. There! Out it boomed. First a warning, musical; then the hour, irrevocable. The leaden circles dissolved in the air.

'Solemn,' which on our first reading of the opening page had only a vague local meaning of 'something awful about to happen,' is now connected with a more particularized terror, the fear of a suspense, of a pause in experience. Each time that 'solemn' is repeated in subsequent descriptions of Big Ben, it carries this additional meaning. The word recurs three times in the afternoon scene in which Clarissa looks across at an old woman in the next house:

> How extraordinary it was, strange, yes, touching, to see the old lady (they had been neighbours ever so many years) move

> away from the window, as if she were attached to that sound, that string. Gigantic as it was, it had something to do with her. Down, down, into the midst of ordinary things the finger fell making the moment solemn.

And a little further on:

> . . . Big Ben . . . laying down the law, so solemn, so just . . . on the wake of that solemn stroke which lay flat like a bar of gold on the sea.

In the early morning scene near the end of the book, Clarissa goes to the window, again sees the old lady, and thinks, 'It will be a solemn sky . . . it will be a dusky sky, turning away its cheek in beauty.' In all but the last passage there is some suggestion in the imagery of Big Ben's stroke coming down and marking an interruption in the process of life. By the end of the book we see the significance in the use of 'solemn' on the first page in a passage conveying a sharp sense of freshness and youth. The terror symbolized by Big Ben's 'pause' has a connection with early life, '. . . one's parents giving it into one's hands, this life, to be lived to the end.' The 'something awful . . . about to happen' was associated with 'the flap of a wave, the kiss of a wave'; the 'solemnity' of life is a kind of 'sea-terror' (so Shakespeare might express it in *The Tempest*). Wave and water images recur in other 'solemn' passages: 'the wave,' 'the wake,' 'the leaden circles dissolved in the air.' So, through various associations, 'solemn' acquires symbolic values for the reader: some terror of entering the sea of experience and of living life and an inexplicable fear of a 'suspense' or interruption.

While following a single symbolic adjective in *Mrs. Dalloway,* we have seen that it was impossible to interpret one continuity apart from several others. Various expressions—'solemn,' 'wave,' 'Big Ben,' 'fear,' and 'pause'—kept leading us toward the key metaphor of the book. The metaphor that links the continuities and gives unity to the dramatic design of *Mrs. Dalloway* is not a single, easily describable analogy, but two complementary and extremely complex analogies which are gradually expressed through recurrent words and phrases and through the dramatic pattern of the various sequences. Though they are salient in the sequences of nearly all the main characters, they are best interpreted from Clarissa's, since her experience forms the center of attention for the reader.

One of the two metaphorical poles of the novel emerges in a passage that comes just after the first account of Big Ben's striking:

> Such fools we are, she thought, crossing Victoria Street. For Heaven only knows why one loves it so, how one sees it so, making it up, building it round one, tumbling it, creating it every moment afresh; but the veriest frumps, the most dejected of miseries sitting on doorsteps (drink their downfall) do the same; can't be dealt with, she felt positive, by Acts of Parliament for that very reason: they love life. In people's eyes, in the swing, tramp, and trudge; in the bellow and the uproar; the carriages, motor cars, omnibuses, vans, sandwich men shuffling and swinging; brass bands; barrel organs; in the triumph and the jingle and the strange high singing of some aeroplane overhead was what she loved; life; London; this moment of June.

The key phrase here is 'they love life,' and what is meant by 'life' and 'loving it' is indicated by the surrounding metaphors—'building it,' 'creating it every moment,' 'the swing, tramp, and trudge'—and also by the various images of sights, sounds, and actions.

'Life' as expressed in Mrs. Dalloway's morning walk (and in the walks of Peter and of her daughter Elizabeth) consists first in the doings of people and things and in the active perception of them. To meet Clarissa's approval, people 'must do something,' as she did in 'making a world' in her drawing room, in 'assembling' and 'knowing' all sorts of individuals, in running her house, and in giving 'her parties,' which were for her 'life.' But the perception, the savoring of these doings of oneself and of others is itself a creation. For Mrs. Dalloway, 'enjoying' and 'loving' is 'creating' and 'building up,' not passive enjoyment. Life is experienced in successively created 'moments'; the sense of succession, of process, is inseparable from Clarissa's feeling about life; it is implicit in her movement along the streets, 'this astonishing and rather solemn progress with the rest of them, up Bond Street.' She thinks of 'all this' as '*going on* without her.' ('This' and 'all this' also become metaphors for life.) Later, in Elizabeth's experience of going up Fleet Street, all these metaphors are explicitly combined: 'this van; this life; this procession.' To live, then, is to enter into the process of action and active perception, to be absorbed in the successive moments: '. . . yet to her it was absolutely absorbing; all this.'

But the sense of being absorbed in the process is inseparable from a fear of being excluded, from the dread that the process may be interrupted. The progress is a 'solemn' one, the adjective suggesting (as elsewhere) the terror of 'plunging' into experience. The sense of being *in* experience is inseparable from the sense of being *outside* of it:

> She sliced like a knife through everything; at the same time was outside, looking on. She had a perpetual sense, as she watched the taxi cabs, of being out, out, far out to sea and alone; she always had the feeling that it was very, very dangerous to live even one day.

Though the terror lies in having to go through with life, paradoxically the escape from terror lies in building up delight and sharing in the process:

> Even now, quite often if Richard had not been there reading the *Times,* so that she could crouch like a bird and gradually revive, send roaring up that immeasurable delight, rubbing stick to stick, one thing with another, she must have perished.

The central metaphor of Clarissa's narrative (and of the novel) is thus twofold: the exhilarated sense of being a part of the forward moving process and the recurrent fear of some break in this absorbing activity, which was symbolized by the 'suspense' before Big Ben strikes. We are to feel all sorts of experiences qualified as at once 'an absorbing progression' and 'a progression about to be interrupted.' Such in crudely schematic terms are the two analogies which make up the metaphorical nucleus of the novel. As my analysis has indicated, this complex metaphor is expressed through countless variant minor metaphors and images.

Both of the major aspects of the metaphor are intricately linked in the wonderful sewing scene in which Clarissa's old lover, Peter Walsh, returns to announce his plans for a second marriage:

> Quiet descended on her, calm, content, as her needle, drawing the silk smoothly to its gentle pause, collected the green folds together and attached them, very lightly, to the belt. So on a summer's day waves collect, overbalance, and fall; collect and fall; and the whole world seems to be saying 'That is all' more and more ponderously, until even the heart in the body which lies in the sun on the beach says too, That is all. Fear no more, says the heart. Fear no more, says the heart, committing its burden to some sea, which sighs collectively for all sorrows, and renews, begins, collects, lets fall. And the body alone listens to the passing bee; the wave breaking; the dog barking, far away barking and barking.

Through the wave simile the opening statement expands in a metaphorical bloom which expresses in little the essence of the novel. The quiet, calm, and content (Clarissa's absorption in what she is doing) and the rhythmic movement of the needle are the points in the immediate situation from which the two main meanings of the key metaphor grow. The comparison between sewing and wave movements draws in these further levels of meaning, thanks to the nice preparation of earlier scenes and the delicate adjustment of those that follow. There are the wave and sea images which have been appearing when Clarissa recalls the terror of early life or when she hears Big Ben's solemn stroke. Much later in the novel, there is Clarissa at her party in her 'silver-green mermaid's dress . . . lolloping on the waves.' Here, in the scene with Peter, as in the final party scene, the waves mainly symbolize Clarissa's complete absorption in her life: 'That is all'—the phrase she had used twice while shopping and which had come back in her musings on 'the solemn progress up Bond Street.' There is for the heart at this moment nothing but the process, and the individual becomes a mere percipient body, intensely aware of the immediate sensation. But the moment has a dual value, as has been suggested by the oblique allusions to solemnity and terror ('waves,' 'ponderously,' 'That is all'). So the reader is perfectly prepared for the return of 'Fear no more,' which it is now clear suggests both freedom from fear and the fear of interruption, meanings which are dramatized in the scene that immediately follows.

Clarissa's quiet is rudely shaken by the sound of the front-door bell:

> 'Who can—what can,' asked Mrs. Dalloway (thinking it was outrageous to be interrupted at eleven o'clock on the morning of the day she was giving a party), hearing a step on the stairs. She heard a hand upon the door. She made to hide her dress, like a virgin protecting chastity, respecting privacy.

The nature of the interruption, the return of her former lover, Peter Walsh, and her gesture, 'like a virgin protecting chastity, respecting privacy,' point to another analogy in *Mrs. Dalloway,* which is simply a special aspect of the 'life' metaphor. We might call it the 'destroyer' theme. Peter's coming in temporarily destroys Clarissa's domesticity, even her marriage. As a lover Peter had allowed her no independence, and as a husband he would have been intolerable, leaving her no life of her own. Clarissa reasserts herself and her life by calling after him as he leaves, 'Remember my party to-night!' Peter is one of those who would cut her off from her way of living by making her into another person: he is one of the 'destroyers of the privacy of the soul.' Compulsion of this sort is a special form of the 'suspense' in life's exhilarating process. The 'suspense' may be fear itself, or the sense of time's passing, or death, or a failure in personal relationships, or, finally, the loss of independence which results from love or hatred or officiousness.

We shall now see to what a remarkable extent the central metaphor penetrates and organizes the novel. The dramatic sequences of the principal characters are all linked with Clarissa's through a shuttling pattern of verbal reminiscences. (Curious readers may amuse themselves by finding dozens more than can be cited here.) Although 'life' is peculiarly the key figure in Clarissa's experience, it is important in that of other characters, including Septimus and Miss Kilman, who are unable to 'live' as Clarissa does.

We may begin with Peter Walsh, who as a lover has the role of one of the 'interrupters' and 'destroyers.' But in the two accounts of his walks through London, he shows much of Clarissa's eager experience of life. He sets off on his morning walk, speaking rhythmically her parting words, 'Remember my party, remember my party.' He then 'marches up Whitehall' as she has gone 'up Bond

Street,' and he too 'makes up' life (his mild 'escapade with the girl'). During his evening walk, he expresses Clarissa's sense of enjoyment:

> Really it took one's breath away, these moments . . . absorbing, mysterious, of infinite richness, this life.

Elizabeth also shares her mother's perceptiveness, and in her bus ride has an experience closely paralleling Clarissa's morning walk. As all three characters pass through the 'procession' of experience, they savor life as a series of exquisite moments, a sensation summed up by the motif of the scene in which Richard brings Clarissa the roses: 'Happiness is this.'

The crude parallel between the roles of Mrs. Dalloway and Septimus is obvious; the finer relations and how they are expressed may be best seen by tracing the links made through the 'life' metaphor. While Clarissa usually feels her inclusion *in* everything and only occasionally feels *outside,* Septimus is almost always 'alone' and unable to connect with the world about him. He had 'felt very little in the war,' and 'now that it was all over, truce signed, and the dead buried, he had, especially in the evening, these thunder-claps of fear. He could not feel.' Rezia, his wife, is his refuge from fear, though like Mrs. Dalloway she too has moments of panic when she cries, 'I am alone; I am alone!' But she is shown as having some of Mrs. Dalloway's gift for active enjoyment, and through her Septimus is for once able to recover his power of feeling and to enter into the real life around him. The moment comes near the end of his narrative, in the late afternoon, as he lies on a sofa while Rezia is making a hat. The writing in this scene shows wonderfully the way in which Virginia Woolf moves from one narrative plane to another via image and metaphor. (The parallel with Shakespeare is obvious.)

Immediately preceding the scene comes the episode of Elizabeth's bus ride, with 'this van; this life; this procession.' These metaphors are then echoed in a long description of cloud movements which cast changing lights on the moving buses; the transition to Septimus takes place as he watches the 'goings and comings' of the clouds. The movements and colors referred to and the verbal rhythm ('watching watery gold glow and fade') prepare us easily for the return of the wave and sea imagery of Clarissa's and Peter's monologues:

> Outside the trees dragged their leaves like nets through the depths of the air; the sound of water was in the room and through the waves came the voices of birds singing. Every power poured its treasures on his head, and his hand lay there on the back of the sofa, as he had seen his hand lie when he was bathing, floating, on the top of the waves, while far away on shore he heard dogs barking and barking far away. Fear no more, says the heart in the body; fear no more.

The last words anticipate the next phase of the scene. Septimus, watching Rezia sew a hat, temporarily loses himself in his interest in her activity: 'She built it up, first one thing, then another, she built it up, sewing.' (The 'building' is an echo of the 'life' metaphor, and the sewing is now symbolic.) Septimus begins to note actual objects around him, as Rezia gives him assurance that real things are real: 'There she was, perfectly natural, sewing.' The words, 'There she was' (also the concluding sentence of the novel) are an exact repetition of one of Peter's earlier remarks about Clarissa, where they signified her 'extraordinary gift, that woman's gift, of making a world wherever she happened to be.' Septimus' participation in life is interrupted, as was Clarissa's, by one of the compellers, Dr. Holmes. His suicide is a protest against having his life forcibly remade by others.

In the figure of Sir William Bradshaw we get an almost allegorical representation of a 'destroyer.' His talk of keeping a 'sense of proportion' and his tactful questions are a screen for his firm intention of getting patients to do what he thinks best. There is a close relation, we are told, between preaching proportion and being a converter, for Proportion has a sister, Conversion, who 'feasts on the wills of the weakly.' Clarissa also is pursued by a compeller of this less lovely type, the horrendous if pious spinster, Miss Kilman. She ruins Clarissa's enjoyment of life and is shown as having herself no capacity for delight (if we overlook her perverse fondness for chocolate éclairs!). In the mock-heroic tea-table scene she fails in her attempt to exert a negative influence over Elizabeth, who leaves to go to her mother's party. As Miss Kilman questions Elizabeth, the reader recalls that Mrs. Dalloway's parting words to Miss Kilman and her daughter had been those she had used to Peter: 'Remember my party!' Her words are symbolic of defiance.

Just after this episode the mysterious old lady makes the first of her two appearances, the value of which can now be seen. The old lady, Clarissa says, was 'merely being herself.' 'There was something solemn in it—but love and religion would destroy that, whatever it was, the privacy of the soul.' 'Solemn' connects this 'privacy' theme, symbolized by the old lady, with the attitudes expressed through the key metaphor of the novel, especially with the precarious and terrifying sense of enjoyment. To experience life, terror and all, we must be left alone.

All of the related analogies that make up the key metaphor are combined near the end of the novel, at the point when Bradshaw tells Clarissa of Septimus' death and when Clarissa, reflecting on its meaning, looks out of the window at the old lady going to bed. Bradshaw, a man 'capable of some indescribable crime—forcing your soul, that was it—,' momentarily ruins her party ('in the middle of my party, here's death, she thought . . .'). But Clarissa immediately recognizes that Septimus' death has a further meaning in relation to his life and hers. By killing himself Septimus had defied the men who make life intolerable, and though he had 'thrown it away,' he had not lost his independence of soul. This (in so far as we can define it) is 'the thing' he had preserved. By contrast Clarissa had sacrificed some of this purity. She had made compromises for the sake of social success, 'She had schemed; she had pilfered.' But she had not given in to Peter, and by marrying Richard she had been able to make a life of her own. The delight, though impure, remained. The old lady, in her second appearance as in her first, symbolizes the quiet maintenance of one's own life, which is the only counterbalance to the fear of 'interruption' whether by death or compulsion.

This scene shows in the highest degree the concentration of various dramatic relationships through a central metaphor. What we would emphasize here is Virginia Woolf's literary feat in achieving this result—literary in the primitive sense of Frost's pun, 'feat of words.' The unity of her design depends on the building up of symbolic metaphors through an exquisite management of verbal devices: through exact repetitions, reminiscent variations, the use of related eye and ear imagery, and the recurrence of similar phrase and sentence rhythms. The novel has as a result a unique closeness of structure which is only slightly dependent on story, though also supported by the time patterns which David Daiches has chosen to emphasize. What is most remarkable is the way in which so many different experiences have been perceived through a single metaphorical vision: the lives of Clarissa, Peter, Richard, Septimus, and Rezia as glimpsed at various periods, and of Elizabeth at the moment of growing up. Most of the characters are seen, too, in some relation to the persons who 'make life intolerable': Miss Kilman, Holmes, Bradshaw, and Peter in his role as lover. Experience, rich and various in its range, has struck the mind of the novelist at a single angle and been refracted with perfect consistency. This singleness in reception and expression, as evidenced in the metaphorical design, is what we mean by integrity of imagination in Virginia Woolf.

But there are certainly points in the novel at which this singleness of vision shows signs of strain. Philistine readers have observed that the men of the novel are not full-blooded or are barely 'men' at all—a type of criticism that could be applied with disastrous results to *Tom Jones,* or *Emma,* or *The Portrait of a Lady*. But the strain that is truly a sign of weakness appears in the relating of dramatic elements through the central metaphorical nucleus. That Peter is no man—whether we mean not lifelike or not masculine—is a relevant comment only because of the symbolic role in which he is sometimes cast. As a lover he stands in Clarissa's thoughts for one of the dark 'forcers of the soul'; but in much of his behavior he is described as a womanish sort of person who has little power to manage himself or to move others. In one rather embarrassing episode, Peter's half-imaginary pursuit of a young girl, Virginia Woolf is apparently attempting to present his passionate side. The lack of lively sensuous detail in this narrative contrasts very badly with the glowing particularity of Mrs. Dalloway's walk through Bond Street or with the vividness of Peter's impressions of a London evening, while by way of a poor compensation there is a good deal of generalized emotional language: 'vast philanthropy,' 'exquisite delight,' 'mournful tenderness,' 'laughing and delightful,' et cetera. Peter calls this 'making up' an 'exquisite amusement,' which is in this instance a painfully accurate label. The metaphor ceases to be an instrument through which experience is connected for us in a new relation and remains a simple declaration of a connection never made.

On occasion Virginia Woolf becomes so fascinated with this instrument that she elaborates the metaphor out of all proportion to its expressive value. (*The Waves* is a kind of metaphorical monster of this sort.) The purest and most interesting example of such elaboration in *Mrs. Dalloway* comes just after Peter's imaginary flirtation, the interlude of 'the solitary traveller.' The passage—which is not a dream, though it covers the time while Peter is sleeping—is an enlarged symbolic version of Peter's experience with the girl and in part an expression of his desire for a more satisfactory relationship with Clarissa. As various echoes show, it is, like the experience on the street, a grand example of 'making up,' a vision of the consolatory woman who gives the kind of understanding which Peter had attributed to the girl and which he had not found in Clarissa. It is in a picturesque sense a beautiful passage, but merely beautiful, a piece which could be detached with little loss. The detailed picture of the woman, the evening, the street, and the adorable landlady does not increase or enrich our knowledge of Peter or of anyone else in the book.

Perhaps the most obvious examples of metaphorical elaboration for its own sake are the super-literary, pseudo-Homeric similes which adorn various pages of *Mrs. Dalloway*. Whether they are in origin Proustian or eighteenth-century Bloomsbury, we could wish that they might be dropped. Here is a relatively short example from the scene following the sewing passage:

> 'Well, and what's happened to you?' she said. So before a battle begins, the horses paw the ground; toss their heads; the light shines on their flanks; their necks curve. So Peter Walsh and Clarissa, sitting side by side on the blue sofa, challenged each other. His powers chafed and tossed in him. He assembled from different quarters all sorts of things; praise; his career at Oxford; his marriage, which she knew nothing whatever about; how he had loved; and altogether done his job.

The contrast between such a literary pastiche and the wave-sewing simile shows us in part what is wrong. The particular sense images, 'paw,' 'toss,' 'light shines,' are not grounded on the dramatic and narrative level, since there is no preparation for this Homeric horse-play in the account of Clarissa's and Peter's talk and gestures. (By contrast the wave motion was anticipated through describing Clarissa's movements as she sewed.) So the reader is unprepared to take the further jump to the psychological levels of the metaphor. The efforts to show any similarity in Peter's internal 'chafings' and 'tossings' come too late. The metaphor is crudely explained; but it doesn't work. Such simulations—like Peter's escapade and the solitary traveler's vision—are verbally inert matter, sending no radiations through the reader's experience of the novel.

But what is vital in the writing of *Mrs. Dalloway* is both more nearly omnipresent and more unobtrusive. To say, as I did at the beginning of this chapter, that Virginia Woolf creates a Shakespearean pattern of metaphor tells us something, of course; but to see how she connects diverse moments of experience by playing on a single analogy, or on a single word, tells us much more. As Clarissa is thinking of the death of Septimus Smith, she says to herself: 'But this young man who had killed himself—had he plunged holding his treasure?' She has just recalled that he had 'plunged' by 'throwing himself from a window,' which in turn echoes his earlier agonies ('falling through the sea, down, down') and his actual death ('flung himself vigorously, violently down'). But Septimus' 'plunge' recalls experiences of a very different sort in Clarissa's social life:

> . . . as she stood hesitating one moment on the threshold of her drawing-room, an exquisite suspense, such as might stay a diver before plunging while the sea darkens and brightens beneath him. . .

'Darkens' suggests that 'plunge' has also a more fearful significance, as we saw on the first page of the novel:

> What a lark! What a plunge! For so it had always seemed to her, when, with a little squeak of the hinges, which she could hear now, she had burst open the French windows and plunged at Bourton into the open air. How fresh, how calm, stiller than this of course, the air was in the early morning; like the flap of a wave; the kiss of a wave; chill and sharp and yet (for a girl of eighteen as she then was) solemn, feeling as she did, stand-

ing there at the open window, that something awful was about to happen . . .

Septimus' plunge from the window is linked with those earlier windows and 'the triumphs of youth' and thereby with the exhilarating and 'solemn' sense of delight in life's process (the 'treasure'). This twofold sense of life is constantly being expressed through the central metaphor of *Mrs. Dalloway*. The recurrence of a single word is a quiet indication of the subtlety and closeness of the structure which Virginia Woolf was 'building up' as she wrote this novel.

Chapter VIII

THE GROVES OF EDEN: DESIGN IN A SATIRE BY POPE

The Groves of Eden, vanished now so long,
Live in description, and look green in song . . .
Not Chaos-like together crushed and bruised,
But, as the world, harmoniously confused:
Where order in variety we see,
And where, though all things differ, all agree.

WINDSOR FOREST

Of all English poets Pope is the most exquisite, 'exquisite' in a sense well defined by Voltaire's remark that 'Poetry is a composition of beautiful details' ('La Poésie n'est faite que de beaux détails.'). He offers a constant display of niceties in image, tone, irony, and rhythm, and if we read Pope at all, we read him, as Dr. Johnson said, 'with perpetual delight.' In Pope's well-known 'Timon' satire ('Of Riches') the distractions are so various and so satisfying that it may seem impertinent to look for an extensive order of any sort. But unless we feel an order we are left with a collection of details and not poetry or a poem. If the satires of Pope are read 'as poems and not as something else' (in Eliot's phrase), they will reveal their own special integrity. Certainly we add nothing to our enjoyment of Pope or to our knowledge of imaginative design, by imposing schemes of the kind that Dr. Warburton provided for the 'Essay on Man' and the Moral Essays. Pope may have been the poet of Reason, but he was most surely not the poet of consecutive reasoning. As was true of Spenser, the structures he talked about and those he realized in writing were often not at all the same.

The design that matters in the Timon satire is implicit in the poem as read and above all poetic; it can be felt, if not described:

EPISTLE IV

To Richard Boyle, Earl of Burlington

Of the Use of Riches

'Tis strange, the Miser should his Cares employ
To gain those Riches he can ne'er enjoy:
Is it less strange, the Prodigal should waste
His wealth, to purchase what he ne'er can taste?
Not for himself he sees, or hears, or eats;
Artists must choose his Pictures, Music, Meats:
He buys for Topham, Drawings and Designs,
For Pembroke, Statues, dirty Gods, and Coins;
Rare monkish Manuscripts for Hearne alone,
And Books for Mead, and Butterflies for Sloane.
Think we all these are for himself? no more
Than his fine Wife, alas! or finer Whore.
  For what has Virro painted, built, and planted?
Only to shew, how many Tastes he wanted.
What brought Sir Visto's ill got wealth to waste?
Some Daemon whispered, 'Visto! have a Taste.'
Heaven visits with a Taste the wealthy fool,
And needs no Rod but Ripley with a Rule.
See! sportive fate, to punish awkward pride,
Bids Bubo build, and sends him such a Guide:
A standing sermon, at each year's expense,
That never Coxcomb reached Magnificence!
  You shew us, Rome was glorious, not profuse,
And pompous buildings once were things of Use.
Yet shall, my Lord, your just, your noble rules
Fill half the land with Imitating-Fools;
Who random drawings from your sheets shall take,
And of one beauty many blunders make;
Load some vain Church with old Theatric state,
Turn Arcs of triumph to a Garden-gate;

Reverse your Ornaments, and hang them all
On some patched dog-hole eked with ends of wall;
Then clap four slices of Pilaster on't,
That, laced with bits of rustic, makes a Front.
Shall call the winds through long arcades to roar,
Proud to catch cold at a Venetian door;
Conscious they act a true Palladian part,
And, if they starve, they starve by rules of art.
Oft have you hinted to your brother Peer
A certain truth, which many buy too dear:
Something there is more needful than Expense,
And something previous even to Taste—'tis Sense:
Good Sense, which only is the gift of Heaven,
And though no Science, fairly worth the seven:
A Light, which in yourself you must perceive;
Jones and Le Nôtre have it not to give.
To build, to plant, whatever you intend,
To rear the Column, or the Arch to bend,
To swell the Terrace, or to sink the Grot;
In all, let Nature never be forgot.
But treat the Goddess like a modest fair,
Nor over-dress, nor leave her wholly bare;
Let not each beauty everywhere be spied,
Where half the skill is decently to hide.
He gains all points, who pleasingly confounds,
Surprises, varies, and conceals the Bounds.
Consult the Genius of the Place in all;
That tells the Waters or to rise, or fall;
Or helps th' ambitious Hill the heavens to scale,
Or scoops in circling theatres the Vale;
Calls in the Country, catches op'ning glades,
Joins willing woods, and varies shades from shades;
Now breaks, or now directs, th'intending Lines;
Paints as you plant, and, as you work, designs.
Still follow Sense, of every Art the Soul,
Parts answ'ring parts shall slide into a whole,
Spontaneous beauties all around advance,
Start even from Difficulty, strike from Chance;

Nature shall join you; Time shall make it grow
A Work to wonder at—perhaps a STOWE.
  Without it, proud Versailles! thy glory falls;
And Nero's Terraces desert their walls:
The vast Parterres a thousand hands shall make,
Lo! COBHAM comes, and floats them with a Lake:
Or cut wide views through Mountains to the Plain,
You'll wish your hill or sheltered seat again.
Even in an ornament its place remark,
Nor in an Hermitage set Dr. Clarke.
  Behold Villario's ten years' toil complete;
His Quincunx darkens, his Espaliers meet;
The Wood supports the Plain, the parts unite,
And strength of Shade contends with strength of Light;
A waving Glow the bloomy beds display,
Blushing in bright diversities of day,
With silver-quiv'ring rills maeandered o'er—
Enjoy them, you! Villario can no more;
Tired of the scene Parterres and Fountains yield,
He finds at last he better likes a Field.
  Through his young Woods how pleased Sabinus strayed,
Or sat delighted in the thick'ning shade,
With annual joy the redd'ning shoots to greet,
Or see the stretching branches long to meet!
His Son's fine Taste an op'ner Vista loves,
Foe to the Dryads of his Father's groves;
One boundless Green, or flourished Carpet views,
With all the mournful family of Yews;
The thriving plants ignoble broomsticks made,
Now sweep those Alleys they were born to shade.
  At Timon's Villa let us pass a day,
Where all cry out, 'What sums are thrown away!'
So proud, so grand; of that stupendous air,
Soft and Agreeable come never there.
Greatness, with Timon, dwells in such a draught
As brings all Brobdignag before your thought.
To compass this, his building is a Town,
His pond an Ocean, his parterre a Down:

Who but must laugh, the Master when he sees,
A puny insect, shivering at a breeze!
Lo, what huge heaps of littleness around!
The whole, a laboured Quarry above ground;
Two Cupids squirt before; a Lake behind
Improves the keenness of the Northern wind.
His Gardens next your admiration call,
On every side you look, behold the Wall!
No pleasing Intricacies intervene,
No artful wildness to perplex the scene;
Grove nods at grove, each Alley has a brother,
And half the platform just reflects the other.
The suff'ring eye inverted Nature sees,
Trees cut to Statues, Statues thick as trees;
With here a Fountain, never to be played;
And there a Summer-house, that knows no shade;
Here Amphitrite sails through myrtle bowers;
There Gladiators fight, or die, in flowers;
Un-watered see the drooping sea-horse mourn,
And swallows roost in Nilus' dusty Urn.
  My Lord advances with majestic mien,
Smit with the mighty pleasure, to be seen:
But soft,—by regular approach,—not yet,—
First through the length of yon hot Terrace sweat;
And when up ten steep slopes you've dragged your thighs,
Just at his Study-door he'll bless your eyes.
  His Study! with what Authors is it stored?
In Books, not Authors, curious is my Lord;
To all their dated Backs he turns you round:
These Aldus printed, those Du Sueil has bound.
Lo, some are Vellum, and the rest as good
For all his Lordship knows, but they are Wood.
For Locke or Milton 'tis in vain to look,
These shelves admit not any modern book.
  And now the Chapel's silver bell you hear,
That summons you to all the Pride of Prayer:
Light quirks of Music, broken and uneven,
Make the soul dance upon a Jig to Heaven.

On painted Ceilings you devoutly stare,
Where sprawl the Saints of Verrio or Laguerre,
On gilded clouds in fair expansion lie,
And bring all Paradise before your eye.
To rest, the Cushion and soft Dean invite,
Who never mentions Hell to ears polite.
  But hark! the chiming Clocks to dinner call;
A hundred footsteps scrape the marble Hall:
The rich Buffet well-coloured Serpents grace,
And gaping Tritons spew to wash your face.
Is this a dinner? this a Genial room?
No, 'tis a Temple, and a Hecatomb.
A solemn Sacrifice, performed in state,
You drink by measure, and to minutes eat.
So quick retires each flying course, you'd swear
Sancho's dread Doctor and his Wand were there.
Between each Act the trembling salvers ring,
From soup to sweet-wine, and God bless the King.
In plenty starving, tantalized in state,
And complaisantly helped to all I hate,
Treated, caressed, and tired, I take my leave,
Sick of his civil Pride from Morn to Eve;
I curse such lavish cost, and little skill,
And swear no Day was ever past so ill.
  Yet hence the Poor are clothed, the Hungry fed;
Health to himself, and to his Infants bread
The Lab'rer bears: What his hard Heart denies,
His charitable Vanity supplies.
  Another age shall see the golden Ear
Embrown the Slope, and nod on the Parterre,
Deep Harvests bury all his pride has planned,
And laughing Ceres re-assume the land.
  Who then shall grace, or who improve the Soil?
Who plants like BATHURST, or who builds like BOYLE.
'Tis Use alone that sanctifies Expense,
And Splendour borrows all her rays from Sense.
  His Father's Acres who enjoys in peace,
Or makes his Neighbours glad, if he increase:

Whose cheerful Tenants bless their yearly toil,
Yet to their Lord owe more than to the soil;
Whose ample Lawns are not ashamed to feed
The milky heifer and deserving steed;
Whose rising Forests, not for pride or show,
But future Buildings, future Navies, grow:
Let his plantations stretch from down to down,
First shade a Country, and then raise a Town.
  You too proceed! make falling Arts your care,
Erect new wonders, and the old repair;
Jones and Palladio to themselves restore,
And be whate'er Vitruvius was before:
'Til Kings call forth th' Ideas of your mind,
(Proud to accomplish what such hands designed,)
Bid Harbours open, public Ways extend,
Bid Temples, worthier of the God, ascend;
Bid the broad Arch the dang'rous Flood contain,
The Mole projected break the roaring Main;
Back to his bounds their subject Sea command,
And roll obedient Rivers through the Land:
These Honours Peace to happy Britain brings,
These are Imperial Works, and worthy Kings.

Before talking of order in this satire, we must respond to the variety and be quite sure we are describing an order felt *within* the 'bright diversity' of the poem. The larger continuities must be perceptible in a moment of the liveliest and most varied reading experience. A good test is to read aloud the scene of Timon's dinner, with the summons to the chapel service that precedes it (lines 141-68):

  And now the Chapel's silver bell you hear,
That summons you to all the Pride of Prayer:
Light quirks of Music, broken and uneven,
Make the soul dance upon a Jig to Heaven.
On painted Ceilings you devoutly stare,
Where sprawl the Saints of Verrio or Laguerre,
On gilded clouds in fair expansion lie,
And bring all Paradise before your eye.

To rest, the Cushion and soft Dean invite,
Who never mentions Hell to ears polite.
  But hark! the chiming Clocks to dinner call;
A hundred footsteps scrape the marble Hall:
The rich Buffet well-coloured Serpents grace,
And gaping Tritons spew to wash your face.
Is this a dinner? this a Genial room?
No, 'tis a Temple, and a Hecatomb.
A solemn Sacrifice, performed in state,
You drink by measure, and to minutes eat.
So quick retires each flying course, you'd swear
Sancho's dread Doctor and his Wand were there.
Between each Act the trembling salvers ring,
From soup to sweet-wine, and God bless the King.
In plenty starving, tantalized in state,
And complaisantly helped to all I hate,
Treated, caressed, and tired, I take my leave,
Sick of his civil Pride from Morn to Eve;
I curse such lavish cost, and little skill,
And swear no Day was ever past so ill.

Reading the lines aloud, we get an impression of constantly shifting balance as we vary pace and stress and as we modulate our voices to make changes of tone or to allow for the fulfilment of sensuous excitements and ironic implications. The special demands that the passage makes on a reader point directly to its surprising range and diversity in images, in patterns of sound, and especially in tones and ironies. Many of these local variations belong to continuities running through the whole poem.

In imagery—to begin with that pattern—we pass from the precious sound of the 'silver bell' to the skipping music which degenerates into 'a jig to heaven.' Next comes a rich impression of baroque painting, of Michelangeloesque saints against gilded, billowing clouds. By a remarkable declension we move to the padded luxury of the chapel seats and the horrid sensation of a dean who 'gives' to the touch. Next, the large-sounding clocks are heard in ironic antiphony to the delicate bell, while the baroque splendors of the ceiling are matched in the rich and *outré* ornaments of the marble hall.

Though we constantly hear the cultivated voice of a guide speaking—rather obliquely—to an audience of equal sophistication, the scale of tones is certainly more varied than that of the imagery. What seemed like a polite comment,

> And now the Chapel's silver bell you hear,

steps up via a more formal vocabulary and alliteration to a pompous announcement:

> That summons you to all the Pride of Prayer.

The view of the ceiling reaches its climax in a tone of Miltonic awe,

> And bring all Paradise before your eye,

which in fact parodies a line from 'Il Penseroso,'

> And bring all Heaven before mine eyes.

The oscillations of tone in the next few lines are most wonderful. The vision of Paradise is gently interrupted by the soothing voice of the social raconteur,

> To rest, the Cushion and soft Dean invite,

and the exquisite deference of the cleric,

> Who never mentions Hell to ears polite.

His rather cozy tone is shattered by the shout of a herald, 'But hark!' Following this hint of heroic narrative the solemnity of a Roman oration is heard in the diction and in the balanced rhetorical questions and replies of

> Is this a dinner? this a Genial room?
> No, 'tis a Temple, and a Hecatomb.

The formality of balance continuing through most of the lines that follow offsets the descent to the personal (the only use of 'I' in the whole poem). In the context of this rather artificial phrasing another Miltonic parody enters unobtrusively, while the irony of the allusion is increased by the contrasting personal tone:

Treated, caressed, and tired, I take my leave,
Sick of his civil Pride from Morn to Eve; *
I curse such lavish cost, and little skill,
And swear no Day was ever past so ill.

All of these diverse tones give rise to irony, not only because they are often incongruous in relation to the events and persons being described (as in Dryden), but because they clash with one another. The accent of Roman cultivation is rudely met by backstairs vulgarity: 'Tritons spew to wash your face.' But the opposition goes beyond differences of tone: high art clashes with physical grossness; ornament, with use. Ironic ambiguities continue to multiply in phrase after phrase. Consider 'fair expansion' in

Where sprawl the Saints of Verrio or Laguerre,
On gilded clouds in fair expansion lie,
And bring all Paradise before your eye.

Read as 'clouds in fair expansion,' the phrase suggests the billowy grandeur of Rubens or Tiepolo. But bigness in this poem is always reminding us of grossness, and the extraordinary length of the word, especially at this point in the line, also helps to magnify the image. The clouds are overexpanded. If we read 'saints in fair expansion lie' (which is equally possible), 'fair' means something more than pleasing to the eye. It includes the awkwardness of 'sprawl' and the indecency of 'stare.' Sacred art becomes exhibitionism: 'This were Paradise' indeed!

The dance of oppositions, of indescribable variety, continues from here to the end of the scene. The herald's cry ('But hark!') introduces something less than an epic action. The innocent rhetorical questions are answered by the expected 'no' and by a most unexpected statement that adds fresh ironies:

Is this a dinner? this a Genial room?
No, 'tis a Temple, and a Hecatomb.

* from morn
To noon he fell, from noon to dewy eve . . .
Paradise Lost, I, 742-3.

Inversion is the order of the day: too much time for drink, not enough for eating; much food and little to eat; kindness which is hateful; civility which is pride.

The inversions and other clashes of meaning are distinctly *heard*. Symmetries and inversions of meaning are matched in the order of accents and words. The matching lines of question and reply divide at exactly the same point; the inversion of propriety is expressed with an inversion of words. Similarly, the inversion of times is matched by chiasmus:

> You drink by measure, and to minutes eat.

This line describing the clock-like precision of the ceremony concludes a series of lines of extraordinarily uniform metrical pattern. Their monotonous regularity is appropriately broken by a couplet that must be read almost in a single breath, its one pause coming in a very odd place:

> So quick retires each flying course, you'd swear
> Sancho's dread Doctor and his Wand were there.

There is quite a different surprise in the reverse break of

> To rest, the Cushion and soft Dean invite,
> Who never mentions Hell to ears polite.

The eternal sleep is not exactly what we anticipated. But Pope moves quite beyond the couplet pattern in the lines describing the vast magnificence of the painted heaven:

> On painted Ceilings you devoutly stare,
> Where sprawl the Saints of Verrio or Laguerre,
> On gilded clouds in fair expansion lie,
> And bring all Paradise before your eye.

If by now the reader feels more confusion than harmony in the passage, I shall have had a more than ironic success. For it is necessary to register fully the richness—sensuous, tonal, ironic, and rhythmic—of Pope's verse, or we shall find it only too easy to bestow on Pope the conventional unity of 'mechanic warblings.' Starting from the instances of variety already described, let us see whether they are linked with other particulars in continuities which unify the whole satire.

Although there is no often repeated image, visual images, particularly of natural objects, have a distinct character and a special value in the design of the poem. Observe the contexts in which they appear. 'Gilded clouds,' which with 'silver' sets the note of luxury in the chapel dinner scene, occurs in a vivid description of painting. Probably the most striking group of visual images in the poem comes in a passage on a garden:

> Behold Villario's ten years' toil complete;
> His Quincunx darkens, his Espaliers meet;
> The Wood supports the Plain, the parts unite,
> And strength of Shade contends with strength of Light;
> A waving Glow the bloomy beds display,
> Blushing in bright diversities of day,
> With silver-quiv'ring rills maeandered o'er . . .

The description has turned the garden into a painting.* Note the symmetrical composition of the scene, the references to the balancing of masses and to contrasting effects of 'Light' and 'Shade.' In this context 'silver-quiv'ring,' 'maeandered,' 'waving glow,' and other visual images become pictorial in a quite limited sense, and we respond accordingly. We get an impression of massed colors, of points of light, and of linear pattern rather than of flowers and streams and trees. Elsewhere in the poem visual imagery of the outdoor world is concentrated in passages which are similarly pictorial both in the use of the technical vocabulary of painting and in the symmetrical composition of the view being described. There is the passage on 'consulting the genius of the place' (lines 57-69), the description of Sabinus' and his son's 'vistas' with their colors and shades (lines 89-93), and finally the scene in Timon's gardens, which is a travesty of art and nature.

* 'All gardening is landscape painting,' he [Pope] said. 'You may distance things by darkening them, and by narrowing . . . towards the end, in the same manner as they do in painting.' Quoted from Spence's *Anecdotes* in E. W. Manwaring: *Italian Landscape in Eighteenth Century England* (New York, 1925), p. 127.

By this recurrent connection Pope creates a vague continuity of metaphor: visual beauties of nature are felt as picturesque. The metaphor was of course conventional for an audience that regarded gardening and architecture as a kind of painting, and Nature as the 'Great Design' or 'Designing Power.' But however conventional, the metaphor is effective at many points in the epistle, not least so in a passage a modern reader might take as 'natural' in a sense most alien to Pope and his public:

> Another age shall see the golden Ear
> Embrown the Slope, and nod on the Parterre,
> Deep Harvests bury all his pride has planned,
> And laughing Ceres re-assume the land.

The recollection in these lines of the 'gilded' * glories of the chapel painting is one small but important sign that these images are to be regarded as pictorial, as belonging to a painter's landscape.

But the epistle hangs together mainly through other continuities, especially of tone and irony. Certain tones recur, which is to say that certain uses of language particularly influential in fixing the tones recur, too. Though every tone is on occasion expressive of irony, there is a value in tracing the tonal continuities apart from their ironic import, for it is largely through them that Pope connects the didactic and the more purely satiric phases of his poem. The voice of the cultivated conversationalist is heard everywhere in the poem as well as throughout the tour of Timon's villa.

To define 'conversational' exactly as used of this tone and to show how Pope gives the illusion of conversation would require a small volume. Of course it is inconceivable, except in a Sitwellian vision of the Augustans, that anyone ever talked like this. We may say in brief that within the dramatic situation of the Horatian epistle Pope introduces just often enough the vocabulary and idiom of talk (by either an eighteenth-century or a modern standard) for us to hear the lines as possible conversation. There are, for example, informal contractions such as 'you'd' and 'you'll' and ''tis,' or expressions such as 'you'd swear' and 'I curse' and 'for all his Lordship

* I owe this point to the perceptive analysis made by William Empson in *Seven Types of Ambiguity* (London, 1930), pp. 161, 162.

knows,' or vulgarisms such as 'spew' and 'squirt,' all of which we—and almost certainly eighteenth-century readers—regard as not quite suitable for written English. The combination of these expressions with many others no Englishman would ever use in speech produces very peculiar conversation indeed. Most of my analysis will go to defining the cultivation of tone which is qualified by such touches of small talk.

The first point to note is the curiously oblique relation between the speaker and his fellow conversationalists, those 'you's' to whom he addresses his observations on men and manners:

> And now the Chapel's silver bell you hear,
> That summons you to all the Pride of Prayer. . .

'You,' in this couplet and in many other passages, hovers on the edge of 'one,' but with the difference of a slight inclination toward the listener. The speaker makes the faintest acknowledgment of solidarity, of sharing with his audience a sense of propriety and a complete aloofness from the object of the satire. The solidarity is in fact immense: that is what makes the faintness possible. By skilfully taking advantage of the ambiguities of 'you' Pope manages both to speak to and for his audience. He glides from a direct formal address to an almost clubby familiarity to the politely didactic and back to the excessively polite, obliquely observant. (The process should be followed in lines 23-104.)

The tone of 'Roman cultivation' is inherent in the dramatic situation of the poem and in the cultural situation of Augustan England: Pope is speaking as Horace to a Burlington-Maecenas. As a *heard* dramatic tone, though obvious, it is not simple, but many-layered. I shall sort out two or three of the minor tones that compose it and indicate how Pope maintains them through the epistle. The precision of his control, often through exact reproduction of verbal patterns, is remarkable.

On the surface there is an air of casual familiarity with things Roman, a manner expressed in the dinner scene by references to 'Tritons' and 'hecatombs' or by the use of words that assume a knowledge of Latin if the wit is to be fully appreciated:

> In plenty starving, *tantalized* in state. . .

The Roman context makes it easy for Pope to move to a solemn oratorical tone which contrasts sharply with the manner of the social raconteur. He adopts the rhetorical questions and answers, the exclamations and exhortations, the balanced phrasing of the Ciceronian orator, examples of which we noted in the grandiloquent lines on Timon's dinner. The ease with which this tone is introduced and the use of the characteristic devices may be seen in the opening lines of the epistle, which emerge casually from a conversation that seems to have already begun:

> 'Tis strange, the Miser should his Cares employ
> To gain those Riches he can ne'er enjoy:
> Is it less strange, the Prodigal should waste
> His wealth, to purchase what he ne'er can taste?
> Not for himself he sees, or hears, or eats;
> Artists must choose his Pictures, Music, Meats . . .

The first satirical portraits are similarly announced by rhetorical questions and answers or by exclamations:

> For what has Virro painted, built, and planted? . . .
> What brought Sir Visto's ill got wealth to waste? . . .
> See! sportive fate, to punish awkward pride,
> Bids Bubo build, and sends him such a Guide.

A kind of tonal expectation is thus built up, which is satisfied very often in very nearly the same way. A rapid glance through the poem will show how many times Pope falls into the same patterns with consequently similar heightening of tone. (Besides the questions, there are: 'Lo! Cobham . . . Lo, what . . . Lo, some . . . Enjoy them, you! . . . His study!' et cetera.)

The 'But hark!' which announced Timon's dinner had a heroic flavor, an accent which was for Pope closely connected with the Roman oratorical manner. Pope's heroic style was also an allusive one, echoing Milton, Dryden, Sandys, and many other poets. Examples of both characteristics are easily found in his translation of the *Iliad:*

> Achilles thus the King of Men address'd:
> 'Why leave we not the fatal Trojan shore,
> And measure back the seas we cross'd before?'

'Augur accurs'd! denouncing mischief still,
Prophet of plagues, forever boding ill!'

Fired with thirst which virtuous envy breeds,
And smit * with love of honourable deeds.

The parodies of Milton in the chapel and dinner scenes are anticipated in the apotheosis of Timon who waits like a demigod to 'bless your eyes':

My Lord advances with majestic mien,
Smit with the mighty pleasure, to be seen.

The heroic note is once imparted by self-parody (one of Pope's fairly common devices):

Conscious they act a true Palladian part,
And if they starve, they starve by rules of art . . .

which recalls

Is it, in heaven, a crime to love too well?
To bear too tender, or too firm a heart?
To act a Lover's or a Roman's part? †

But the heroic element should not be exaggerated in this or any of Pope's epistles. It is only one note in the cultivated Roman manner, and not, as so often in Dryden, the prevailing tone. Pope moves through a wider range of tones than Dryden and is constantly passing up and down his tonal scale, a movement that is characteristic and indispensable for his ironic mode.

The recurrence of certain tones in the epistle entails also the recurrence of certain ironies. Pope has only to talk of Villario or Timon rather than of Boyle for the accent of cultivation to become satiric. I shall note one or two examples to indicate the kinds of irony that arise. The aloof politeness of 'your' in

Greatness, with Timon, dwells in such a draught
As brings all Brobdignag before your thought

* Compare: 'Smit with the love of sacred song.' . . .
Paradise Lost, III, 29.

† 'Elegy to the Memory of an Unfortunate Lady.'

indirectly stresses the horror of this monstrous vision. ('I should regard this dispassionately?' says the auditor. 'Certainly not!') The high Miltonic tone of the parody expresses a similar ironic contrast with the scene being described, a contrast that is crudely underlined by the anticlimax of 'all *Brobdignag* before your thought.' The constant incongruity of the Roman tone whether merely learned and Latinate or oratorical and semi-heroic needs no further illustration.

But as we observed in discussing such incongruities in the dinner scene, the irony involved is more than an inappropriateness of literary manner. By constantly surrounding these men with Amphitrites and Dryads or quincunxes and pilasters, Pope symbolizes the culture which they miss while aping it. Just so their Latin names keep reminding us of how very un-Latin they are. The symbol of classical civilization is almost always balanced by a reference to something commonplace or obscene or physically disgusting:

> For Pembroke, Statues, dirty Gods, and Coins. . .
> Two Cupids squirt before. . .
> And swallows roost in Nilus' dusty Urn.

Expressions of grandeur regularly become ambiguous in exactly the same way:

> A hundred footsteps scrape the marble Hall. . .
> The whole, a laboured Quarry above ground. . .
> First through the length of yon hot Terrace sweat;
> And when up ten steep slopes you've dragged your
> thighs. . .

Exaggerations of praise are as common as exaggerations of size, both being nicely combined in

> So proud, so grand; of that stupendous air
> Soft and Agreeable come never there.

The oratorical exclamations often express ironic wonder, the 'lo's,' 'hark's,' 'see's,' and the like preparing us for a display of elegance, but admiration is always checked by a further surprise. In a similar way the rhetorical questions with their inevitably shocking answers lift us up to survey some noble social or cultural achievement only to let us down with its opposite:

For what has Virro painted, built, and planted?
Only to shew, how many Tastes he wanted.

His Study! with what Authors is it stored?
In Books, not Authors, curious is my Lord.

So Pope displays the clash between certain intellectual, aesthetic, and social values and the antics of a Virro or a Villario or a Timon. We emerge from reading the poem a bit breathless, as if we had been running on a treadmill of antitheses. Pope has taken us through almost the whole possible range of antithetical meanings, from the mildly incongruous to negation of opposites to inversion which produces a sort of ironic nonsense.

In tracing different sorts of continuity in the poem—of pictorial imagery, tone, and irony—we have seen that the recurrence of a similar meaning, for example, of a particular tone, is often accompanied by the recurrence of a similar or even the identical verbal pattern. Although the same word is not often repeated, very similar arrangements of words are met with frequently. (The arrangements or patterns may be grammatical, rhetorical, or metrical, or any combination of the three.) Obviously, similar patterns of sounds (i.e. rhythms) are therefore also recurrent. I am concerned here with the coincidence between a recurrent meaning and a recurrent sound pattern, not with mere uniformities of meter or word order apart from what is being expressed.

In the passages where pictorial imagery predominates, in those symmetrical compositions of natural beauties, Pope's phrasing and meter often fall into the most extreme balance. As he plays light against shade and beauty against beauty, he breaks the lines with sharp pauses at the fourth, fifth, and sixth syllable and often balances the two half-lines by using exactly the same order of words in each. But at the points where the more particular color and line images cluster, the balance is less marked, and the movement tends to run beyond the couplet unit. As in the lines on the chapel painting, there is a kind of widening out of the sound pattern in the most sensuously active moments of description. Consider by contrast the deadly uniformity of the picture of Timon's gardens, a passage to which we shall return later.

I pointed out earlier that the Roman oratorical tone was introduced repeatedly by the same rhetorical and grammatical devices, with the effect of seeming to reproduce the same sounds and rhythms. Four times a rhetorical question in the first line of the couplet is balanced by the answer in the second. There is also a much more complex couplet pattern, in which one question balances another in the first line, followed in the second by balanced answers that come in the reverse order:

> Is this a dinner? this a Genial room?
> No, 'tis a Temple, and a Hecatomb.

The same pattern is heard in:

> Who then shall grace, or who improve the Soil?
> Who plants like BATHURST, or who builds like BOYLE.

The oratorical exclamations and exhortations tend to come at the same point in the verse, producing rhythmic as well as tonal parallels between passages otherwise very different. For example,

> Enjoy them, you! Villario can no more;

has its exact metrical parallel in the line which opens the grand address to Burlington:

> You too proceed! make falling Arts your care. . .

Recurrent ironies of various types (in addition to those of tone) are marked by even more striking parallels in word order and rhythm. The explosion of some sort of grandeur by linking it with something vulgar is expressed—perhaps too many times—in a line ending on an anticlimactic monosyllable:

> First through the length of yon hot Terrace sweat. . .
> Smit with the mighty pleasure, to be seen. . .
> Shall call the winds through long arcades to roar. . .
> Tired of the scene Parterres and Fountains yield,
> He finds at last he better likes a Field.

August polysyllables expressing ironic praise, sometimes with a play on a Latin meaning or an allusion, appear regularly in the same rhythmic pattern:

On gilded clouds in fair expansion lie. . .
Conscious they act a true Palladian part. . .
So proud, so grand; of that stupendous air. . .
His Gardens next your admiration call. . .

When the ironic meanings become most violently antithetical, Pope sharpens the contrast by using the patterns of exact balance through which he accentuated the symmetries of art in descriptive passages. There is the same obnoxious symmetry of word order and metrical stress in the account of the clock-like service at Timon's dinner as in the ironic picture of his gardens. The inversion of times is expressed by the same rhetorical figure used in depicting the inversion of nature:

Trees cut to Statues, Statues thick as trees

and

You drink by measure, and to minutes eat.

With the return of the familiar ironic contrast we hear a swing and pause, a grouping of accents and syllables already associated with that particular type of irony. We can appreciate now the importance in Pope of the recurrence of certain verbal patterns along with the recurrence of certain tones or ironies or descriptive modes. To the connections made by one or more of the other continuities is added an analogy of rhythm.

The garden passage (lines 113-126) offers a good example of how Pope's continuities work, both to impress the seal of his individual mode of irony and to produce a sense of unity in the whole poem. There is a large pictorial impression with its balanced beauties so beguiling as to seem hardly ironic. There is the tone of politely aloof comment and of public awe; the air of classic learning and the occasional accent of pungent vulgarity. Along with the familiar ironies of tone go other equally familiar blends: the ambiguous praise and marveling, the combination of classical grandeur and meanness, the inversions of taste and use. Finally, there is the recurrence (noted above) of equally familiar verbal patterns: 'We have heard this before.'

How do these continuities work in our reading of the whole

satire? At least two or three ways may be pointed out. First, as implied in our analysis, they work horizontally, sending lines of relation across the poem. The tone and rhythm heard in the address to Burlington is beautifully continuous with that heard in hailing Timon's pompous achievements. And yet in the most intense moments of the satire all of the continuities seem to affect us simultaneously. The pictorial imagery, the aristocratic-Roman tone, and the related ironies—with the accompanying sound patterns—tend to move together as a literary constellation and to recur in close community with one another. In the more purely ironic passages, there is also a somewhat regular sequence in the reappearance of the continuities within each section or poetic paragraph. The shorter portraits and the separate paragraphs of the Timon portrait ordinarily develop in much the same way. They open at the top of Pope's tonal scale, often with an exclamation or some semi-heroic note, and descend at the end to the semi-vulgar conversational level. Toward the middle of the paragraph comes a pictorial phase with the balanced beauties which so easily become balanced incongruities. In the final couplet or two, beauty or consistency is no longer attributed, as nobility and politeness of tone disappear:

> The thriving plants ignoble broomsticks made,
> Now sweep those Alleys they were born to shade.
>
> I curse such lavish cost, and little skill,
> And swear no Day was ever past so ill.

The curve of the accompanying sound patterns has been fairly well indicated. Some such development, with many fine variations in detail, may be traced in nearly all of the more satirical paragraphs of the poem. So we come to anticipate in each of Pope's tirades a more or less regular gamut made up of familiar elements. (An expectation is set up similar to that experienced in reading Corneille.) In the large compositional rhythm which is thus created we have something like a key design in the epistle to Burlington; it is the design that mainly shapes the total attitude Pope is expressing.

The continuities that make up the smaller patterns and the large design of the poem are more than a series of rhetorical hoops through which the reader obediently hops. Otherwise, they would hardly affect us much or convey any integrated sense of life. To recall James's remark a second time, Pope's irony, like all irony, is 'operative' through vibrant reference to 'the sincerities, the lucidities, the utilities that stand behind it.' The continuities we have been tracing are the very stuff of Pope's active satire, the more-than-medium through which Pope expresses his vision of wealthy builders and cultivators of the arts. Each of the continuities becomes expressive fully and precisely only in relation to a cultural ideal, the point of view from which Pope observes so many eccentricities of behavior.

But what is the ideal, and what is the relation of the satire to it? These questions may easily be answered in the wrong way, as Warburton's example reminds us. We can make up a definition of taste partly from the text and partly from eighteenth-century usage and trace a more or less accurate logical connection between the definition and each section of the poem: Pope presents a series of *exempla* of bad taste. Though it would be absurd to deny a connection of this sort, the answer is not very satisfying in relation to a lively reading of the poem. It hardly accounts for any link between the ideal and the imagery and tone in the moments of richest irony. We can find a more illuminating and more pertinent answer by describing the ideal as it is defined in the dramatic texture of the poem, in Pope's whole address to Burlington:

> You show us Rome was glorious, not profuse,
> And pompous buildings once were things of Use. . .
> 'Tis Use alone that sanctifies Expense,
> And Splendour borrows all her rays from Sense.

Here is the poem's imaginative germ, the nucleus of most of its felt relationships. The ideal that ratifies the ironies and makes them meaningful is not simply the group of propositions stated in these lines, but the type of aesthetic and social behavior implicit in addressing Burlington as an aristocrat and restorer of Roman and Renaissance principles of architecture, implicit too in the Latinate accent of 'profuse' and 'pompous,' in the balancing of values, and in the corresponding formality of verbal pattern. As further expressed in the closing section of the poem (lines 181-end), the ideal is that of the responsible aristocrat who builds and plants for socially useful ends, whose whole style, both in acting as a public benefactor and in designing and building, is Roman. Unlike the Imitating Fools he considers the propriety of classical design to its modern use. His 'pompous buildings' owe their 'Splendour' to his 'Sense.'

Good Sense, the faculty indispensable for classical propriety, is equally necessary for the exercise of a larger propriety, for 'following Nature.' Such terms, like similar rallying cries in other periods, are of course never exactly definable, their potency depending in part on their obscurity. The slippery ease with which Pope glides from 'following Sense' to 'following Nature' should warn us against expecting a philosopher's precision in definition. But if Dr. Johnson could say that 'the most valuable passage' in the epistle 'is perhaps the Elegy on "Good Sense,"' we can hardly dismiss the term as without serious meaning. The relevant meaning can be gathered from the metaphor and imagery of the 'Elegy' as much as from the direct statements. It is, for example, worth noting that 'Sense . . . only is the gift of Heaven,' not acquired by learning, but an inborn power. It is essentially aristocratic. It is also significant that 'the Genius of the Place' (Nature as revealed in a particular place) is described in imagery borrowed from painting and draughtsmanship. To 'follow Nature' is to work with the artistry of Nature the Designer, the metaphor implied in nearly every descriptive passage of the poem. Vaguely enough for us, but in terms clear to his audience, Pope is alluding also to nature as the principle of order in all things, an order that includes spontaneous variety. The architect-landscaper must first of all work according to the order (e.g. in the landscape) which nature has achieved. If he works as she works,

> Parts answ'ring parts shall slide into a whole,
> Spontaneous beauties all around advance. . .

This generous concept of a propriety of design which imitates the grand artistry of nature and which is consistent with 'surprise' is not separable for Pope from the Roman-aristocratic code with its stress on appropriateness of design to use. To sum up what really should not be summed up as so many concepts, we may describe Pope's ideal as that of the aristocratic builder who works in the

Roman tradition with a sense of propriety to use and who aims also at a larger propriety, at designing with the varied order which is nature's.

Let me suggest briefly how the main continuities in the poem are related to this complex ideal. From many anticipatory asides, it must be clear that they both derive from it and embody it in expressive forms. The major tones of the poem, to begin with the most obvious point of relation, are 'sanctified' (in Pope's sense of the word) by the dramatic symbol of the ideal builder-benefactor. Pope's peculiar approach to his audience depended on his sharing their standards of propriety. Speaking both for and to them, he adopts the politeness and easy cultivation appropriate to the aristocrat and the unpedantic amateur. It is quite natural for such a conversationalist to assume the public oratorical tone—or even the heroic—for these tones are his by social prerogative and education. And unlike the proper man of the middle class, he can publicly indulge in a piece of smacking vulgarity or obscenity.

The force of the irony that depends on these tones is intensified enormously by constant reference to the Roman-aristocratic ideal. The incongruity of either the polite or the oratorical tone cruelly measures Timon and his kind by the implied standard of civilized behavior. As has been suggested, other ironies that sharply contrast the classical and the vulgar or the grand and the obscene or high praise and actual achievement are more than local hits. They remind us that the pomp is out of relation to use or is wasteful or that it has been created by disregarding or inverting a more 'natural' order. Machine-like symmetries of design are more than amusing as a type of dullness: they allow no place for Nature's 'spontaneous beauties.' I have anticipated the connection between Pope's imagery and the ideal of emulating Nature the Designer. It is significant that we rarely encounter a visual impression of any object in physical nature except in a description which reminds us that Nature is a painter of 'order in variety.'

It would be impossible to demonstrate any simple relation between Pope's ideal standard in the poem and the fact that recurrent ironies or tones are often accompanied by the recurrence of certain sound patterns. We can feel, of course, that the increased sense of order that results has its appropriateness to the concept of art being expressed. We can feel too that the frequent balancings of word patterns and of sounds are exactly right for the propriety in expense and art which is being praised and for the corresponding improprieties which are rejected.

That the other continuities are expressive of the cultural ideal and that they become more largely significant and more fully coherent in relation to it is clear. This is not a relation between ideas, or between ideas and devices, but of connections felt in the resonances of words, a peculiarly poetic experience of language. The finest examples of this active relationship come in the noble epitaph with which Pope closes the satire on Timon's monstrosities:

> Another age shall see the golden Ear
> Embrown the Slope, and nod on the Parterre,
> Deep Harvests bury all his pride has planned,
> And laughing Ceres re-assume the land.

The impersonality and formality of tone with its Latinate 'laughing Ceres' and 're-assume the land' belong to the voice of the idealized aristocrat: it is not Pope who speaks. The pictorial imagery brings to mind the 'design' of Nature and the noble builder's aim of imitating its varied order in his creations. The future scene will be one of useful art, of fields that are picturesque in cultivation, not stupidly landscaped nor abandoned to 'wild disorder.' 'Gold,' symbolic in Timon's villa of waste and impropriety, is in this setting a symbol of 'Splendour' that 'borrows all her rays from Sense.' 'Laughing Ceres' signifies among other things the Nature of cultivated fields smiling in triumph over waste and the 'inversion' of nature. This is a triumph of eighteenth-century order, and certainly not prophetic of the coming revolution, as William Empson rather ingeniously suggests. In using a phrase that echoes the *laeta seges* of Virgil's *Georgics,* Pope reminds us that his vision of nature and art and society has a historical model.

By such energy of language Pope realizes the links between the ideal and the continuities in imagery, tone, and irony which we have been tracing. So they become richly expressive of a whole style of living, and so their recurrence in a characteristic pattern is indicative of something more than a rhetorical habit. We may describe Pope's satirical gamut as a key design if we emphasize the poetically achieved connection between the continuities and the cultural ideal. Whatever term we use, we may agree that in the 'bridge' of this relationship as constantly renewed in the detail of language lies the imaginative order of Pope's poem.

Chapter IX

LIGHT AND BRIGHT AND SPARKLING: IRONY AND FICTION IN 'PRIDE AND PREJUDICE'

The work is rather too light, and bright, and sparkling; it wants shade; it wants to be stretched out here and there with a long chapter of sense, if it could be had; if not, of solemn specious nonsense . . .

JANE AUSTEN

Many pages of *Pride and Prejudice* can be read as sheer poetry of wit, as Pope without couplets. The antitheses are almost as frequent and almost as varied; the play of ambiguities is certainly as complex; the orchestration of tones is as precise and subtle. As in the best of Pope, the displays of ironic wit are not without imaginative connection; what looks most diverse is really most similar, and ironies are linked by vibrant reference to basic certainties. There are passages too in which the rhythmical pattern of the sentence approaches the formal balance of the heroic couplet:

> Mr. Bennet was so odd a mixture of quick parts, sarcastic humour, reserve, and caprice, that the experience of three and twenty years had been insufficient to make his wife understand his character. *Her* mind was less difficult to develope. She was a woman of mean understanding, little information, and uncertain temper. When she was discontented she fancied herself nervous. The business of her life was to get her daughters married; its solace was visiting and news.

The triumph of the novel—whatever its limitations may be—lies in combining such poetry of wit with the dramatic structure of fiction. In historical terms, to combine the traditions of poetic satire with those of the sentimental novel, that was Jane Austen's feat in *Pride and Prejudice.*

For the 'bright and sparkling,' seemingly centrifugal play of irony is dramatically functional. It makes sense as literary art, the sense with which a writer is most concerned. The repartee, while constantly amusing, delineates characters and their changing relations and points the way to a climactic moment in which the change is most clearly recognized. Strictly speaking, this union of wit and drama is achieved with complete success only in the central sequence of *Pride and Prejudice,* in the presentation of Elizabeth's and Darcy's gradual revaluation of each other. Here, if anywhere, Jane Austen met James's demand that the novel should give its readers the maximum of 'fun'; at the same time she satisfied the further standard implied in James's remark that the art of the novel is 'above all an art of preparations.' That she met these demands more continuously in *Emma* does not detract from her achievement in *Pride and Prejudice.*

Her blend of ironic wit and drama may be seen in its simplest form in the first chapter of the novel, in the dialogue between Mr. and Mrs. Bennet on the topic of Mr. Bingley's leasing Netherfield Park. Every remark which each makes, Mrs. Bennet petulantly, and Mr. Bennet perversely, bounces off the magnificent opening sentence:

> It is a truth universally acknowledged, that a single man in possession of a good fortune, must be in want of a wife.

The scene that follows dramatizes the alternatives implied in 'universally,' Mrs. Bennet reminding us of one; and Mr. Bennet, of the other:

> 'My dear Mr. Bennet,' said his lady to him one day, 'have you heard that Netherfield Park is let at last?'
>
> Mr. Bennet replied that he had not.
>
> 'But it is,' returned she; 'for Mrs. Long has just been here, and she told me all about it.'
>
> Mr. Bennet made no answer.
>
> 'Do not you want to know who has taken it?' cried his wife impatiently.

'*You* want to tell me, and I have no objection to hearing it.'

This was invitation enough.

'Why, my dear, you must know, Mrs. Long says that Netherfield is taken by a young man of large fortune from the north of England; that he came down on Monday in a chaise and four to see the place, and was so much delighted with it that he agreed with Mr. Morris immediately; that he is to take possession before Michaelmas, and some of his servants are to be in the house by the end of next week.'

'What is his name?'

'Bingley.'

'Is he married or single?'

'Oh! single, my dear, to be sure! A single man of large fortune; four or five thousand a year. What a fine thing for our girls!'

'How so? how can it affect them?'

'My dear Mr. Bennet,' replied his wife, 'how can you be so tiresome! You must know that I am thinking of his marrying one of them.'

'Is that his design in settling here?'

'Design! nonsense, how can you talk so!'

A parallel appears in the opening of Pope's Epistle, 'Of the Characters of Women':

> Nothing so true as what you once let fall,
> 'Most Women have no Characters at all,'

a pronouncement immediately followed by a series of portraits showing that women have 'characters' in one sense if not in another. It is also easy to find counterparts in Pope's satirical mode for Mr. Bennet's extreme politeness of address, his innocent queries, and his epigrammatic turns. The character that emerges from this dialogue is almost that of a professional satirist: Mr. Bennet is a man of quick parts and sarcastic humor, altogether a most unnatural father. Mrs. Bennet speaks another language; *her* talk does not crackle with irony and epigram; *her* sentences run in quite another mold. They either go on too long or break up awkwardly in impulsive exclamations; this is the talk of a person of 'mean understanding' and 'uncertain temper.'

But though the blended art of this scene is admirable, a limitation appears. Mr. and Mrs. Bennet are so perfectly done that little more is left to be expressed. Variety or forward movement in the drama will almost surely be difficult, which obviously proves to be the case. The sequences that depend most closely on the opening scene—those concerned with the business of getting the Bennet daughters married—are all amusingly ironic, but relatively static as drama. As Mrs. Bennet contrives to join Jane and Bingley, to marry one daughter to Mr. Collins, and to further Lydia's exploits with the military, father, mother, and daughters remain in very nearly the same dramatic positions. True enough, the last of these sequences ends in a catastrophe. But the connection between Lydia's downfall and the earlier scenes of ironic comedy in which Mr. and Mrs. Bennet are opposed is not fully expressed. Lydia's behavior 'leads to this' in a Richardsonian moral sense, but Lydia is too scantly presented in relation to her parents or to Wickham to prepare us adequately for her bad end. We accept it if at all as literary convention. Incidentally, we might conjecture that the marriage-market sequences belong to the early version of *Pride and Prejudice,* or at least that they are examples of Jane Austen's earlier manner. In the central sequence of *Pride and Prejudice,* especially in its more complex blend of ironic and dramatic design, we can see anticipated the more mature structure of both *Mansfield Park* and *Emma.*

In portraying the gradual change in Elizabeth's estimate of Darcy and in his attitude to her, Jane Austen achieves a perfect harmony between the rich ambiguity of ironic dialogue and the movement toward the climactic scenes in which the new estimate is revealed. I shall limit my discussion to scenes from the Elizabeth-Darcy narrative through the episode in which Elizabeth recognizes her 'change in sentiment.' Let us first read Jane Austen's dialogue as poetry of wit, disregarding for the time being any forward movement in the drama, and observing the variety of the irony and the unity of effect achieved through recurrent patterns and through assumptions shared by writer and reader. As in our reading of Pope, we may in this way appreciate the extraordinary richness of ironic texture and the imaginative continuity running through the play of wit. In analyzing the ironies and the assumptions, we shall see how intensely dramatic the dialogue is, dramatic in the sense of defining characters through the way they speak and are spoken about.

The aura of implications which surrounds many of the dialogues between Elizabeth and Darcy is complex enough to delight the most pure Empsonian. Take for example the dialogue in which Sir William Lucas attempts to interest Mr. Darcy in dancing:

> . . . Elizabeth at that instant moving towards them, he was struck with the notion of doing a very gallant thing, and called out to her,
>
> 'My dear Miss Eliza, why are not you dancing?—Mr. Darcy, you must allow me to present this young lady to you as a very desirable partner.—You cannot refuse to dance, I am sure, when so much beauty is before you.' And taking her hand, he would have given it to Mr. Darcy, who, though extremely surprised, was not unwilling to receive it, when she instantly drew back, and said with some discomposure to Sir William,
>
> 'Indeed, Sir, I have not the least intention of dancing.—I entreat you not to suppose that I moved this way in order to beg for a partner.'
>
> Mr. Darcy with grave propriety requested to be allowed the honour of her hand; but in vain. Elizabeth was determined; nor did Sir William at all shake her purpose by his attempt at persuasion.
>
> 'You excel so much in the dance, Miss Eliza, that it is cruel to deny me the happiness of seeing you; and though this gentleman dislikes the amusement in general, he can have no objection, I am sure, to oblige us for one half hour.'
>
> 'Mr. Darcy is all politeness,' said Elizabeth, smiling.
>
> 'He is indeed—but considering the inducement, my dear Miss Eliza, we cannot wonder at his complaisance; for who would object to such a partner?'
>
> Elizabeth looked archly, and turned away.

'Mr. Darcy is all politeness': the statement, as Elizabeth might say, has a 'teazing' variety of meanings. Mr. Darcy is polite in the sense indicated by 'grave propriety,' that is, he shows the courtesy appropriate to a gentleman—which is the immediate, public meaning of Elizabeth's compliment. But 'grave propriety,' being a very limited form of politeness, reminds us forcibly of Mr. Darcy's earlier behavior. His 'gravity' at the ball had been 'forbidding and disagreeable.' 'Grave propriety' may also mean the bare civility of 'the proudest, most disagreeable man in the world.' So Elizabeth's compliment has an ironic twist: she smiles and looks 'archly.' 'All politeness' has also quite another meaning. Mr. Darcy 'was not unwilling to receive' her hand. He is polite in more than the public proper sense; his gesture shows that he is interested in Elizabeth as a person. Her archness and her smile have for the reader an added ironic value: Elizabeth's interpretation of Darcy's manner may be quite wrong. Finally, there is the embracing broadly comic irony of Sir William's action. 'Struck with the notion of doing a very gallant thing,' he is pleasantly unconscious of what he is in fact doing and of what Elizabeth's remark may mean to her and to Darcy.

A similar cluster of possibilities appears in another conversation in which Darcy asks Elizabeth to dance with him:

> . . . soon afterwards Mr. Darcy, drawing near Elizabeth, said to her—
>
> 'Do not you feel a great inclination, Miss Bennet, to seize such an opportunity of dancing a reel?'
>
> She smiled, but made no answer. He repeated the question, with some surprise at her silence.
>
> 'Oh!' said she, 'I heard you before; but I could not immediately determine what to say in reply. You wanted me, I know, to say "Yes," that you might have the pleasure of despising my taste; but I always delight in overthrowing those kind of schemes, and cheating a person of their premeditated contempt. I have therefore made up my mind to tell you, that I do not want to dance a reel at all—and now despise me if you dare.'
>
> 'Indeed I do not dare.'
>
> Elizabeth, having rather expected to affront him, was amazed at his gallantry; but there was a mixture of sweetness and archness in her manner which made it difficult for her to affront anybody; and Darcy had never been so bewitched by any woman as he was by her. He really believed, that were it not for the inferiority of her connections, he should be in some danger.
>
> Miss Bingley saw, or suspected enough to be jealous; and her

> great anxiety for the recovery of her dear friend Jane, received some assistance from her desire of getting rid of Elizabeth.
>
> She often tried to provoke Darcy into disliking her guest, by talking of their supposed marriage, and planning his happiness in such an alliance.

Again Mr. Darcy's request may be interpreted more or less pleasantly, depending on whether we connect it with his present or past behavior. Again Elizabeth's attack on Darcy and her archness have an irony beyond the irony intended by the speaker. But the amusement of this dialogue lies especially in the variety of possible tones which we detect in Darcy's speeches. Elizabeth hears his question as expressing 'premeditated contempt' and scorn of her own taste. But from Mr. Darcy's next remark and the comment which follows, and from his repeating his question and showing 'some surprise,' we may hear in his request a tone expressive of some interest, perhaps only gallantry, perhaps, as Elizabeth later puts it 'somewhat of a friendlier nature.' We could take his 'Indeed I do not dare' as pure gallantry (Elizabeth's version) or as a sign of conventional 'marriage intentions' (Miss Bingley's interpretation), if it were not for the nice reservation, 'He really believed, that were it not for the inferiority of her connections, he should be in some danger.' We must hear the remark as spoken with this qualification. This simultaneity of tonal layers can be matched only in the satire of Pope, where, as we have seen, the reader feels the impossibility of adjusting his voice to the rapid changes in tone and the difficulty of representing by a single sound the several sounds he hears as equally appropriate and necessary. Analysis such as I have been making shows clearly how arbitrary and how thin any stage rendering of *Pride and Prejudice* must be. No speaking voice could possibly represent the variety of tones conveyed to the reader by such interplay of dialogue and comment.

It would be easy enough to produce more of these dialogues, especially on the subject of music or dancing, each with its range of crisply differentiated meanings. Similar patterns of irony recur many times. Mr. Darcy makes his inquiries (polite or impolite), asking with a smile (scornful or encouraging) questions that may be interpreted as pompous and condescending or gallant and well-disposed.

So Mr. Darcy cross-examines Elizabeth in the scene in which their 'superior dancing' gives such pleasure to Sir William:

> 'What think you of books?' said he, smiling.
>
> 'Books—Oh! no.—I am sure we never read the same, or not with the same feelings.'
>
> 'I am sorry you think so; but if that be the case, there can at least be no want of subject.—We may compare our different opinions.'
>
> 'No—I cannot talk of books in a ball-room; my head is always full of something else.'
>
> 'The *present* always occupies you in such scenes—does it?' said he, with a look of doubt.

When connected with a hint of Darcy's changing attitude, that 'look of doubt,' Elizabeth's arch comments take on the added ironic value we have noted in other conversations.

Earlier in this dialogue, Darcy and Elizabeth run through the same sort of question and answer gamut, and with very nearly the same ironic dissonances:

> He smiled, and assured her that whatever she wished him to say should be said.
>
> 'Very well.—That reply will do for the present.—Perhaps by and bye I may observe that private balls are much pleasanter than public ones.—But *now* we may be silent.'
>
> 'Do you talk by rule then, while you are dancing?'
>
> 'Sometimes. One must speak a little, you know. It would look odd to be entirely silent for half an hour together, and yet for the advantage of *some,* conversation ought to be so arranged as that they may have the trouble of saying as little as possible.'
>
> 'Are you consulting your own feelings in the present case, or do you imagine that you are gratifying mine?'
>
> 'Both,' replied Elizabeth archly; 'for I have always seen a great similarity in the turn of our minds.—We are each of an unsocial, taciturn disposition, unwilling to speak, unless we expect to say something that will amaze the whole room, and be handed down to posterity with all the eclat of a proverb.'

'This is no very striking resemblance of your own character, I am sure,' said he.

When Darcy himself is being quizzed he frequently remarks on his own behavior in a way that may be sublimely smug or simply self-respecting, as for example in his comment on his behavior at the first of the Hertfordshire balls:

'I certainly have not the talent which some people possess,' said Darcy, 'of conversing easily with those I have never seen before. I cannot catch their tone of conversation, or appear interested in their concerns, as I often see done.'

But these conversations are not simply sets of ironic meanings; they are in more than a trivial sense *jeux d'esprit,* the play of an adult mind. (The sophistication they imply is of a kind which, as John Jay Chapman once remarked, is Greek and French, rather than English.) The fun in Jane Austen's dialogue has a serious point; or rather, the fun *is* the point. The small talk is the focus for her keen sense of the variability of character, for her awareness of the possibility that the same remark or action has very different meanings in different relations. What most satisfies us in reading the dialogue in *Pride and Prejudice* is Jane Austen's awareness that it is difficult to know any complex person, that knowledge of a man like Darcy is an interpretation and a construction, not a simple absolute. Like the characters of Proust, the chief persons in *Pride and Prejudice* are not the same when projected through the conversation of different people. The *snobisme* of Darcy's talk, like Swann's, is measured according to the group he is with. Mr. Darcy is hardly recognizable as the same man when he is described by Mr. Wickham, by his housekeeper, or Elizabeth, or Mr. Bingley.

But it is only the complex persons, the 'intricate characters,' that require and merit interpretation, as Elizabeth points out in the pleasant conversation in which she tells Bingley that she 'understands him perfectly':

'You begin to comprehend me, do you?' cried he, turning towards her.

'Oh! yes,—I understand you perfectly.'

'I wish I might take this for a compliment; but to be so easily seen through I am afraid is pitiful.'

'That is as it happens. It does not necessarily follow that a deep, intricate character is more or less estimable than such a one as yours.'

'Lizzy,' cried her mother, 'remember where you are, and do not run on in the wild manner that you are suffered to do at home.'

'I did not know before,' continued Bingley immediately, 'that you were a studier of character. It must be an amusing study.'

'Yes; but intricate characters are the *most* amusing. They have at least that advantage.'

'The country,' said Darcy, 'can in general supply but few subjects for such a study. In a country neighbourhood you move in a very confined and unvarying society.'

'But people themselves alter so much, that there is something new to be observed in them for ever.'

Elizabeth's remark with its ironic application to Darcy indicates the interest that makes the book 'go' and shows the type of awareness we are analyzing. 'Intricate characters are the *most* amusing,' because their behavior can be taken in so many ways, because they are not always the same people. The man we know today is a different man tomorrow. Naturally, we infer, people will not be equally puzzling to every judge. Mr. Bingley and Jane find Mr. Darcy a much less 'teazing' man than Elizabeth does. It is only the Elizabeths, the adult minds, who will observe something new in the 'same' people.

Such are the main assumptions behind the irony of *Pride and Prejudice,* as they are expressed through conversational studies of Darcy's character. In marked contrast with the opening scene of the novel, there is in these dialogues no nondramatic statement of the ironist's position, a further sign that in shaping the Elizabeth-Darcy sequence Jane Austen was moving away from the modes of satire toward more purely dramatic techniques.

While Jane Austen's irony depends on a sense of variability and intricacy of character, her vision is not one of Proustian relativity. The sense of variability is balanced by a vigorous and positive belief.

Elizabeth, in commenting on Charlotte Lucas' choice of Mr. Collins, expresses very emphatically this combination of skepticism and faith:

> 'My dear Jane, Mr. Collins is a conceited, pompous, narrow-minded silly man; you know he is, as well as I do; and you must feel, as well as I do, that the woman who marries him, cannot have a proper way of thinking. You shall not defend her, though it is Charlotte Lucas. You shall not, for the sake of one individual, change the meaning of principle and integrity, nor endeavour to persuade yourself or me, that selfishness is prudence, and insensibility of danger, security for happiness.'

Though as usual Elizabeth's affirmations have an ironic overtone for the reader, they express a belief that is implied throughout *Pride and Prejudice*. There are persons such as Mr. Collins and Mrs. Bennet and Lady Catherine, about whom there can be no disagreement among people who 'have a proper way of thinking.' These fixed characters make up a set of certainties against which more intricate exhibitions of pride and prejudice are measured. They are the 'fools' which James says are almost indispensable for any piece of fiction. For Jane Austen there can be no doubt about the meaning of 'principle and integrity' and similar terms of value. Right-thinking persons know what pride is and when to apply the term. In common with her contemporaries Jane Austen enjoys the belief that some interpretations of behavior are more reasonable than others. The climactic scene of the novel, in which Elizabeth arrives at a new view of Darcy, shows us what is meant by a more reasonable interpretation: it is a reasoned judgment of character reached through long experience and slow weighing of probabilities. The certainty is an achieved certainty.

So the local ironies in Jane Austen, as in Pope, are defined and given larger significance through assumptions shared by the writer and public. The trivial dialogues are constantly being illuminated by a fine sense of the complexity of human nature and by a steady belief in the possibility of making sound judgments. At the same time the playfulness is always serving for 'the illustration of character.' (The term is Elizabeth's, though in applying it to Darcy, she is as usual unaware of its aptness to her own behavior.) Both she and Darcy are 'illustrated' by their ambiguous questions and answers and the alternate interpretations which are so deftly indicated: the poetry of wit in *Pride and Prejudice* is completely dramatic. Certainly nothing could be more dramatic than the assumptions we have been describing: they reflect the practical dramatist's interest in human beings and their behavior, his awareness that character is expressed by what men say and do. The assumption that more reasonable interpretations of conduct are attainable provides for the movement toward a decisive change in relationships at the climax of the novel. It also lays the ground for the resolution of ambiguities and the cancellation of irony at the same moment.

We can now appreciate how beautifully the ironies of the dialogue function in the curve of the main dramatic sequence. The conversations have been skilfully shaped to prepare us for Elizabeth's revised estimate of Darcy, for her recognition that Darcy regards her differently, and for her consequent 'change of sentiment' toward him. The preparation for this climax is made mainly through the controlled use of ambiguity that we have been observing. Though we are always being led to make double interpretations, we are never in confusion about what the alternatives are. It is important also that in these ironic dialogues no comment is included that makes us take Darcy's behavior in only an unpleasant sense. When there is comment, it is mainly used to bring out the latent ambiguity without in any way resolving it. So in general the earlier Darcy scenes are left open in preparation for a fresh estimate of his character. The pleasanter interpretation of one of Darcy's or Elizabeth's remarks or of one of the author's comments allows for the later choice and for the consequent recognitions. The pleasanter possibility also gives in passing a hint of Darcy's changing attitude to Elizabeth. For instance, the more favorable meaning of Elizabeth's 'Mr. Darcy is all politeness' or of the comment on his 'grave propriety' points forward to Darcy's perfect courtesy at Pemberley and to Elizabeth's admission that he was right in objecting to her family's 'impropriety of conduct.'

This exquisite preparation pays wonderfully at the climactic moment of the novel, when Elizabeth reconsiders the letter in which Darcy justified his conduct toward Bingley and Jane and Wickham. Since more kindly views of Darcy have been introduced through the flow of witty talk, Darcy does not at that point have to be remade, but merely reread. (The tendency to remake a character appears in an obvious form only in the later and lesser scenes of the novel.)

The passages in which Elizabeth reviews the letter present an odd, rather legalistic process. After the more obvious views of Darcy's behavior and the possible alternatives are directly stated, the evidence on both sides is weighed and a reasonable conclusion is reached:

> After wandering along the lane for two hours, giving way to every variety of thought; re-considering events, determining probabilities, and reconciling herself as well as she could, to a change so sudden and so important, fatigue, and a recollection of her long absence, made her at length return home . . .

To illustrate her manner of 'determining probabilities' we might take one of several examples of Darcy's pride. Immediately after Darcy has proposed to her, she describes his treatment of Jane in rather brutal language:

> . . . his pride, his abominable pride, his shameless avowal of what he had done with respect to Jane, his unpardonable assurance in acknowledging, though he could not justify it.

A little later, she rereads the passage in which Darcy explains that Jane had shown no 'symptom of peculiar regard' for Bingley. A second perusal reminds Elizabeth that Charlotte Lucas had a similar opinion, and she acknowledges the justice of this account of Jane's outward behavior. In much the same way she reviews other charges, such as Darcy's unfairness to Wickham or his objection to her family's 'want of importance,' and she is forced by the new evidence to draw 'more probable' conclusions.

Jane Austen does not make us suppose that Elizabeth has now discovered the real Darcy or that an intricate person is easily known or known in his entirety, as is very clearly shown by Elizabeth's reply to Wickham's ironic questions about Darcy:

> 'I dare not hope,' he continued in a lower and more serious tone, 'that he is improved in essentials.'
>
> 'Oh, no!' said Elizabeth. 'In essentials, I believe, he is very much what he ever was.'

> While she spoke, Wickham looked 'as if scarcely knowing whether to rejoice over her words, or to distrust their meaning. There was a something in her countenance which made him listen with an apprehensive and anxious attention, while she added,
>
> 'When I said that he improved on acquaintance, I did not mean that either his mind or manners were in a state of improvement, but that from knowing him better, his disposition was better understood.'

It is wise not to be dogmatic about 'essentials,' since in any case they remain 'as they were.' A sensible person contents himself with 'better understanding.'

This process of judgment is not merely odd or legalistic, because it is dramatically appropriate. It fits exactly the double presentation of Darcy's character through ironic dialogue and comment, and it fits perfectly the picture of Elizabeth as 'a rational creature speaking the truth from her heart,' one who adapts her statements to her knowledge. She is quite clear about the meaning of 'pride' and 'vanity,' and she judges herself with complete honesty:

> 'Had I been in love, I could not have been more wretchedly blind. But vanity, not love, has been my folly.—Pleased with the preference of one, and offended by the neglect of the other, on the very beginning of our acquaintance, I have courted prepossession and ignorance, and driven reason away, where either were concerned. Till this moment, I never knew myself.'

We feel that Elizabeth's judgment of Darcy and of herself is right because the preparation for it has been so complete. The foundations for Elizabeth's choices and her acknowledgment of error were laid in the ambiguous remarks of the earlier scenes of the novel.

The dialogue has been preparing us equally well and with perhaps greater refinement for Elizabeth's realization that she and Darcy now regard one another with very different feelings. The ironic remarks and commentary have included hints that revealed ever so gradually Darcy's developing interest in Elizabeth. Mr. Darcy's 'politeness,' his 'repeated questions,' his 'gallantry,' his 'look of doubt,' if interpreted favorably, indicate his increasing warmth of feeling. Elizabeth's pert remarks and impertinent questions bear an amusing relation to this change in Darcy's sentiments. Besides being more ambiguous than she supposes, they backfire in another way, by increasing Darcy's admiration. Her accusation of 'premeditated contempt' brings out his most gallant reply, and her 'mixture of sweetness and archness' leaves him more 'bewitched' than ever. In this and other ways the repartee provides local 'amusements' while pointing forward to the complete reversal of feeling that follows the meeting at Pemberley.

The judicial process by which Elizabeth earlier 'determined probabilities' in judging Darcy's past conduct is matched by the orderly way in which she now 'determines her feelings' toward him:

> . . . and the evening, though as it passed it seemed long, was not long enough to determine her feelings towards *one* in that mansion; and she lay awake two whole hours, endeavouring to make them out. She certainly did not hate him. No; hatred had vanished long ago, and she had almost as long been ashamed of ever feeling a dislike against him, that could be so called. The respect created by the conviction of his valuable qualities, though at first unwillingly admitted, had for some time ceased to be repugnant to her feelings; and it was now heightened into somewhat of a friendlier nature, by the testimony so highly in his favour, and bringing forward his disposition in so amiable a light, which yesterday had produced. But above all, above respect and esteem, there was a motive within her of good will which could not be overlooked. It was gratitude.—Gratitude, not merely for having once loved her, but for loving her still well enough, to forgive all the petulance and acrimony of her manner in rejecting him, and all the unjust accusations accompanying her rejection. He who, she had been persuaded, would avoid her as his greatest enemy, seemed, on this accidental meeting, most eager to preserve the acquaintance, and without any indelicate display of regard, or any peculiarity of manner, where their two selves only were concerned, was soliciting the good opinion of her friends, and bent on making her known to his sister. Such a change in a man of so much pride, excited not only astonishment but gratitude—for to love, ardent love, it must be attributed; and as such its impression on her was of a sort to be

> encouraged, as by no means unpleasing, though it could not be exactly defined. She respected, she esteemed, she was grateful to him, she felt a real interest in his welfare . . .

In this beautifully graded progress of feeling, from 'hatred' or any 'dislike' to 'respect' to 'esteem' to 'gratitude' and 'a real interest' in Darcy's 'welfare,' each sentiment is defined with an exactness that is perfectly appropriate to Elizabeth's habit of mind as presented earlier in the novel. She defines her sentiments as exactly as her moral judgments.

As all ambiguities are resolved and all irony is dropped, the reader feels the closing in of a structure by its necessary end, the end implied in the crude judgment of Darcy in the first ballroom scene. The harsh exhibit of the way character is decided in this society prepares us to view Mr. Darcy's later actions as open to more than one interpretation:

> . . . Mr. Darcy soon drew the attention of the room by his fine, tall person, handsome features, noble mien; and the report which was in general circulation within five minutes after his entrance, of his having ten thousand a year. The gentlemen pronounced him to be a fine figure of a man, the ladies declared he was much handsomer than Mr. Bingley, and he was looked at with great admiration for about half the evening, till his manners gave a disgust which turned the tide of his popularity; for he was discovered to be proud, to be above his company, and above being pleased; and not all his large estate in Derbyshire could then save him from having a most forbidding, disagreeable countenance, and being unworthy to be compared with his friend.
>
> . . . His character was decided. He was the proudest, most disagreeable man in the world, and everybody hoped that he would never come there again.

These comments convey above all the aloof vision of the ironist, of Jane Austen herself, who had been described years before as a little girl 'who is a judge of character and who remains silent.' In the very grammar of the sentences (the passive voice, the *oratio obliqua*), there is an implication of a detached and superior mind that reports both judgments of Darcy, knowing quite well which is the more true, and fully aware that true judgment is considerably more difficult than most people suppose. The display of alternatives in ironic dialogue, the projection by this means of intricate characters, and the movement toward a sounder evaluation of first impressions—all this and more is implicit in the initial view of Darcy and his judges.

Once we have reached the scenes in which the promise of the introduction is fulfilled, the literary design both ironic and dramatic is complete. Thereafter, it must be admitted, *Pride and Prejudice* is not quite the same sort of book. There are fewer passages of equally bright and varied irony and consequently rarer exhibitions of intricacy of character. Mr. Darcy now appears as 'humble,' not 'proud,' and even as 'perfectly amiable.' There are single scenes of a broadly satiric sort, in which Mr. and Mrs. Bennet express characteristic opinions on their daughters' alliances and misalliances. But the close and harmonious relation between ironic wit and dramatic movement is disturbed. A great deal happens, from seductions and mysterious financial transactions to reunions of lovers and weddings. But these events seem to belong to a simpler world where outright judgments of good and bad or of happy and unhappy are in place. The double vision of the ironist is more rarely in evidence.

Occasionally, we feel a recovery of the richer texture of amusement and of the more complex awareness of character revealed in the central sequence. One glancing remark suggests that the final picture of Darcy might have been less simply ideal (Darcy has just been commenting on how well Bingley had taken his confession of having separated Bingley and Jane):

> Elizabeth longed to observe that Mr. Bingley had been a most delightful friend; so easily guided that his worth was invaluable; but she checked herself. She remembered that he had yet to learn to be laughed at, and it was rather too early to begin. In anticipating the happiness of Bingley, which of course was to be inferior only to his own, he continued the conversation till they reached the house.

It is perhaps not 'rational,' as Elizabeth would say, to expect the same complexity when a drama of irony has once arrived at its resolution. But it is probably wise for the novelist to finish up his story as soon as possible after that point has been reached. In *Emma,* the crucial scene of readjustment comes very near the end of the novel. Jane Austen does not run the risk of presenting many scenes in which Emma appears as a wiser and less fanciful young woman. To be sure, the risk is lessened somewhat because the initial and governing vision in Emma is less purely ironic than in *Pride and Prejudice.*

The triumph of *Pride and Prejudice* is a rare one, just because it is so difficult to balance a purely ironic vision with credible presentation of a man and woman undergoing a serious 'change of sentiment.' Shakespeare achieves an uneasy success in *Much Ado About Nothing,* and Fielding succeeds in *Tom Jones* because he does not expect us to take 'love' too seriously. The problem for the writer who essays this difficult blend is one of creating dramatic speech which fulfils his complex intention. In solving this problem of expression, Jane Austen has her special triumph.

Chapter X

THE TWILIGHT OF THE DOUBLE VISION: SYMBOL AND IRONY IN 'A PASSAGE TO INDIA'

. . . the twilight of the double vision . . .
A Passage to India

In *A Passage to India,* as in all of E. M. Forster's novels, there are admirable scenes of social comedy that remind us of the sunny repose of Jane Austen. We can enjoy the behavior of Mrs. Turton, the great lady of a British civil station, with the same satisfaction with which we view the absurdities of Mrs. Bennet and Lady Catherine de Bourgh. Here is Mrs. Turton commenting on her Indian guests at the Bridge Party given for Adela Quested and Mrs. Moore soon after their arrival in India:

> 'They ought never to have been allowed to drive in; it's so bad for them,' said Mrs. Turton, who had at last begun her progress to the summer-house accompanied by Mrs. Moore, Miss Quested, and a terrier. 'Why they come at all I don't know. They hate it as much as we do. Talk to Mrs. McBryde. Her husband made her give purdah parties until she struck.'
>
> 'This isn't a purdah party,' corrected Miss Quested.
>
> 'Oh, really,' was the haughty rejoinder.
>
> 'Do kindly tell us who these ladies are,' asked Mrs. Moore.
>
> 'You're superior to them, anyway. Don't forget that. You're superior to everyone in India except one or two of the Ranis, and they're on an equality.'
>
> Advancing, she shook hands with the group and said a few words of welcome in Urdu. She had learnt the lingo, but only

to speak to her servants, so she knew none of the politer forms and of the verbs only the imperative mood. As soon as her speech was over, she enquired of her companions, 'Is that what you wanted?'

'Please tell these ladies that I wish we could speak their language, but we have only just come to their country.'

'Perhaps we speak yours a little,' one of the ladies said.

'Why, fancy, she understands!' said Mrs. Turton.

'Eastbourne, Piccadilly, High Park Corner,' said another of the ladies.

'Oh yes, they're English-speaking.'

'But now we can talk: how delightful!' cried Adela, her face lighting up.

'She knows Paris also,' called one of the onlookers.

'They pass Paris on the way, no doubt,' said Mrs. Turton, as if she was describing the movements of migratory birds. Her manner had grown more distant since she had discovered that some of the group was Westernized, and might apply her own standards to her.

From a politically liberal, cosmopolitan point of view we may be amused at Mrs. Turton's having 'learnt the lingo' or at the charming rudeness of her grammar. But we shall not be able to maintain this comfortable frame of mind for long. Or if we suppose so, like Adela we have been taken in by a surface simplicity and by our own excellent principles. Reading a little further, we realize that our enlightened point of view has itself been undermined:

> Miss Quested now had her desired opportunity; friendly Indians were before her, and she tried to make them talk, but she failed, she strove in vain against the echoing walls of their civility. Whatever she said produced a murmur of deprecation, varying into a murmur of concern when she dropped her pocket-handkerchief. She tried doing nothing, to see what that produced, and they too did nothing.

The scene leaves us in a most discomforting state of mind. The essence of its irony is expressed in a metaphor, 'the echoing walls of their civility': friendly conversational gestures are so perfectly reproduced as to prove that nothing whatever has been communicated. But the phrase sends out tentacles of connection well beyond the immediate context. We are reminded of the more sinister echoes of a Marabar cave or of the image that came to Mrs. Moore after telling her son that the British must love the Indians because it 'satisfies God':

> Mrs. Moore felt that she had made a mistake in mentioning God. . . She must needs pronounce his name frequently, as the greatest she knew, yet she had never found it less efficacious. Outside the arch there seemed always an arch, beyond the remotest echo a silence.

'The echoing walls' adds a new level of irony to the dialogue of the Bridge Party and at the same time introduces one of the major symbols of *A Passage to India.*

It is characteristic of *A Passage to India,* as it is utterly uncharacteristic of *Pride and Prejudice,* that the irony should be expressed through metaphor and that the meaning of an ironic expression can be appreciated only in relation to other expressions that are clearly symbolic. The central design of Forster's novel is composed of a group of symbolic metaphors, and his irony is inherent in the meaning of his symbols. By interpreting them and seeing how they unify the experience of the novel, we can also understand the peculiar character of Forster's irony, how like and how unlike it is to that of Jane Austen.

The main symbols of *A Passage to India* are named in the titles to the three Parts of the novel: Mosque, Caves, and Temple. Each is more or less closely related to a corresponding variant: Arch, Echo, and Sky. To anyone familiar with the book the three title words * are immediately and richly expressive. Each conveys a generalized impression of a salient object or event in the narrative, an impression

* It would be hard to find purer examples of symbolic expressions. They are obviously 'iconic'; the reader is to think of something (the subject) in terms of the Mosque or the Caves or the Temple (i.e. the generalized impressions). And the 'subject' is not otherwise stated. Throughout this chapter expressions of the type, 'the Mosque,' 'the Caves,' et cetera, refer to the iconic half of the metaphor. The terms without the article, Mosque, Caves, et cetera, refer to the symbol as a complete metaphor.

that stands for and is inseparably connected with various large meanings. To get a sense of Forster's total design it is necessary to see how the meanings of these symbols are built up through the dramatic structure. What follows is an attempt to display the kind of design—symbolic, ironic, and dramatic—peculiar to *A Passage to India.* (I shall also indicate where and why the design seems to break down.)

The most general meaning of the Mosque symbol is perhaps best expressed in the scene between Mrs. Moore and Aziz, the young Indian doctor whom she meets in a mosque near the civil station. In a dialogue which is a blend of minor mistakes and underlying sympathy Mrs. Moore and Aziz reach a surprisingly intimate relationship, Aziz declaring that the Englishwoman is 'an Oriental.' Although in a later scene Mrs. Moore calls him her friend, there is something precarious about their intimacy. In spite of his affectionate declarations Aziz quickly forgets that he has promised to take Mrs. Moore and Adela to visit the Marabar Caves. From the scene in the mosque and from similar episodes, the Mosque comes to symbolize the possibility of communication between Britons and Indians, and more generally the possibility of understanding relationships between any two persons. And in every instance this larger meaning always implies its opposite or near-opposite, an ambivalence finely suggested by the first description of the mosque. Aziz is especially pleased by the dualism of 'black and white' in the frieze above the arches, and he appreciates the stillness and beauty of the building in contrast with 'the complex appeal' of the night. At the end of the scene,

> As he strolled downhill beneath the lovely moon, and again saw the lovely mosque, he seemed to own the land as much as anyone owned it. What did it matter if a few flabby Hindus had preceded him there, and a few chilly English succeeded?

In relation to this and various other points in the narrative, the Mosque represents the ambiguous triumph of Islam, the belief Aziz shares with his Moslem friends 'that India was one; Moslem; always had been; an assurance that lasted until they looked out of the door.'

The Mosque also expresses Fielding's friendship with Aziz and more generally Fielding's conviction that 'The world . . . is a globe of men who are trying to reach one another and can best do so by the help of good will plus culture and intelligence . . .' But this Anglo-Indian relationship is a precarious one, too, its instability being finely expressed in the crisscross of the conversation when Fielding visits Aziz during his illness. After his friend leaves, the Indian goes to sleep, dreaming happily of 'good Fielding,' in a Moslem paradise with domes 'whereunder were inscribed, black against white, the ninety-nine attributes of God.' The ironic dualism of color echoes the halfhearted comment on his rapprochement with Fielding: '. . . affection had triumphed for once in a way.'

Miss Quested's blundering attempts to 'know' Indians and her shifting relationship with her fiancé, Mrs. Moore's son, Ronny, reinforce the negative meanings of the symbol. She naïvely imagines that Mrs. Moore in meeting Aziz at the mosque had seen 'the real India,' a remark that imparts to the symbol still another ironic connotation. Ronny, who interprets the same episode as a piece of native insolence, reveals as always the reduction of human intercourse to the automatic responses of a governing class.

The opening section of the novel is thus composed as a series of dramatic variations on Mosque themes. While the connection between the narratives and the symbol is always clear, there is hardly ever a point where, as in *The Longest Journey,* we feel the cold hand of allegory. Our attention is always more engaged by what is happening than by any generalized significance. The dialogue is always sufficiently confusing; it mirrors the complex play of interests, amusements, and mistakes that is fairly typical of social intercourse. There is also in the Mosque section complexity of a sort that is more important in the structure of the whole novel. Through the oddly interrupted episodes run lines of symbolic meaning that point to the scene in the Marabar Caves.

By focusing attention on this episode, particularly on Mrs. Moore's curious 'vision,' we can see how admirably Forster has prepared us for a moment of dramatic change through building up meanings of various major symbols. What does the experience of hearing the echo mean for Mrs. Moore? The sentence that best sums up her situation and its significance is one describing her state of mind as she 'surrenders to her vision':

> Then she was terrified over an area larger than usual; the universe, never comprehensible to her intellect, offered no repose to her soul, the mood of the last two months took definite form at last, and she realized that she didn't want to write to her children, didn't want to communicate with anyone, not even with God.

The change in Mrs. Moore's relation to her family and friends is the most obvious effect of her jarring experience. She 'loses all interest, even in Aziz,' and in her later conversations with Adela and Ronny she exhibits the most snappish and capricious irritability and a complete indifference concerning the 'unspeakable attempt' in the cave, an attitude that extends to marriage and love in general:

> 'Why all this marriage, marriage? . . . The human race would have become a single person centuries ago if marriage was any use. And all this rubbish about love, love in a church, love in a cave, as if there is the least difference, and I held up from my business over such trifles!'

All distinctions of feeling and of moral value have become confused and meaningless:

> . . . the echo began in some indescribable way to undermine her hold on life. Coming at a moment when she chanced to be fatigued, it had managed to murmur, 'Pathos, piety, courage—they exist, but are identical, and so is filth. Everything exists, nothing has value.'

The doctrines of Western religious faith become equally empty:

> But suddenly, at the edge of her mind, Religion appeared, poor little talkative Christianity, and she knew that all its divine words from 'Let there be Light' to 'It is finished' only amounted to 'boum.'

Finally, the comforting belief in a universe or in some eternal setting for human life is shaken; and at the same time serene acceptance of this world as an end in itself is impossible:

> She had come to that state where the horror of the universe and its smallness are both visible at the same time—the twilight of

> the double vision in which so many elderly people are involved. If this world is not to our taste, well, at all events there is Heaven, Hell, Annihilation—one or other of those large things, that huge scenic background of stars, fires, blue or black air. All heroic endeavour, and all that is known as art, assumes that there is such a background, just as all practical endeavour, when the world is to our taste, assumes that the world is all. But in the twilight of the double vision, a spiritual muddledom is set up for which no high-sounding words can be found; we can neither act nor refrain from action, we can neither ignore nor respect Infinity.

Mrs. Moore has had a somewhat more than adequate glimpse of complete muddle, an exposure to chaos in personal relations and in the universe.

These are certainly large and varied meanings for a novelist to press from the story of an old woman's visit to some not so 'extraordinary' Indian caves. Forster's surprising success in bringing us to accept the strange and wonderful significance of the event depends on his earlier building up of symbolic meanings of Cave, Sky, and Echo. Throughout the preceding narrative, beginning with the opening sentence of the novel, he has imparted to the caves a twofold significance, suggestions of mystery and order that are constantly countered by suggestions of disillusionment and muddle. At the moment of climax the more unpleasant alternatives emerge with the force of truths already experienced and half acknowledged.

The preparation begins in the Mosque symbolism, through which hints of communication between persons and peoples have been accompanied by 'clinging forms' of uncertainty. The Cave symbol is not (as I once supposed) simply the antithesis of the Mosque, but in part a parallel symbol repeating the same oppositions. When at Fielding's tea party Aziz first proposes a trip to the Marabar, it seems that the expedition will be a triumph of Anglo-Indian friendship. And during the ecstatic moments of the later tea party outside the caves, this possibility is apparently about to be realized. Once the horrid tour has taken place, the Caves symbolize the failure of all communication, the collapse of human relationships ironically foreshadowed in the less pleasant meaning of the Mosque symbol.

That the Caves should symbolize 'mystery' as well as 'muddle' depends on preparations that are fairly subtle, particularly in relation to Mrs. Moore. From her first appearance in the novel Mrs. Moore has been presented as ready for 'a mystery,' for some revelation of unity. Shortly after meeting Aziz in the mosque, she has a minor mystical vision:

> She watched the moon, whose radiance stained with primrose the purple of the surrounding sky. In England the moon had seemed dead and alien; here she was caught in the shawl of night together with earth and all the other stars. A sudden sense of unity, of kinship with the heavenly bodies, passed into the old woman and out, like water through a tank, leaving a strange freshness behind.

This mood is recalled much later, when Mrs. Moore is caught 'in the twilight of the double vision' and able neither to 'ignore nor respect Infinity':

> Mrs. Moore had always inclined to resignation. As soon as she landed in India it seemed to her good, and when she saw the water flowing through the mosque-tank, or the Ganges, or the moon, caught in the shawl of night with all the other stars, it seemed a beautiful goal and an easy one. To be one with the universe! So dignified and simple. But there was always some little duty to be performed first, some new card to be turned up from the diminishing pack and placed, and while she was pottering about, the Marabar struck its gong.

The Sky (or the 'heavenly bodies') as a symbol of the universe and of infinity had also been introduced in other, nondramatic contexts: in the picture of the 'overarching sky' at the very beginning of the novel,

> . . . the stars hang like lamps from the immense vault. The distance between the vault and them is as nothing to the distance behind them, and that farther distance, though beyond colour, last freed itself from blue . . .

and in the ironic setting for the Bridge Party:

> Some kites hovered overhead, impartial, over the kites passed the mass of a vulture, and with an impartiality exceeding all, the sky, not deeply coloured but translucent, poured light from its whole circumference. It seemed unlikely that the series stopped here. Beyond the sky must not there be something that overarches all the skies, more impartial even than they? Beyond which again . . .

But in Mrs. Moore's reflections on God and love the infinite series of arches had also been associated with an echo, an association that anticipates the later link between Sky and Caves. God, the traditional Christian order that had sheltered and contained her world, oddly recedes in her thoughts like a fading echo. (The Sky, like the other symbols, has its antithetical and ironic connotations.) Imagery used in various descriptions of the caves also tends to link the two symbols. They are circular, perhaps numberless, and 'when a match is struck' and reflected in the 'marvellously polished walls . . . two flames approach and strive to unite' in something like an ecstasy of love. The caves take on some of the mysterious qualities of the night sky, and the reader is not altogether surprised that Mrs. Moore finds cosmic significance in making a visit to them. It is quite appropriate that she should have a vision of infinity, though it turns out to be less acceptable than she had imagined.

The preparation for the caves episode as a revelation of 'muddle' extends through nearly every phase of the narrative up to the moment of Mrs. Moore's panic. All of the kinds of muddledom that she consequently experiences are anticipated and connected more or less subtly with the Marabar. The conversation in which she first hears that 'India's a muddle' is a nice example of this twofold preparation. Miss Quested has been describing a tiny social muddle that began at the Bridge Party in a 'shapeless discussion' with two Hindus, Mr. and Mrs. Bhattacharya. The 'couple with the unpronounceable name' (a significant comment) change their plans in order to have Mrs. Moore and Adela visit them, and then on the appointed day fail to send their carriage for their guests. Adela wants Fielding to help her clear the matter up:

> 'I do so hate mysteries,' Adela announced.
> 'We English do.'

> 'I dislike them not because I'm English, but from my own personal point of view,' she corrected.
>
> 'I like mysteries but I rather dislike muddles,' said Mrs. Moore.
>
> 'A mystery is a muddle.'
>
> 'Oh, do you think so, Mr. Fielding?'
>
> 'A mystery is only a high-sounding term for a muddle. No advantage in stirring it up, in either case. Aziz and I know well that India's a muddle.'
>
> 'India's— Oh, what an alarming idea!'
>
> 'There'll be no muddle when you come to see me,' said Aziz, rather out of his depth. 'Mrs. Moore and everyone—I invite you all—oh, please.'
>
> The old lady accepted: she still thought the young doctor excessively nice; moreover, a new feeling, half languor, half excitement, bade her turn down any fresh path.

In a few moments Aziz shows that he is as unstable as the Hindus. Having issued his invitation, he thinks with horror of his detestable bungalow and changes the place to the Marabar Caves.

Another symbolic connection is anticipated a little later in a conversation that takes place between Aziz and Professor Godbole, the 'Deccani Brahman.' The echo, we recall, produced in Mrs. Moore a curious spiritual confusion. What she had known as religion became meaningless, and yet she had had an experience that was somehow religious, a glimpse of evil, of 'the undying worm itself.' The Caves, it appears, stand for a type of religious experience accessible only to a peculiar type of Oriental intelligence. When Aziz questions Godbole about the Marabar Caves, he gets nowhere. But it is perfectly clear that the Hindu was 'concealing something.' Adela, who listens without understanding, does 'not know that the comparatively simple mind of the Mohammedan was encountering Ancient Night.' Just after the caves are mentioned again Godbole sings a Hindu song, the effect of which is described in imagery that suggests the baffling caves and their echoes:

> His thin voice rose, and gave out one sound after another. At times there seemed rhythm, at times there was the illusion of a Western melody. But the ear, baffled repeatedly, soon lost

> any clue, and wandered in a maze of noises, none harsh or unpleasant, none intelligible. It was the song of an unknown bird.

Somehow—and the 'how' cannot be very well defined—we are made to feel that the Marabar may be the scene of a revelation, perhaps confused and murky, but comprehensible to the Hindu mind.

Mrs. Moore's indifference to values and her moral confusion focused in her loss of faith in Christian marriage. The dramatic appropriateness of this is obvious, especially in relation to Adela's discovery on entering the second cave, that she has left out love in deciding to marry Ronny. Mrs. Moore has observed the unsteady course of her 'young people's' relations with growing signs of irritation and disillusionment. She hears the word of their engagement with no joy: '. . . though it was all right now she could not speak as enthusiastically of wedlock or of anything as she should have done.' The connection between the caves and the unsatisfactoriness of marriage is made at various points in the narrative of Adela's and Ronny's engagement. They quarrel rather bitterly over Aziz's invitation, while Mrs. Moore listens to them with extreme annoyance:

> 'I've never heard of these caves, I don't know what or where they are,' said Mrs. Moore, 'but I really can't have'—she tapped the cushion beside her—'so much quarrelling and tiresomeness!'

Adela, declaring (with unconscious irony) that what she has to say has 'nothing to do with the caves,' proceeds to tell Ronny that she will not marry him. It is symbolically a little too neat that they get re-engaged during an accident while driving at night on the Marabar Road. The car in which they were riding hits a hyena or a ghost or . . . ?

But the most subtle preparation for Mrs. Moore's disillusioning vision of marriage comes in the superb account of the approach to the caves. Here the main symbols—Mosque, Caves, and Sky—all appear, unobtrusively woven into a narrative that has a predominant tone of dullness and nightmarish confusion. The party itself is made up of an incredible jumble of persons whom Aziz barely succeeds in holding together; in fact Fielding and Godbole arrive only when Adela is rushing away in panic. As the 'train half asleep' moves along in a scene of 'timeless twilight,' Mrs. Moore and Adela apathetically discuss plans for Adela's married life. Mrs. Moore's reflections indicate an approaching crisis in her uncertainty about marriage:

> She felt increasingly (vision or nightmare?) that, though people are important, the relations between them are not, and that in particular too much fuss has been made over marriage; centuries of carnal embracement, yet man is no nearer to understanding man. And to-day she felt this with such force that it seemed itself a relationship, itself a person who was trying to take hold of her hand.

The sky, with appropriate irony, brightens up as if for a 'miracle,' but there is no sunrise, only a 'false dawn.' There is '. . . a spiritual silence which invaded more senses than the ear. Life went on as usual, but had no consequences, that is to say, sounds did not echo or thoughts develop.' There was, for example, '. . . a confusion about a snake which was never cleared up.' (The echoes are later described as serpent-like in their coiling movement.) It is again suggested that the mystery of the Marabar could be understood only by a Hindu:

> . . . he [Aziz] had no notion how to treat this particular aspect of India; he was lost in it without Professor Godbole, like themselves.

For a few minutes before entering the caves, the happy Mosque relationship between Mrs. Moore and Aziz is revived, and understanding between individuals and even peoples seems possible. But Aziz warns Adela of the deceptions of 'Akbar's universal religion': 'Nothing embraces the whole of India,' he tells her, 'nothing, nothing, and that was Akbar's mistake.' As the oddly assorted members of the party go into the first cave, we get a final and tremendous impression of annihilation of human relationships and distinctions:

> The small black hole gaped where their varied forms and colours had momentarily functioned. They were sucked in like water down a drain. Bland and bald rose the precipices; bland and glutinous the sky that connected the precipices; solid and white, a Brahminy kite flapped between the rocks with a clumsiness

that seemed intentional. Before man, with his itch for the seemly, had been born, the planet must have looked thus. The kite flapped away. . . Before birds, perhaps. . . And then the hole belched and humanity returned.

The pressure felt behind each of the details in this narrative, their power of evoking at once a sequence of dramatic relationships and a rich variety of feelings, is due to the kind of far-reaching preparation we have been tracing. When the echo comes, it seems to the reader as to Mrs. Moore that this is what he has been waiting for all along. As the 'echoes generate echoes,' the layers of meaninglessness unfold and the whole range of 'muddles,' in personal relationships, in moral and religious values, and in concepts of the universe, is revealed. The symbolic values of Caves, Mosque, and Sky were being built up for this moment, the perfect aptness of their ironic character now being clear.

The Echo, though less ambiguous than the other symbols, has a dual value for the reader. As an image linked with the receding arches of the sky and with Mrs. Moore's glimpses of infinity it recalls the possibility of a revelation. But through its monotonous meaningless 'bou-oum' the echo brings to the surface uglier levels of experience already associated with the Marabar and hinted at in the less sinister symbols of Mosque and Sky. The vision turns out to be a nightmare. Forster's success in making it so convincing and so meaningful arises from his handling of a complex design which is at once dramatic, symbolic, and ironic. As an artist he has earned the right to attribute large and various meanings to Mrs. Moore's curious experience and to express a significance that goes well beyond the immediate dramatic moment. While presenting a seemingly personal crisis Forster has expressed the vision perhaps most characteristic of the twentieth century, the discovery that the universe may not be a unity but chaos, that older philosophic and religious orders with the values they guaranteed have dissolved. The vision of *A Passage to India* has its counterparts in *The Education of Henry Adams* and in 'Gerontion' and 'The Waste Land.' All these visions are—with differing emphases—the result of various kinds of over-exposure, to too many civilizations (which seem to make nonsense of one another), to too many observations of complexity in the mind and in the physical world—

> After such knowledge, what forgiveness?

We are not concerned here with the proper action after such a vision, but with Forster's novel and with how he completes the structure which he began with such art. I think there can be few readers who will say that the concluding Temple section of *A Passage to India* gives them no pause. Is this section of the novel merely a *tour de force,* or does it have an integrity of design comparable to that of the earlier sections? Is its structure complementary to the design we have been tracing? We can answer these questions best by asking and answering a question of the sort we have put to each of the other symbols: what does the Temple symbol mean in dramatic terms?

It signifies most clearly Hinduism, the religion of Godbole, who presides over the ceremony at Mau in which the worshippers 'love all men, the whole universe' and in which 'the Lord of the Universe' is born. But from a Western point of view, the narrator observes, 'this . . . triumph of India was a muddle . . . a frustration of reason and form.' Forster's account of the ceremony is shot through with comic, sometimes farcical touches, with the result that of all the symbols the Temple seems the most crudely ironic. Its twofold meaning is expressed very well in the final picture of Fielding's and Aziz's relationship. For a brief time, after being reconciled during the jumble of the Hindu ceremony, they are friends; but their friendship, like the unity of India, is unstable. In the concluding words of the novel we are told that the 'temples' as well as 'the tank' (i.e. the Mosque), and 'the sky' do not want them to be friends. This, we may say, is a finely poised irresolution, the only possible conclusion for a novel of irony. The Temple is a symbol of Hindu unity in love which is no unity.

But if we try to interpret the Temple symbol in terms of the dramatized experiences of Mrs. Moore and of her children, we get into difficulties. We find 'muddle' in the relations between symbolic and dramatic designs and at some points a kind of dramatic vacuum. For example, the temple ceremony has an odd meaning in the account of what has happened to Fielding's wife and her brother, Ralph. Fielding tells Aziz that his wife now 'believes that the Marabar is wiped out,' and after adding that Ralph 'rides a little behind her, though with her,' he says:

> 'From her point of view, Mau has been a success. It calmed her —both of them suffer from restlessness. She found something soothing, some solution of her queer troubles here.'

Though there is a notable lack of irony in Fielding's remarks, it is not wholly out of character for him to describe such changes as conceivable, for he has several times shown tolerance for religious experiences that he cannot himself share. For example, he has asked Aziz to sing of 'something in religion . . . that the Hindus have perhaps found.' But for some reason we are embarrassed by the injection of such vague and solemn mysticism at this point in the novel. We are embarrassed not because the possibility of mystical experience is to be rejected, but because we cannot believe in it here as a part of the fictional experience. Something has gone wrong, or perhaps something is wanting, in the literary structure. The test again is to ask what the metaphors mean in the dramatic context. How has 'Mau' (the temple ceremony) 'calmed' Fielding's wife, and what is this 'wiping out of the Marabar'? If 'the Marabar' was 'muddle' and panic, the 'calming' is apparently an experience of unity and peace, a Hindu vision in which chaos is reduced to order. But once we refer these mystical effects to the narrative of the Mau celebration and recall the glorious muddle of Godbole's 'vision,' we can no longer solemnly accept 'Mau' as a symbol of a soothing revelation of unity.

The 'peace of Mau' also seems to be induced through some queer telepathic influence of Mrs. Moore and her children, who have apparently inherited something more marvelous than their mother's 'restlessness.' In the operatic scene in which Aziz and Ralph hear the chant of 'Radhakrishna Radhakrishna,' Aziz forgets the wrong done him at Marabar and 'focusing his heart on something more distant than the caves, something beautiful,' he becomes reconciled with Mrs. Moore's son and discovers that he, like his mother, is 'an Oriental.' The imagery reminds us of the 'distant' sky, of the ultimate unity, but the dramatic preparation for the mystical effect of Mrs. Moore's influence is lacking or unconvincing. More than once after the caves episode we hear that Mrs. Moore 'knew something' inaccessible to Fielding and Adela. The queer girl also believes that 'only Mrs. Moore could drive' the sound of the echo 'back to its source and seal the broken reservoir. Evil was loose . . .' Mrs. Moore can somehow restore the broken unity and give peace to those who, like her children and Aziz, are in communication with her as Esmiss Moore, a sort of Hindu demigoddess. The impression created before the Marabar visit, that the caves were comprehensible only to a Hindu, prepared us for Mrs. Moore's bafflement but hardly for her 'reincarnation.' When we recall in contrast with such fragmentary hints what has been so completely and wonderfully presented, the cave nightmare, we can hardly accept this about-face in Mrs. Moore's role and its symbolic value. We cannot at the end of the novel regard Mrs. Moore as in tune with the infinite and conveniently forget the mocking denial of her echo. 'To be at one with the universe! So dignified and simple.' The exquisite irony of that comment has been too vividly realized in 'the muddle' of the Caves.

Put crudely, there is little dramatic evidence that Mrs. Moore or her children ever had any experience of cosmic unity and the peace that passeth understanding. There are some marvelously clever bits of sleight of hand, oblique allusions to being 'calmed' and to 'knowing something,' but not much more. It can be said that Forster, like his characters, was up against the inexpressible: visions of unity are not to be dramatized. Or perhaps they are not easily presented in fiction. They lend themselves better to self-dramatization, as in the poetry of Wordsworth or Vaughan or St. John of the Cross. But it is always unwise to say what cannot be done in literature; in the present instance it is better to say that Forster did not succeed in giving dramatic meaning to the Temple as a symbol of unity. By contrast, the positive meaning of the Mosque—the attainment of closer understanding—is portrayed with sharp particularity as in the scenes between Aziz and Mrs. Moore or between Aziz and Fielding. As Forster's other novels triumphantly prove, he commands this area of experience: he is above all the novelist of personal relations.

It is fortunate that Forster did not succeed in recovering for Temple and Sky single meanings of peace and unity, for the total design of his novel moves toward no such clear resolution. Whenever he emphasizes these simply serious connotations, he is in effect attempting to transcend the limits of his own ironic vision. (Sweet are the uses of ambiguity to the ironist, especially to one who presents experience through richly ambiguous symbols.) In the best of *A Passage to India* Forster enjoys to the full the freedom of giving varied and even opposite meanings to his symbolic metaphors. In the Mosque-Cave sequences the narrative precisely and fully defines the double meanings of the symbols, and there is complete harmony between symbolic and dramatic designs: we saw how beautifully Forster built up the unpleasant implications of Mosque, Caves, and Sky to prepare for the climactic moment when their full force was realized.

The contrast between his ironic-fictional design and Jane Austen's is now clear. Her balancing of possible interpretations, since it depended on well-defined beliefs, led inevitably to a choice and a resolution. Hers was the irony that moves toward the cancellation of irony. Forster's pattern leads to no such resolution. Playing, sometimes capriciously, with every possible meaning of an experience, he cannot reach conclusions. For his basic assumption, best expressed through Fielding, is that anything may be true, that the unreasonable explanation may be as valid as the reasonable one. Only one allegiance remains unshaken throughout the novel, a belief in the possibility and value of communication between individuals, a belief accompanied by the reservation that human relationships are always on the verge of breakdown. The hope of communication is generous, but skeptical, and hints of unity among all men or all nations or all things can hardly be accepted without an ironic smile. The design of Forster's fiction suffers only when he deviates into solemnity.

Chapter XI

THE FLOWER OF LIGHT: INTEGRITY OF IMAGINATION

It was the plant and flower of light,
In small proportions we just beauties see;
And in short measures, life may perfect be.

BEN JONSON

The dream of integrity of imagination haunts both the writer and the reader; but like all absolutes it exerts a fascination which may be either fruitful or sterile in its effect. It may lead to Mallarmé's blank sheet of paper: the ineffable reality defies expression. Or as in the case of Keats, it may supply the dissatisfaction necessary for growth. For the reader, too, the influence of this 'divine Idea' may be a mixed blessing. It may entice him into rejecting the vigor of Dickens and accepting instead the 'perfect art' of a Landor or a Pater. If he happens to have a bent for systematic criticism, he may mistake one manifestation of integrity for Integrity, and under the spell of the absolute he may suppose that he has defined for all time the essential nature of imagination.

My own aim as a definer is less ambitious: it is to outline some meanings for integrity of imagination that emerge from this experiment in reading, particularly meanings of the term as applied to the longer literary forms. Since the same methods have been used in interpreting both shorter and longer works, the general definition of integrity of imagination will be the same, whether used of a sonnet by Donne or a play by Shakespeare.

What common meanings have we found for this confusing and

yet almost indispensable term? In writing of *Mrs. Dalloway,* I spoke of the way in which so many different experiences have been perceived through a single metaphorical 'vision': 'this singleness in reception and expression of experience, as evidenced in the metaphorical design, is what we mean by integrity of imagination in Virginia Woolf.' Integrity of imagination is used here of the writer's 'vision,' of the way Virginia Woolf's mind functioned in writing *Mrs. Dalloway.* Like all critical statements about what a writer knows or does, such a remark represents an elaborate series of inferences. There is no access to what went on in Virginia Woolf's mind in the act of composition: we have only our reading experience, the evidences of order which we traced in analysis. From the reader's point of view integrity of imagination is the singleness of the design discovered in reading *Mrs. Dalloway.* We can best describe this singleness or integrity by isolating the main characteristics of the metaphorical design of the novel.

In the first place, it is a key design, a group of analogies that serve as a bond between items so various as to seem like mere scatterings of memories and impressions in separate narratives. The key analogies are kept up in the sequences of Clarissa and Peter, of Septimus and Rezia, through special uses of language—the recurrences of 'Fear no more,' of sea and wave imagery, of metaphors of building and 'making it up.'

These connections are more than mechanical uniformities: infatuation with the sound of one's own words is not a sign of imaginative power. Furthermore they are not merely sensuous or emotive analogies such as could be conveyed by the same expressions quoted out of context. Any two persons speaking of 'fear' or 'solemnity' or 'waves,' may seem vaguely, if absurdly, similar. We feel more than a superficial likeness between 'moments' in *Mrs. Dalloway* because the analogies are also being expressed through other uses of language and other relationships, dramatic and narrative. When Clarissa speaks of Septimus as having 'plunged holding his treasure,' we feel immediately a general likeness to 'plunges' in her own life. But the analogy does not end there; the similarities are defined and amplified through briefly recollected events in the sequences of both characters or through occasional bits of more objective dramatization. There is Septimus helping Rezia trim the hat shortly before he escapes from Holmes and Bradshaw by leaping to his death. There is Clarissa sewing her dress and hearing Peter come up the stairs, or thinking of her parties just as Miss Kilman appears to carry off Elizabeth. The likeness evoked by the image of the exhilarating and fearful plunge of a sea diver is complemented by dramatic parallels.

The fullest awareness of connection comes at the climax of the novel, when Clarissa evaluates the relation between her life and Septimus' and between her present and her past self. At this moment we feel a meeting and completion of various designs, metaphorical, dramatic, and chronological. The sensuous and emotive analogies, the dramatic parallels, the memories of numerous points in time (of the day and of the characters' lives) focus to a remarkable degree in our reading of the single word 'plunged': all sorts of 'plunges,' 'fallings down,' impressions of 'divine vitality' and 'solemn' breaks in the process of living come to mind. This sense of extraordinary concentration depends directly on the economy of expression: one word does the work of pages of narrative:

> But this young man had killed himself—had he *plunged* holding his treasure?

The word strikes us as unexpected at first, because of the shift from 'killed' to the image. It is also expected, if we think of Septimus' leap from the balcony and earlier anticipations of 'falling.' But the sense of surprise is there, too, because we had thought many of the implied relationships had been left behind.

The appearance of one of these 'focal' words or expressions is perhaps the best single proof of integrity of imagination in the writer, of his singleness of vision. Coming on the unexpected word and finding that its meaning has been anticipated in so many ways and that it belongs to a rich network of connections, we say, 'Here was a literary mind that worked with a unique sense of the growing order of composition. Virginia Woolf knew what she was doing.' That is to say, she knew what she was to do and had done. The simultaneity which the reader experiences is a sign of a rare simultaneity of vision in the writer.

We are using 'vision' here in a special, and perhaps not wholly definable sense. Virginia Woolf herself disclaimed conscious intention in the composition of *Mrs. Dalloway:*

> . . . the idea started as the oyster starts or the snail to secrete a house for itself. And this it did without any conscious direction. The little note book in which an attempt was made to forecast a plan was soon abandoned, and the book grew day by day, week by week, without any plan at all, except that which was dictated each morning in the act of writing.

The exception is large enough to allow for an important kind of planning—the hidden pressure exerted by the writer's organism to select and relate experience through words, and the further pressure exerted by what is already written, which keeps accumulating as the writer commits himself to particular words and meanings. The pressure to select and relate, to produce meaningful symbols in art by words or sounds or lines or colors is simply 'given.' We can call this planning so long as we do not suppose it is a simple activity or wholly under 'conscious direction.' It is the writer's vision in action. Although we cannot explain how vision functions, we can point to the order discovered in the completed work. We then assume—and it is a large assumption—that the integrity of imagination experienced by the reader is a sign of a corresponding integrity of vision in the writer.

I have been describing three main signs of imaginative integrity: the presence of a key design maintained through the work by special uses of language; the harmonious relation between designs and especially the convergence (and completion) of several designs at a point of marked dramatic change; and the appearance of focal words. Through the convergence of designs and through focal expressions, the reader experiences what we may call an effect of simultaneity. With these statements as guides we can explore what we mean by integrity of imagination in the other works we have been reading.

The Tempest is the purest conceivable example of singleness of design achieved through a key metaphor. Through all the varying analogies—of sea and tempest, of music and harmony, of sleep and dream, and so on—there is a constant and vivid reference to 'sea-change.' There is also the most intimate relation between dramatic and metaphorical designs because the analogies are so thoroughly embedded in the drama. The meaning of each recurrent metaphor depends very closely on who is speaking to whom and when; and metaphorical expressions are varied with the nicest sense of fitness to the individual tone of the speaker. Ariel sings of 'a sea-change / Into something rich and strange'; while Caliban says

> From toe to crown he'll fill our skins with pinches,
> Make us strange stuff.

The point in *The Tempest* of the most decisive change in dramatic relationships, Prospero's restoration speech, is also a point of highest concentration in lines of analogy. The marvelous union of continuities in the 'dissolving-cloud' metaphor of the masque speech is recapitulated in Prospero's words announcing the many changes of the last act:

> The charm *dissolves* apace . . .

It would be hard to find in another work an expression that brings into focus more lines of relationship and more distinct moments of reading experience. But we are continually coming on focal words in *The Tempest:* that is what makes it so Shakespearean.

'Dissolves' appears more remarkable if we think of Shakespeare in the act of writing the play. He seems to have his eye on the stage-fact, the dispelling of the charm, and he brings in a conceit that at first seems only pleasantly adequate. That 'dissolves' (and 'melting') should come to Shakespeare and introduce analogies and dramatic echoes that are so apt is almost certainly beyond 'conscious direction.' Connectedness of this sort must be, as Proust says, beyond the mechanical exercise of memory. To paraphrase Dryden's remark, all the implications of Shakespeare's images were present to him as he wrote. The potentialities of storm images as symbols of inner confusion and healing were implicit in his initial dramatization of the storm. These further meanings are a part of what Shakespeare 'saw' in the subject of an island shipwreck.

But what do we mean by integrity of imagination in speaking of a work like Pope's Essay on Riches? Our general statements must be considerably redefined to fit a piece of sustained irony in the epistolary style of the eighteenth century. If, for example, we say that there is a harmonious relationship in Pope's Essay between dramatic and other designs, we are thinking of a dramatic design very different from that of a Shakespearean play or a novel. But though the dramatic use of language in the Essay is limited almost entirely to shaping the voice of the speaker, it plays an important part in the total effect of the poem. Many of the ironies acquire their meaning and edge through the poet's speaking role and what it symbolizes, and Pope's ridicule is felt above all in the refinement of the tone in which he records Timon's monstrosities.

The sense of a larger integrity in Pope's poem rises from the recurrent constellation—or group of continuities in imagery, irony, and rhythm—that is not wholly unlike a recurrent set of Shakespearean metaphors. Pope's design when understood has a singleness of relation comparable to Shakespeare's, in the all-important bridge between the grouped continuities and his cultural ideal. It is this further connection that makes Pope a poet of the first order and sets him above all other eighteenth-century verse satirists except Johnson. Edward Young, the author of a number of successful satires, had learned many of Pope's tricks of ironic contrast in tone and logical pattern. But what he could not do was to fuse his scattered points in any large relationship. He had not mastered any vision of the society he was criticizing, and so he offers alternate patches of morality and satire. 'He plays, indeed,' Dr. Johnson observes, 'only on the surface of life; he never penetrates the recesses of the mind, and therefore the whole power of his poetry is exhausted by a single perusal; his conceits please only when they surprise.' By contrast, Pope's 'conceits,' his play of wit, have the large significance which Johnson finds missing in Young. His language keeps alluding to the aesthetic and social standard that he and his contemporaries called 'following Good Sense' or 'following Nature.'

Pope's art of combining surprise and depth appears in single words or phrases in which many-layered ironies carry overtones of the ideal order on which his satirical attack is based. These are Pope's focal expressions; they bring together very different kinds of design, comprehending Pope's entire satirical mode. Probably the finest example in the Timon Essay is 'laughing Ceres' in

> Deep Harvests bury all his pride has planned,
> And laughing Ceres re-assume the land.

'Laughing Ceres' is expressive of a dominant tone in the poem and of typical ambiguities and contrasts of tone; at the same time it presents an image of characteristic pictorial grandeur and a symbol of high Roman cultivation and Good Sense. Coming at the end * of the Timon episode, the ironic picture of Ceres serves also as a kind of epilogue to the day at Timon's villa. But the characteristic dramatic movement of the poem is not a progress, but a fluctuation of tones against a dominant tone. Pope's almost purely ironic design is about as far removed as possible from that of a play or a novel.

Pride and Prejudice has a very special structure produced by combining large controlling ironies with the traditional dramatic movement toward a climax. The key design of the novel consists in this peculiarly blended relationship; in an Aristotelian sense, it is the formal cause of *Pride and Prejudice*. As for focal expressions, we think immediately of the packed ironies of dialogue and incidental comment, of words that bring together familiar oppositions and tacitly remind us of basic beliefs—as Pope's focal expressions do—while they are all the time pointing forward. Like 'sea-change' in Ariel's song, they are inclusive by anticipation. They anticipate not by planting a cell which becomes the source of almost inexhaustible analogies, but by posing sharply defined alternatives. On Darcy's first appearance in *Pride and Prejudice* we hear that 'His character was decided.' The narrator's attitude toward such easy judgments is implied, the possible views of Darcy's character are formulated, and the course of the drama is indicated in advance.

Though the irony centers in 'decided,' it is the sentence, not the word which is focal, a fact that is fairly characteristic of Jane Austen's genius. She writes with the warmest feeling, but she moves serenely within the bounds of grammar, and she has few rivals in compactness. No one can write a sentence that seems more unitary, more completely together. The style is Racinian, not Shakespearean. There are occasional sentences in *Pride and Prejudice* that sum up wonderfully a particular role while expressing the ever-present sense of the inconsistency of all human characters:

> Miss Bingley's congratulations to her brother, on his approaching marriage, were all that was affectionate and insincere.

* The lines originally '. . . came just before the Timon passage. . .' *The Best of Pope,* ed. George Sherburn (New York, 1940), p. 432.

But there is no sentence in the novel that equals the comment at the climax of *Emma:*

> Her way was clear, though not quite smooth.

These words are more than a concentration of what Emma has learned and of the balanced sympathy and irony of Jane Austen's attitude toward her heroine; like Shakespeare's metaphors, they invite us to explore ranges of experience well beyond the work itself.

The key design of *A Passage to India* might be described as a rather fluid system of ironic symbols. Unlike the metaphors of *The Tempest,* they are not united through a key metaphor, nor are they connected by implicit reference to a belief or standard of behavior, as are the crisply differentiated ironies of Pope or Jane Austen. The symbols of Forster's novel are all alike in one respect: they are curiously ambiguous. (Compare those of Yeats's 'Two Songs.') Each symbol, whether Mosque or Caves or Sky or Temple, combines meanings that are conflicting, and often completely opposite. 'Nothing is but what is not.' All express unity and disunity, and they are also loosely linked by images of 'circling' and 'arching'; but the 'circle of unity' metaphor does not permeate the language of the novel very thoroughly. We have seen how skilfully Forster makes use of these vague analogies and oppositions in preparing for Mrs. Moore's vision, and how the convergence of designs at this point is felt to be absolutely right.

If it is asked whether there are focal expressions in *A Passage to India,* the answer is not simple. We do come on words that are surprising in a Shakespearean way; for example in the scene when Aziz shows Fielding his wife's picture:

> The lady faced the world at her husband's wish and her own, but how bewildering she found it, the echoing contradictory world!

'Echoing' introduces meanings that are wonderfully apt: at a time of nearly successful communication between the two friends, it reminds us of the confusing maze of Indian and other human societies and of the ever-imminent breakdown of understanding. In the narrative preceding the cave nightmare there are words that have a similar power:

> Bland and bald rose the precipices; bland and glutinous the sky that connected the precipices; solid and white, a Brahminy kite flapped between the rocks with a clumsiness that seemed intentional.

Coming just before the entrance into the caves, 'sky' recalls the ambiguous meanings of the symbol and links two major stages of the drama. No longer blue and distant and offering hints of unity, the sky is now too near, it connects only to efface distinctions. The symbol looks back to Mrs. Moore's early dreams and uncertainties, and ahead to her vision of chaos.

But these and similar expressions in *A Passage to India* send us down only one line of symbolic and dramatic meaning, and in general there are few expressions that focus many analogies and many lines of dramatic development. One further consequence of Forster's symbolic manner appears in the later sections of the book. Since the meaning of certain expressions has been vividly dramatized, they can now be used with great force and economy. Consider 'mosque' and 'caves' in Aziz's reflections on calling Ralph Moore 'an Oriental':

> 'Then you are an Oriental.' . . Those words—he had said them to Mrs. Moore in the mosque in the beginning of the cycle, from which, after so much suffering, he had got free. Never be friends with the English! Mosque, caves, mosque, caves. And here he was starting again.

The two words convey an immediate sense of the early phases of the novel, but the economy has been gained at a loss of surprise. The link by which the symbolic words are introduced is too obvious, and because the expression of the symbols is not modified to fit Aziz's thought at this moment, we feel no shock whatever but rather automatically supply fixed meanings. By contrast, Shakespeare's 'dissolve' or 'sea-swallowing' images present new and difficult metaphors peculiar to their dramatic context. The tempest analogy is revived, then and there.

Key design, harmony and convergence of designs, and focal expressions do not have quite the same meanings when used of *The Tempest,* or of *Mrs. Dalloway,* of Pope's Timon Essay, of *Pride and Prejudice,* or *A Passage to India.* It would not be too difficult to draw out the definitions of integrity common to all five works, but I leave the charms of making general definitions to the philosophic reader. I am assuming that the 'common' reader will be more interested in exploration than in definition. I shall be pleased if the reader, 'common' or 'uncommon,' accepts my implied definitions of imagination and integrity as among the possible true ones. It is more important for him to see their value as guides to the discovery of design, a value which can be appreciated through following the complete analyses, and not from rough summaries or generalized formulas. 'The reader,' as Coleridge said in defining a poem, 'should be carried forward, not merely or chiefly by the mechanical impulse of curiosity, or by a restless desire to arrive at the final solution; but by the pleasureable activity of mind excited by the attractions of the journey itself.'

The equivalent in criticism to 'a restless desire to arrive at the final solution' is an overeagerness to arrive at judgments. Though not aimed primarily at evaluation, the analyses lead, it is hoped, to the Arnoldian type of judgment 'which almost insensibly forms itself in a fair and clear mind, along with fresh knowledge.' Distinctions have already appeared between the earlier and later sections of *Pride and Prejudice,* and between ambiguity in Jane Austen and in E. M. Forster. Our experiments in discovery of design show where defects in composition point to defects in the writer's vision, and where by contrast there is almost perfect integrity in vision and design.

Forster's tendency to use symbols mechanically is another sign of the gap between symbolic and dramatic design which we noted in our reading of the final chapters of *A Passage to India.* Hints of ultimate unity point to a resolution that lies outside the ironic and symbolic pattern. Forster's vision is double; but the double vision imposes as strict demands as other views of experience. Altering James's metaphor slightly, we may say that if a writer is not content with the outlook from 'the window at which he is posted,' he is in danger of communicating no view at all.

Mrs. Dalloway is a less ambitious book than *A Passage to India;* it is an expression of a nineteenth-century sensibility jarred but not quite undermined by the twentieth-century world. The steadiness and wholeness of Virginia Woolf's vision, its purity and simplicity, are expressed through a design almost perfectly centered in a single metaphor. But when metaphorical expressions in *Mrs. Dalloway* become overcomplex in relation to the drama, the result is 'beautiful' writing, literary passages that lie outside the vision so clearly projected through the narratives of Clarissa and Septimus.

Pride and Prejudice deals with an even more restricted area of social experience than *Mrs. Dalloway;* but the novel shows how a limited yet penetratingly ironic vision may embrace a surprising degree of complexity. When the ironic doublings diminish, the controlling sense of life certainly becomes simpler. But integrity is never altogether lost because Jane Austen's view of experience led so logically to a resolution of irony. In describing the final phase of *Pride and Prejudice* as simple, it is well to remember that all simplicity is not the same. To be sure there are in the later chapters stock fictional escapades and happy endings; but there is also an attained simplicity that rests on the whole Elizabeth-Darcy sequence. Elizabeth's beautiful remark to Darcy, 'Think only of the past as its remembrance gives you pleasure,' comes from a woman who says that her *feelings* are now 'widely different from what they were.' The expression is precise: it is her 'feelings,' not her character, that have changed. We are reminded of the reasoning by which she arrived at her 'change of sentiment' toward Darcy; Elizabeth's serene view of the past has not been easily won. If her attitude is sentimental, it is marvelously temperate and not quite simple.

Pope's Timon Epistle has an imaginative integrity as complete in its kind as that of Donne's judgment day sonnet or Keats's ode 'To Autumn'—that is, if we read it as we read the poems of Donne or Keats, with a readiness to see and accept its special design. What is rare is that such complexity and such sinuous subtlety should have found an expression so poised and so fully ordered. If there is a flaw in the composition, it comes in the simplest lines of the poem, where Pope expresses most directly his doctrines of Sense and Taste. But even here Pope is not merely didactic (as he is at times in the 'Essay on Man' or in the Epistle 'Of the Characters of Men'). He never sacrifices the easy sophistication of tone or the well-bred lack of solemnity which belong to his role. Donne's 'Third Satyre' (on religion) is nobly and continuously didactic; in 'Seeke true religion . . .' we hear the voice of the preacher, impetuous and urgent. The integrity of both Pope and Donne appears in their sure consciousness of their role, as evidenced in a perfect consistency of tone. Pope's vision of experience is a worldly one, but it is as unwavering as Donne's. His integrity appears in the way he at once strikes the right note of casual conversation and moderate surprise:

> 'Tis strange, the Miser should his Cares employ
> To gain those Riches he can ne'er enjoy. . .

To have struck that note in relation to what follows is as much a sign of wholeness of imagination as to have written the opening lines of *The Tempest,* which perfectly anticipate the 'noises, / Sounds, and sweet airs' that are to come.

It has surprised no one, I suppose, that Shakespeare comes off best in a comparison of relative integrity in design and vision. *The Tempest* is in its completeness and harmony the 'very plant and flower of light.' Although in other plays of Shakespeare metaphors grow out of proportion to the dramatic context and to the human actions and relationships being represented, examples of such Shakespearean nonsense are not easily found in *The Tempest.* As so often in Jane Austen, the apparently incidental and trivial expression is later seen to be dramatically right. The King's talk of how 'the thunder, / That deep and dreadful organ-pipe . . . did bass my trespass' may on a first reading seem to be a piece of conceited rhetoric. But the metaphor of musical harmony has a special aptness at this moment in the play: Ariel has just pointed out the moral purpose of the tempest, and in these words Alonso first acknowledges his guilt. He has understood the meaning of Prospero's storm, and his confession marks the beginning of the transformations of the last two acts. The integrity, Shakespeare's awareness of his meaning in relation to the character speaking and to the movement of the drama, appears in the particular form of the metaphor he uses here.

There is another kind of integrity of which I have said little and in which *The Tempest* easily surpasses the other works we have considered—integrity in the sense of the relative completeness in the kinds of experience included within a work. Pope and Jane Austen have a comparable complexity within the much narrower areas they embrace, and Forster and Virginia Woolf have a twentieth-century awareness of areas of consciousness almost unexplored by the Elizabethans, but none of the four brings into the total imaginative design experiences from so many different levels of life. Almost the entire scale of conceivable beings, from Caliban and the loudmouthed boatswain to Kings and sages, airy nymphs and divinities, is represented in the characters of *The Tempest.* But no Calibans or Trinculos come into the imaginative worlds of *Pride and Prejudice* or *Mrs. Dalloway* or *A Passage to India.* (Forster's novel has its deities, but they do not always seem to be present in fact.) And in spite of the small compass of his plot, Shakespeare manages to express through his varied characters a remarkable range of feeling and emotions. At one extreme there are fishy jokes and horse-pond humor, and at the other, Miranda's innocent wonder and Prospero's 'rarer action' that lies in 'virtue rather than in vengeance.' Of the writers we have considered, Pope alone commands the lower end of this scale, but unlike Jane Austen he is excluded from the upper.

Though there are exquisite images in both *Mrs. Dalloway* and in Pope's Timon Essay, it is doubtful whether either work offers more kinds of sensuous appeal than *The Tempest.* Shakespeare knows many things with his senses, as a random group of images will show. There are for example: 'the nimble marmoset,' 'the green sour ringlets whereof the ewe not bites,' 'the dreadful organ pipe,' 'twangling instruments,' 'th' earth . . . baked with frost,' 'apes with foreheads villainous low,' and 'flat meads thatch'd with stover.' Although Forster probably touches on more topics of a purely intellectual sort, and though Pope has a wide range of reference to 'monuments of intellect,' Shakespeare combines a considerable variety of intellectual interests with knowledge of many 'trades their gear and tackle and trim.' *The Tempest* shows Shakespeare's interest in geography and in the wonders of exploration, in ideal states and in the nature of freedom and sovereignty, in moral sanity, in distinctions between reality and unreality. (He of course never expresses his knowledge in such terms.) Shakespeare also knows a good deal about ships and sailing and something about fishing, hunting, and farming, and in general about 'country matters' of the sort that enliven Caliban's talk of 'barren place and fertile.'

But one could probably make longer and more imposing lists of 'things touched on' from Akenside's 'Pleasures of Imagination,' the finest of ironic monuments to a lack of imaginative power. Shakespeare surpasses the other writers we have been reading by *including in his design* a wider range of experience. His knowledge—in the broadest sense of the term—is absorbed into the tissue of his dramatic fiction and communicated through it. It is the manner of including the variety that counts. To include must mean to use words so that diverse items of experience are fully and constantly connected in the total design of a work; it means to use words so that several kinds of connection are being made at one and the same time. The completeness that counts in imaginative design is inseparable from the sense of simultaneity.

One or two comparisons with Virginia Woolf and E. M. Forster will show Shakespeare's superiority. Here and there in *Mrs. Dalloway* 'Calibanish' characters turn up, 'frumps' whose 'downfall' is 'drink,' battered women of the London streets. The imagery used in depicting these creatures is often vivid and sometimes vaguely reminiscent of the central metaphorical themes of the novel. But the language of their speech or of their internal monologues is not very convincing: no sharply individualized tone is heard, and their relationship with other persons in the narrative is slight, often little more than a matter of coincidence in time or space. As an example of variety of another sort, there is Peter's 'passionate' escapade with a young girl. Familiar metaphors of 'making it up' and 'building it up' appear, but they are not renewed in fresh images or given any precise meaning in Peter's actions and thoughts. The working in of this episode or of various low characters convinces no one; the emotional and sensuous and social experiences that they are apparently meant to express do not quite belong to the *felt* order of *Mrs. Dalloway.*

Forster is a novelist of ideas, a writer who possesses a finely observant and reflective intelligence. There are thoughts in all of his books that stay with the reader: 'Death destroys a man; the idea of Death saves him' (*Howards End*) or, 'where there is officialism, every human relationship suffers' (*A Passage to India*). In *A Passage to India,* Forster more often indulges in reflections on less personal themes. He produces aphorisms on Western civilization: 'The Mediterranean is the human norm.' Or he comments on the nature of mystical experience:

> Not only from the unbeliever are mysteries hid, but the adept himself cannot retain them. He may think, if he chooses, that he has been with God, but as soon as he thinks it, it becomes history, and falls under the rules of time.

These somewhat portentous observations are rather too easily detached from their context. Unlike the sense of 'muddle,' they are not inseparable from a character and a symbolic event. And unlike the focal sentences of Jane Austen, they are not closely connected with any particular moment in the novel. We may say, of course, that they belong to the role of the author, but in their unironic solemnity they are not altogether in character for the narrator of *A Passage to India.*

Shakespeare is equally quotable, but his language is continuously dramatic even when he is most philosophic. The language in *The Tempest* that is richest in philosophic implications and in sensuous appeal is not out of character and not without reference to the inner drama and to what is happening on the stage. Shakespeare's variety is borne by dramatic speech and is not separable from the total design he is building.

Shakespeare's superior power of combining the most diverse levels of experience can be seen wonderfully in Caliban's speech after *Ariel plays the tune on a Tabor and Pipe:*

> *Caliban.* Art thou afeard?
> *Stephano.* No, monster, not I.
> *Caliban.* Be not afeard: the isle is full of noises,
> Sounds and sweet airs, that give delight, and hurt not.
> Sometimes a thousand twangling instruments
> Will hum about mine ears; and sometime voices
> That, if I then had wak'd after long sleep,
> Will make me sleep again: and then, in dreaming,
> The clouds methought would open and show riches
> Ready to drop upon me; that, when I wak'd,
> I cried to dream again.

In these lines we feel first the clumsy humor of Caliban soothing the fears of Stephano and Trinculo; and then immediately following come impressions of inexhaustible riches, both of musical sounds and visual beauties. There are feelings of magic and of the mystery of sleep, of intense sensuous delight, and of a childlike love of a dream-world. The main levels of being—sub-human, human, and divine—are all present by implication in these consoling and visionary words of the 'man-monster.' The speech also bears an increment of philosophic meaning: the merging of sleep and dream and waking suggesting as always in *The Tempest* the slightness of the distinction between real and unreal.

The words that convey so wide a range of experience are also renewing and maintaining the lines of relation that make up the total design of *The Tempest.* The mere repetition of 'sleep' and 'dream' recalls an important motif in the play. The recurrent images of sound and sight ('noises,' 'clouds,' 'riches ready to drop') echo the storm scenes and anticipate the heaven-sent riches of the masque. They point also to the large metaphorical patterns of music and noise, tempest and clearing, and magical transformation. And Shakespeare makes these connections of image and metaphor without sacrificing his dramatic design. Caliban's tone is not lost: we hear his voice in 'twangling' and 'hum,' and in the slightly awkward naïveté of 'hurt not' and 'ready to drop *upon me*' and '*I cried* to dream again.' The speech is not out of character since Caliban is a half-god (though of the devilish variety) and therefore a creature who might hear, but not understand, the divine music of the island. He is, in his own way, 'given to visions.' His comment on meeting Stephano and Trinculo is:

> These be fine things an if they be not sprites.
> That's a brave god and bears celestial liquor:
> I will kneel to him.

Greeting Stephano a little later, he says,

> Hast thou not dropped from heaven?

(Caliban speaks in verse, thus suggesting his middle state in the dramatic world of *The Tempest.*) In the 'noises and sweet airs' speech Shakespeare finely adjusts Caliban's usual speech rhythm to blend with the dreamy repetitive movement characteristic of the more visionary passages of the play.

While expressing through Caliban's speech the most varied emotions and sensations, Shakespeare keeps in mind the developing order of his work. He is in fact able to express a wider range of meanings just because his sense of design is so unwavering. The humor that qualifies the splendor and mystery of Caliban's unexpected revelation depends on a nice suggestion of Caliban's characteristic tone. The philosophic meaning arises from the links made through imagery with the key metaphor of sea-change. So Shakespeare is not guilty of 'introducing characters' or of 'working in' sensuous images or of 'making reflections.' He is continually shaping a complete poetic design and using words to make the connections that build up that design. Whether we mean by integrity of imagination singleness of design or relative completeness in the kinds of experience included, Shakespeare is superior to the other writers we have been reading. He easily surpasses them because he can make the individual word bear at once so many different relationships: 'Within that circle none durst walk but he.' In Shakespeare we see most clearly that singleness and comprehensiveness of imaginative vision are inseparable from mastery of language.

Index

GALAXY BOOKS

Author	Title	No.
Aaron, Daniel	*Men of Good Hope*	GB58
Abrams, Meyer H., ed.	*English Romantic Poets*	GB35
Barker, Ernest, ed. & tr.	*The Politics of Aristotle*	GB69
ed.	*Social Contract: Essays by Locke, Hume, Rousseau*	GB68
	Reflections on Government	GB15
Bate, Walter Jackson	*The Achievement of Samuel Johnson*	GB53
Berlin, Isaiah	*Karl Marx: His Life and Environment*	GB25
Bowra, C. M.	*Ancient Greek Literature*	GB30
	The Romantic Imagination	GB54
Brower, Reuben A.	*The Fields of Light*	GB87
Bruun, Geoffrey	*Nineteenth Century European Civilization*	GB36
Clark, George	*Early Modern Europe*	GB37
	The Seventeenth Century	GB47
Clifford, James L.	*Biography as an Art*	GB70
ed.	*Eighteenth-Century English Literature*	GB23
Cochrane, Charles Norris	*Christianity and Classical Culture*	GB7
Collingwood, R. G.	*The Idea of History*	GB1
	The Idea of Nature	GB31
	The Principles of Art	GB11
Cruickshank, John	*Albert Camus and the Literature of Revolt*	GB43
Dean, Leonard, ed.	*Shakespeare*	GB46
Dixon, W. MacNeile	*The Human Situation*	GB12
Evans-Wentz, W. Y., ed.	*The Tibetan Book of the Dead*	GB39
Feidelson and Brodtkorb, eds.	*Interpretations of American Literature*	GB26
Gerould, Gordon Hall	*The Ballad of Tradition*	GB8
Gerth, H. H., and Mills, C. Wright, eds. & trs.	*From Max Weber: Essays in Sociology*	GB13
Gilby, Thomas, ed. & tr.	*St. Thomas Aquinas: Philosophical Texts*	GB29
Grierson, Herbert, ed.	*Metaphysical Lyrics and Poems of the Seventeenth Century*	GB19
Halsband, Robert	*The Life of Lady Mary Wortley Montagu*	GB44
Heiler, Friedrich	*Prayer,* translated by Samuel McComb	GB16
Herklots, H. G. G.	*How Our Bible Came to Us*	GB4
Highet, Gilbert	*The Classical Tradition*	GB5
	Juvenal the Satirist	GB48
Kaufmann, R. J., ed.	*Elizabethan Drama*	GB63
Knox, Ronald A.	*Enthusiasm*	GB59
Langer, Susanne K., ed	*Reflections on Art*	GB60
Lewis, C. S.	*The Allegory of Love*	GB17
	A Preface to Paradise Lost	GB57
Lindsay, A. D.	*The Modern Democratic State*	GB86
Lowrie, Walter, tr.	*Kierkegaard: Christian Discourses*	GB49
Livingstone, Richard, ed. & tr.	*Thucydides: The History of the Peloponnesian War*	GB33
MacNeice, Louis, tr.	*Goethe's Faust*	GB45

GALAXY BOOKS

Author	Title	No.
Malinowski, Bronislaw	*A Scientific Theory of Culture*	GB40
Matthiessen, F. O.	*The Achievement of T. S. Eliot,* third edition	GB22
Matthiessen, F. O., and Murdock, Kenneth B., eds.	*The Notebooks of Henry James*	GB61
Mills, C. Wright	*The Power Elite*	GB20
	White Collar	GB3
Muller, Herbert J.	*The Uses of the Past*	GB9
Murray, Gilbert	*The Rise of the Greek Epic*	GB41
Otto, Rudolf	*The Idea of the Holy*	GB14
Peterson, Merrill D.	*The Jefferson Image in the American Mind*	GB71
Price, Don K.	*Government and Science*	GB72
Radhakrishnan, S.	*Eastern Religions and Western Thought*	GB27
Roberts, David E.	*Existentialism and Religious Belief,* edited by Roger Hazelton	GB28
Rostovtzeff, M.	*Rome*	GB42
Russell, Bertrand	*The Problems of Philosophy*	GB21
	Religion and Science	GB50
Schorer, Mark, ed.	*Modern British Fiction*	GB64
Schumpeter, Joseph A.	*The Theory of Economic Development,* translated by Redvers Opie	GB55
Shapiro, Harry L., ed.	*Man, Culture, and Society*	GB32
Shaw, T. E., tr.	*The Odyssey of Homer*	GB2
Sinclair, John D., ed. & tr.	*Dante's Inferno*	GB65
	Dante's Purgatorio	GB66
	Dante's Paradiso	GB67
Tillich, Paul	*Love, Power and Justice*	GB38
Toynbee, Arnold J.	*A Study of History, Volume 1*	GB74
	A Study of History, Volume 2	GB75
	A Study of History, Volume 3	GB76
Turberville, A. S.	*English Men and Manners in the Eighteenth Century*	GB10
Wagenknecht, Edward, ed.	*Chaucer*	GB24
Ward, John William	*Andrew Jackson: Symbol for an Age*	GB73
Wedgwood, C. V.	*Seventeenth-Century English Literature*	GB51
Whitehead, Alfred North	*An Introduction to Mathematics*	GB18
Woodward, C. Vann	*The Strange Career of Jim Crow*	GB6
Wright, Austin, ed.	*Victorian Literature*	GB52
Young, J. Z.	*Doubt and Certainty in Science*	GB34
Zaehner, R. C.	*Mysticism Sacred and Profane*	GB56
Zimmern, Alfred	*The Greek Commonwealth*	GB62